MW00440336

NEVER BE WRONG AGAIN

NEVER BE WRONG AGAIN

FOUR STEPS TO MAKING BETTER DECISIONS IN WORK AND LIFE

by

AUTHOR: MICHAEL ANGELO COSTA

EDITOR: LESLEY MARLO

Publisher: Thoreau Press

Copyright © 2015 Michael Angelo Costa
Published by Thoreau Press

All rights reserved. No part of this publication may be reproduced, stored in a retrieval system or transmitted, in any form, or by any means, electronic, mechanical, recorded, photocopied, or otherwise, without the prior written permission of both the copyright owner and the above publisher of this book, except by a reviewer who may quote brief passages in a review.

The scanning, uploading, and distribution of this book via the Internet or via any other means without the permission of the publisher is illegal and punishable by law. Please purchase only authorized electronic editions and do not participate in or encourage electronic piracy of copyrightable materials. Your support of the author's rights is appreciated.

Cover Design: Antonio García Aprea
Interior Design: Vince Pannullo
Printed in the United States of America

ISBN: Paperback 978-0-9861306-1-8
ISBN: Hardcover 978-0-9861306-0-1
ISBN: ePub 978-0-9861306-2-5
ISBN: Mobi 978-0-9861306-3-2

DEDICATION

To Claudia, Mickey and Cristina

CONTENTS

SECTION 2: The Four-Point Framework for Making Better Decisions

Always Done It That Way • How Do You Choose Which
Decisions to Reevaluate? • Stewing versus Jumping Ship •
Undoing a Previous Decision • Recap • Timing Checklist

Data versus Instinct • Statisticians 10, Poets 0 • Moneyball
• Calculating Value • High Stakes Imbalance • "Rough
Justice" for a Large Potential Payoff • Determining
Acceptable and Unacceptable Risk • Risk of Inaction •
Balance in Relationships • Responsibility = Authority •
Determining and Sticking to Your Risk Parameters • Risk
Unbalanced in Your Favor • High Stakes Risk • Black
Swan Events and Human Nature • Determining the Cost
to Succeed • Recap • Balance Checklist

Establishing and Clearly Defining Targets • Expected
Happenings, Outcomes, and Values • A Hit or a Miss •
Gambling • 100% Probability, Variable: When • 100%
Probability, Variable: Who • Less than 100% Probability •
Size Matters • Recap • Probabilities Checklist

Training Your Brain to Connect the Dots • Knowledge
versus Understanding • The Importance of Analysis •
Step 1: Finding Correlation • Jumping to Conclusions •
Apply All Data That Matters • Assumptions and Statistics
• Step 2: Determining Whether Relevance Exists • 100%
Correlation ≠ Relevance; Drinking Milk *Correlates* with
Drug Addiction • Relevance Found in "WHY" • Step
3: Finding Causation • When Correlation + Relevance
≠ Causation; Sushi and Same-Sex Marriage • When
Correlation + Relevance = Causation; Finding Patterns

through Data Analysis • Italy • Japan • The French Paradox • Blue Zones • Managing Vast Data • Recap • Pattern Recognition Checklist

SECTION 3: The Framework in Action

Acknowledgements

I would like to personally thank the following people for their contributions, support, and other help in creating this book:

First and foremost, I am deeply grateful to my family for their patience and support, especially my loving wife Claudia whose constant motivation kept spirits high as this book consumed many late nights and weekends and seemed as though it might never be finished.

I am blessed to have been raised by two loving parents, William and Lida Costa, who stressed education and taught me to always think about things. Back then, I thought all nine-year olds were reading *Advise and Consent* by Allen Drury. My father, who passed away during the creation of this book, was my hero. One of my biggest regrets is that he never had the chance to hold it in his hands. My mother, who is also my greatest cheerleader, offered helpful high-level observations and specific grammar changes, all while learning to send texts on her first smart phone.

My children, Mickey and Cristina, despite being busy building their own lives and successful careers, provided invaluable insights and opinions on everything from the content to the cover, while my siblings, Barbara and Bill offered language suggestions for clarity.

The tireless work of my editor, Lesley Marlo, and her team at Expert Copy went well beyond the normal effort. She didn't focus solely on grammar but ensured that I kept the content focused and delivered on my promise to help readers make better decisions. Even though she caused me great angst by cutting over 200 pages of my hard work, upon reflection, she was right every time.

I am fortunate to have worked with many very smart people in a number of organizations over the years. I began this book when I was with Ernst & Young as a partner, a position I owe in large part to my great mentors Bill Lipton, Gary Pompan, Jack Wilson, and Jake Blank. I am grateful to many of my fellow partners for their advice, most notably Gerry Grese, who is one of the smartest people I have ever met and whose insights into my early thinking about decision making were invaluable. While at Deutsche Bank I was also able to observe two great decision makers, Seth Waugh and Stuart Clarke.

It was my good friend, golfing partner, and trader extraordinaire, Larry Trainor, who suggested that I put something in the book about investing based on his wise observation that most people are very good at making money from their own profession but very bad at investing and protecting the money they earn. Marilyn Trainor and Christy Ruvituso offered excellent suggestions on the book's cover design.

Three good friends, Gene Cobuzzi, Saleh Lootah, and Ben Emanuel, made time in their busy lives to read the book and offer improvements, which I incorporated into the latest version.

I also want to thank my friend, Kathy Travis, who took time out of her demanding schedule to sit down with me to provide guidance on how to translate my ideas into a book and whose referrals lead me to Lesley Marlo.

I have been fortunate to have many friends and colleagues who have influenced me along the way, and I apologize to all those who are not mentioned by name.

THE EPIPHANY

It was a bright, sunny day in southern California. I'd flown in from New York to propose a complex two-billion-dollar transaction to the board of directors of a publicly traded company. On the flight out, I reviewed the resumes of the board members and while they all had different backgrounds, each had a stellar educational pedigree and impressive business experience. The fact that they had been asked to be on this board proved they had previously excelled at something, whether it was business or academia.

I gave a relatively smooth presentation and received a number of questions that I handled with ease. After my presentation, three board members near me were discussing whether to proceed with the transaction. This was an important decision that would have a meaningful impact on the company's financial statements. I took a seat and listened. Although aware of my presence, the board members spoke candidly, tossing their differing opinions back and forth.

Two people argued their rationale in favor of the transaction and one person argued his case against the deal. As I listened to the conversations, I heard three different views. Even though the decision had only two possible outcomes (in this case, approve the deal or not), each member had vastly different reasons for reaching his or her own conclusion. The two people in favor of the deal had incompatible reasons for their conclusions, and for his own reasons, the third person did not think the transaction should proceed.

Just like their resumes indicated, all three were intelligent and thoughtful people. As they articulated their independent views, I sat silently observing. How could these three successful people, who had just heard the exact same information at the same time, have such differing opinions? When their conversation began, it had been no more than three minutes since my presentation ended and only twenty-three minutes since it started. It dawned on me that, regardless of their point of view, each of the three members had based his or her decision on some form of very quick, instinctive reaction. Shortly thereafter, their initial reaction hardened into a final conclusion about whether the deal should go forward or not. This was a deal that would impact the company's financial statements and stock price, but the decision makers hadn't allowed themselves enough time to give this decision any real thought.

As they talked, I reflected on the prior week's presentation to another board when I had faced some really thoughtful but difficult questions. This board also asked probing questions, but not the same ones as the other board of directors. Then it clicked. Shouldn't there be some sort of framework, guide, or method for making such a substantial financial decision, or any important decision for that matter? How could these three people just be "winging" this? It was too important. Then I realized that I didn't have a decision-making process either. I knew this deal well, but if I was in their position how would I go about analyzing it?

What questions would I ask? What if the deal was completely outside of my realm of expertise? I think I'm smart and have had a degree of professional success, but what would I do? Would I just assume that because I am smart, or at least think I'm smart, I would automatically get to the right answer?

Perhaps if I were on this board, I would defer the decision to the next meeting in order to have time to think about it. But what would I think about? Sure, I would be thinking about whether to approve the deal or not, but what would I be thinking? *How* would I go about deciding? I have sufficient self-confidence in my ability to examine the problem and think about possible solutions, but did I have a clear plan or method for thinking through the decision? I didn't. I was just like those board members. As I embarked on a decade-long research project on decision making at all levels, I realized that it wasn't just those board members and me; no one seemed to have a structured decision-making process.

The Decision-Making Epidemic

A *New York Times* article titled, "Shake Up at Shell to Speed Decision-Making"[1] focused on the global mega-corporation undertaking realignment in order to make better decisions on a timely basis. One could argue that Shell is an old company that is apt to have multiple layers of management, so of course it could use help in decision making. I haven't personally done a study on Shell, so I don't know whether the organization operates efficiently or not, but this is one of the largest companies in the world, with sophisticated management and access to the best external consultants.

We might assume that problems like Shell's would not extend to a tremendously successful technology company with a worldwide reputation for inspiring and rewarding forward thinking, but we would be wrong. In a 2011 *Wall Street Journal* article titled, "For Google CEO Larry Page, A Difficult Premiere Role,"[2] the journalist recounted that Google's co-founder announced he would shake up the internet giant to accelerate decision making there. This is a modern, highly innovative, high-tech giant that is very young by corporate standards, not old and stodgy. Still, Google and Shell share the struggle of efficient decision making in their organizations.

This isn't a case study on Shell, Google, or myriad other corporations that have experienced the same problem. Even start-ups suffer the same malaise. Start-up companies usually have only a few well-defined decision makers who are, most often, the founders. The need to "pivot" is critical, and changes can often be executed overnight if needed. Almost all of the early decisions in a start-up are based on biases and heuristics (covered in detail in the next chapters), with the co-founders relying heavily on

---

[1] Saltmarsh, Matthew. "Shake-up at Shell to Speed Decision-Making." *New York Times*, May 28, 2009.

[2] Efrati, Amir. "For Google CEO Larry Page, a Difficult Premier Role." *Wall Street Journal*, August 30, 2011.

gut-level instinct. If their instincts are right, their company may become a viable start-up, receive the requisite financing, and grow.

This is when the seeds for bad decision-making habits are unknowingly sown. If there was never a framework for decision making and these smart creative people got the several important first decisions right, they may develop a sense that they naturally get things right. After all, they may have just received Series A financing or are further down the line and about to reap huge rewards by going public. Their assumption is that they are excellent decision makers, which is validated by the amount of money they have. The start-up then hires more and more people, who in turn do not have any framework for decision making because it's just not taught, and the cycle continues.

What do the old corporations and the newer, expanding companies have in common? Size and people. Once an organization reaches a certain size, it doesn't matter if another one is much larger. It doesn't matter if a company has ten people in its legal department or one hundred lawyers. It doesn't matter if it has four people writing code or five hundred coders. There are now internal departments for legal, accounting, marketing, financing, research and development, and mergers and acquisitions—and a lot more people.

While the typical person who wants to work for Shell may be different than the typical person who wants to work for Google, both of them are still people. If they aren't aware of the influencers on their decisions, they will be inclined to decide based on biases and assumptions. Employees of both companies are also likely to avoid making decisions for the same reasons—primarily, the risk of being wrong and the inability to convince a room full of other people to agree with them. This is how two companies with vastly different corporate cultures could end up with the same problem.

Choosing The "Best" Option

A few years ago, I gave a presentation on decision making to a group of executives at a prominent international financial services company. After the presentation, one senior executive came up to me and announced that his group had already solved their decision-making problems. Intrigued, I asked him how they did it. It turned out that the company's decision-making solution was to detail the troubling situation or problem in an e-mail and then send that e-mail to the top one hundred people in the company, soliciting their solutions to the problem.

Like a modern-day electronic suggestion box, this is a great way to gather a multitude of gut reactions, but then what? The senior executive said that someone would then decide on the "best" option of all of those presented. I asked him how the "best" option was chosen, and he did not know. While I appreciate the organization's attempt to seek more inputs, without a structured, unbiased way to analyze the suggestions from this group of intelligent employees, how could anyone be certain that the most optimal path would be chosen? They couldn't. This is an incredibly common issue.

Score More Points Than the Other Team

A team in the National Football League is searching for a new head coach. Through a connection, you have landed an interview with the current owner. After shaking hands you begin the meeting by telling him that you will lead the team to an unprecedented number of Super Bowl victories. You say, "My plan is to make sure we always score more points than our opponents." The owner's initial thought is to find out which friend of his (now a former friend) arranged this meeting. He then politely tells you that what you have described is not a plan. Yes, it's true. If you score more points than your opponent you will win. Scoring more points than your opponent is always the objective. That's how you define winning. But that's the objective, not a plan. Great coaches are those who have a plan for *how* to achieve that goal.

When I ask people how they make decisions, either on an individual or organizational level, most people's answer is a variation of, "I consider all the options and then choose the best one." Considering all of the options and choosing the best one is NOT a process; it is the overall objective. Choosing the best option is the goal in decision making, but is not a plan for *how* to achieve that goal. It is the exact equivalent of saying you should be head coach because your plan is to score more points than your opponents.

Development of the Framework

The personal "aha" moment after the board presentation launched my ten-year journey to research, observe, and interview individuals and groups of people who made decisions. My research has encompassed over ten thousand pages of books, periodicals, and academic articles in addition to personal experience. While a number of well-written, commercially available books point out the common pitfalls we make, none I found presented the most effective method for making optimal decisions. My varied business experiences have given me access to educated, successful people who are in significant decision-making roles. My discussions and interviews with them have allowed me to hone my theories and test the framework that follows while quietly observing missteps in decisions as they were made.

During my thirty-year career as a lawyer and investment banker, I spent more than twenty thousand hours with "C-suite" executives and boards of directors at major international companies. As a result, I have seen just about every possible outcome that can result from a decision-making process (or a lack of one.) Some of the research for this book came from the meetings I had with these boards of directors, CEOs, COOs, CFOs, and other executives. When I first started my meetings and interviews, I assumed that these influential people would have a very clear decision-making process. As it turned out, while my clients and others were all smart and well educated, I consistently observed flaws in their decision making, even at the highest levels.

The examples I cite throughout the book are taken from real-life transactions and decisions with which I am personally familiar or that are public knowledge. When an example I cite is based on private information, minor details have been changed to protect the identity of the individual or corporation involved, but the pertinent facts have been maintained to protect the integrity of the analysis. For any public information, I clearly refer to the journal, periodical, newspaper, or other source of information.

Most of the commercially available books that I have read and may refer to in these pages don't directly relate to decision making, per se, except for *Blink*,[3] *Thinking, Fast and Slow*,[4] and, to a certain extent, *Judgment*.[5] In each case, I clearly refer to the books and their information. I encourage you to read some of these books because they raise intellectual issues and are great for sharpening your decision-making skills.

I came up with the framework by observing and analyzing both good and bad decisions. When I started, I had no idea whether my research and analysis would lead me to a three, four, six, eight, or fifteen step process or whether I would able to find a clear decision-making process at all. Did people make good decisions without using a structured decision-making framework? Sure. What decision-making process did they employ? Usually none, because they didn't have one. I call it "accidental correctness." Accidental, because the same people and organizations would later make very poor decisions, not considering all of the variables that they had in a prior problem. Not only was the outcome bad, but the approach was flawed.

The purpose of a structure or checklist is to provide certainty of a thought process when addressing complex problems. A well-thought-out structure provides a way to replicate good decision making. After thinking and analyzing what people did right and what they did wrong, I was able to distill the framework for good decision making, even about complex matters, into the four points that I will discuss in the next section.

The epiphany inside the boardroom that day convinced me that I didn't want to rely solely on my gut instinct for a big decision, regardless

[3] Gladwell, Malcom. *Blink* (New York: Little, Brown and Company, 2005).

[4] Kahneman, Daniel. *Thinking, Fast and Slow* (New York: Farrer, Straus and Giroux, 2011).

[5] Tichy, Noel M. and Warren G. Bennis. *Judgment: How Winning Leaders Make Great Calls* (New York: Penguin Group, 2007).

of my prior successes. There is always a risk of not getting the result you want in a decision, but what is really a shame are the times we get it wrong when we shouldn't have – those times that we go with our gut instead of employing a more analytical approach.

WHAT MAKES A GOOD DECISION?

People are judged every day by the decisions they make, but how would you define whether a decision is good or bad—by the outcome? There is no question that the goal of any specific decision or decision-making process is to get the best result, but is the outcome the only way to define a good decision? The answer is no.

If your financial advisor made you a 50% return on your money last year, you would be ecstatic. That is an outstanding result. If you ask him how he did it and he replies that he picked your investments by throwing darts at the stock listings in a newspaper, would you continue letting him manage your money? Your entire reason for reading this book is to get better results, so we all agree that results count, but results are not the only indicator of whether a decision is good or bad.

The Roulette Wheel

Imagine that you are in a Las Vegas casino waiting to meet your friend by the roulette wheel. A man who is frustrated with his current position in life stands nearby. He begins by telling you his life story and tales of woe. He has come to Las Vegas to gamble his way to wealth. He has a total of $10,000, which has taken years to accumulate. He believes that if he can significantly increase the amount of cash he has, his life will get better.

He steps up to the roulette table and bets all of his money on his lucky number—seven. If the roulette ball lands on seven, his payoff of 36 to 1 will win him $360,000. If the ball lands on any other number, he will lose everything instantly. The roulette wheel begins to spin, and the croupier lets the ball drop.

Do you think he has made a good decision or a bad decision by betting his life savings on a roulette spin? The ball bounces from number to number as the wheel spins and our gambler anxiously awaits the result. You hope he will win, but you know that the odds are stacked against him. He only has a 1 in 38 chance of winning (around 2.6%).[6] The chances that he will lose everything are overwhelming (97.4%).

If he wins, will you think he made a good decision by gambling his life savings on a roulette spin? Most people would agree that this is a very risky decision and probably not the smartest. If he wins, everybody will congratulate him, but this cannot be considered a good decision when there is such high risk and unfavorable odds.

Can You Really Never Be Wrong Again?

It's true that you can never be wrong again. While this seems like an outrageous claim, I am willing to stand behind it completely. You can never be wrong again in your decision-making thought process. Our dart-throwing investment advisor and the roulette playing desperate man have clearly demonstrated that making a good decision is not defined solely by the outcome, because the outcome can be influenced by things such as luck and unexpected events. If the roulette ball landed on his chosen number, our gambler would have won big, but he would have just been extremely lucky. He would not have made a good decision. Making a good decision is about the process, not the outcome. A better process drives better results.

Nothing can guarantee a specific result for two basic reasons. First, there are factors beyond your control. The overheated housing market in the United States and resulting lack of confidence in mortgage-backed securities was the catalyst for the Great Recession. I am guessing that you had nothing to do with either of those things and, unless you were among a

---

[6] The typical casino roulette wheel in the United States has 38 numbers (1-36 plus 0 and 00). Notice that the risk is 1 out of 38, but the payoff is only 36:1, which is why casinos want gamblers to come visit and stay for a long time.

handful of experts, never saw it coming. Nevertheless, it probably impacted your life and some decisions you made before the financial crisis happened. Say, for example, that you and your spouse both had good jobs and decided to purchase a larger home in a nicer area than where you were living at the time. With two salaries, the price of the house was well within your means. Then the Great Recession happened and, through no fault of his own, your spouse lost his job and is still currently unemployed. If you had known that there would be a substantial economic downturn that would adversely impact your household income, you probably would not have purchased the new home.

Second, no decision is 100% assured. Let's say that after reading this book, you undertake a thoughtful decision-making analysis and, after considering all aspects, determine that you have an 80% chance of getting the result you want, which is a very high percentage. By definition, that means there still is a 20% chance that the outcome will not be the one you want. Every decision has some level of risk. You always want to increase your chances of getting the outcome you desire, but you should not judge a decision by the result.

That said, the entire point of learning to make better decisions is to get better outcomes. A good decision-making process will lead to better results. Your goal should be to never have a flaw in your decision-making process, which in turn, increases the chances of achieving your desired outcome. The "right" decision is the decision that optimizes your chances of obtaining the result you desire. You are "wrong" when you don't get the outcome you want but could have with a better thought process. Using the four-point framework in this book will maximize your chances for the optimal result and lead you to the right decision every time, which also means that you will never be wrong again.

The Science Behind the Art of Decision Making

It's often said that decision making is an art. I agree that it is not a hard science in that even the best decision process cannot guarantee that you will achieve your goal. But people mistakenly jump to the conclusion that since decision making is not a hard science, it is 100% art.

In fact, there is a science to the art of good decision making. Do you know what else is an art? Art. I will posit that there is nothing more art than art itself. Almost all of the great artists trained under others to learn, among other things, the impact of lighting and shading, how to mix the proper color, and how to create textures. When artists want to create a certain shade of color, they use their knowledge of which combination and proportion of two or three other colors will create the exact hue they want. There is skill to be learned in becoming a better artist. Just as Leonardo da Vinci studied science as a method to improve his art, there is a method to becoming better at the art of decision making.

Research in academic papers and in published books is overwhelmingly clear: While sometimes comical and sometimes quite sad, the fact is that the human mind still reacts and decides the same way it did thousands of years ago when we were farming in the grasslands or hunting in the jungle.

Very simply, few of us have actually developed a consistent thought process for making decisions. When you pause and reflect on that, it is really quite staggering. At this point in your life, you have made countless decisions but have relied, for the most part, solely on your gut instinct. From the largest, most successful organizations to individuals facing an important choice, having a clear structure and practice for thinking through important decisions cannot only help cause a better outcome, but also make the decision process more efficient.

Your gut instinct may prove to be the right one, but when the stakes are high and the outcome of your decision matters, doesn't common sense dictate that we should have a check and balance system to test our first visceral reaction?

Complex Decisions Require a Structured Analysis

In the book *The Checklist Manifesto*, author Atul Gawande points out that there are three categories of problems or tasks: simple, complicated, and complex. A simple task would be learning how to pack a grocery bag

– heavy items on the bottom, eggs on top. This is something you could figure out on your own or with minimal training. Sending a rocket into space, however, is extremely complicated and requires a deep knowledge of physics, math, liquid fuels, materials, and so on. However, once you have solved the equations needed, you could probably replicate them with only a minimal amount of new knowledge needed for your second launch, which makes this a complicated task. A complex problem is a complicated problem that is not necessarily capable of being easily replicated.

Gawande is a medical doctor, so his analysis centers on the complex problem of diagnosing and treating patients. If I go to a hospital with chest pains, the doctors may immediately get an accurate diagnosis of my issues and come up with the proper solution, but the problem and proposed solution for the next person who comes to the hospital with chest pains could be completely different from mine. What worked for me may not work for the next guy. The overarching point of *The Checklist Manifesto* is that complex problems require a checklist instead of reliance on gut instinct and memory recall.

Every important decision in our lives is like a patient in Gawande's example—unique and with individual facts, assumptions, and overall scenarios that may vary. Important decisions need to be examined independently. The best solution to one problem may be very different from a previous solution to a similar problem. If you jump to the conclusion that an important problem in front of you is exactly like the last problem you faced and therefore should be treated the same, you are like a doctor who assumes all chest pains should get treated the exact same way. Important decisions, which are defined as decisions with high stakes, usually present complex problems and need a structured solution. We need to use a decision-making "checklist" of sorts so that we don't solely use our preliminary conclusions and end up making poor decisions.

What Type of Book is This?

Never Be Wrong Again is a self-help book if you use it to become a better decision maker in personal matters. It is a business management book if you use it to help make business and investment decisions. Mostly, it is a how-to book. How-to books teach you how to do something, and this book is intended to teach you how to reach the best decision possible every time you are faced with an important choice. By providing a proven structure for decision making, *Never Be Wrong Again* helps you do just that. You can never be wrong if you are making decisions that offer the greatest chances for getting the result you want.

Whatever your goal is, the decision-making framework presented in these pages will help you think through important decisions to achieve that goal. Having a structure to follow will also help you make decisions more efficiently and mitigate some of the stress involved in making those important decisions. In the end, it is my hope that *Never Be Wrong Again* will help many people and organizations make better decisions, faster, with less stress.

How to Use This Book

Decision making can be stressful and time consuming, but it doesn't need to be. Using a structured framework is not about discarding your initial visceral reaction, but instead presents a process for validating it. If your gut reaction contradicts a more analytical information-based approach, one of them is wrong. Using a clear decision-making framework, you can achieve better decisions more efficiently and more confidently.

My initial focus primarily addressed business scenarios, but as I made presentations to groups of investment professionals, the feedback was consistent: People also wanted to know how to apply these concepts to life decisions. Based on this, I have deliberately included examples of choices that are more personal—matters like marriage, legalization of marijuana, and playing the lottery.

The first section of this book is designed to shed light on the common pitfalls we face in decision making. Having an efficient decision-making structure will increase your chances for a good result, but it does not inoculate you against subtle and not-so-subtle emotional stumbling blocks.

Raising your awareness of these forces will help protect you from getting unconsciously manipulated by them.

The middle section of the book details the four-point framework: Timing, Balance, Probabilities, and Pattern Recognition. Each chapter begins with an overview of what you can expect to learn in that chapter and ends with a checklist of reminders for that section.

In the final section of the book, I apply the four-point framework to various scenarios to reach a final conclusion. You may not agree with my conclusions, but we will agree exactly on where we disagree.

Let's start with a decision that is important to the participant but is not complex: "Deal or No Deal."

DEAL OR NO DEAL – PART 1

Gary was a hard-working guy with a huge heart who loved two things: his family and NASCAR. Gary and his wife of twenty-seven years had an open-door policy in their humble home. If there was ever a child who was down and out and needed a place to stay, Gary and his wife welcomed him or her in like family. Some stayed three days. Some stayed three years.

Gary, a long-haul trucker, was often away from home and struggled to find a balance between time on the road and time with the family. While family was his priority, the down economy found him short on a few bills. His wife needed a new car because hers was in disrepair and, as Gary referred to it, "a potential deathtrap."

Every weekend, the extended relatives gathered for pizza at Gary's, which was another cost the couple willingly accepted. The continuous shortfall was becoming a serious problem. The couple desperately needed money and entered a contest to be on a popular television game show called *Deal or No Deal*.

Amidst flashing lights, a live audience, and an elaborate stage, *Deal or No Deal* presents its contestants with the ultimate choice between a known quantity and the potential for more. Everyone wants more. More is great, particularly when it comes to money. If you had the choice between receiving $100 or $1,000, that wouldn't be a difficult decision, but it also wouldn't make for good television.

Now, what if I told you that you could walk away with a guaranteed $1,000 or take a chance to win even more money? Of course, with chance comes risk. You have the chance to walk away with more than $1,000, but if you continue on, you risk only winning $1. That is better television.

On *Deal or No Deal*, contestants must choose a single case from among twenty-six briefcases. Each one contains a card representing a set amount of money ranging from one cent to one million dollars. A contestant doesn't get to open his case and see the amount until the end of the game, but the other twenty-five cases are gradually opened a few at a time, showing the contestant the dollar amounts they forfeited. The game is simple. The contestant tries to guess the amount in their case by process of elimination. As each case is eliminated, the amount shown in that briefcase is ruled out as the possible amount in the contestant's case.

Periodically throughout the game, a "banker" offers the contestant a sum of money in exchange for his unopened briefcase. Accepting the offer ends the game and guarantees the contestant that amount of money. Remember, the contestant still does not know the value of his case, and taking the banker's offer means relinquishing whatever amount the case contains. The contestant is actually "selling" his case to the banker and must decide whether to take the banker's offer or reject it in hopes of getting a higher offer later in the game or of finding a higher amount in the case he already holds.

When faced with this decision, the contestant will need to estimate the odds of his case being worth more than the banker's offer. How are the odds estimated? If the eliminated cases hold lower amounts, the odds increase that the contestant's case holds a higher figure. If cases containing higher amounts are eliminated, it becomes less likely that the contestant's case also holds a large payoff. The banker's offers correspond with the probabilities about what is inside the case, increasing and decreasing as cases are eliminated and the odds become clearer. Contestants decline the banker's offer by shouting, "No deal!" With every shout of "No deal," the contestant gambles on the opportunity to win more money but risks getting a lower offer the next time.

Back to Gary: Gary starts off lucky. He is playing a new version of the game and the television producers are offering two cases worth $1 million, not just one. After choosing his own case, Gary begins the process of choosing which cases to eliminate. Right away, he eliminates both cases containing $1 million, destroying any hope that his case holds the biggest jackpot. He also eliminates the $100,000 and $300,000 cases, whittling down his chances for a big payoff.

The banker makes his first offer to Gary for $44,000. Gary says he didn't come on the show for just $44,000 and shouts, "No deal!" A few more cases are opened, and the banker's next offer is for $52,000. Gary tells the host that he and his wife have discussed an amount of money that they would accept, and $52,000 is too low. Again, he shouts, "No deal!"

Gary selects a few more of the remaining cases to open, including the cases containing $200,000 and $400,000. The only big-money case that is left contains $500,000, and there is no guarantee that Gary's case holds this amount. The banker throws a curveball. He offers Gary $30,000. The offers are going down, but to sweeten the deal, the host offers Gary a NASCAR prize package including a chance to meet NASCAR legend Jimmy Johnson, drive a pace car, and go on a $2,000 NASCAR shopping spree. Gary says he would love the NASCAR package, but it only benefits him and not his whole family. The $30,000 isn't enough, so he rejects the offer.

More cases are opened, but all of them hold low dollar amounts. The chance that Gary holds the $500,000 case is looking better. The banker's next offer is $63,000. Gary acknowledges that $63,000 is "a life-changing amount of money." If he declines the $63,000 and the next case holds the $500,000 card, he can expect the banker's offers to bottom out.

Gary decides that he would like his life to change even more than it would with the $63,000 and says, "No deal!" Gary selects another case to open, and it reveals the $1,000 card. He gets an offer from the banker for $85,000, and his family advises him to take the deal. Gary tells the host that he has a "gut" feeling that his case holds $500,000, but he can't escape the realization that $85,000 could change his life even more significantly than the "life-changing amount" of $63,000. Risking his prior position has paid off. Can he afford to keep pushing his luck?

If Gary eliminates more cases that don't contain the $500,000, he will be offered more money from the banker, but if he is unlucky and chooses the $500,000 case, the offers will drop dramatically. *Deal or No Deal* is a classic case of balancing risk against potential reward and gauging your gut reaction (or hope) against the mathematical odds of success.

Do you think Gary is thinking things through in a methodical way or just going with his gut? If he goes with his gut reaction and it pays off, is that wrong? If you were Gary and in his economic position with the same chances of risk and reward based on the amounts left, what would you do, and why? Of course more money is better than less, but would you risk ending up with less than a guaranteed "life-changing" amount of money? Would you judge whether your decision was good or bad by the result after you have seen what is actually in the briefcase? Would you consider it a smart decision if the next offer is higher and a poor decision if the next offer is lower?

Later in the book I will tell you what Gary did and how it worked out, but first it is your turn to decide: Deal or no deal?

SECTION 1

HOW WE DECIDE NOW

Your brain is a computer, and the way you think is an operating system. No matter how good a software package is, bad inputs cannot result in great outputs because as the old saying goes, "Garbage in, garbage out." The garbage in this case is bad input in the form of skewed information, subconscious emotions, habits, and more.

The world's best global positioning system (GPS) cannot get you to your desired destination if you don't know your starting point. Your starting point in this case is how you make decisions today. You need to clearly understand the subtle forces at work when you are faced with important decisions, because if you are unaware of them, they will hijack your decision-making process, which will lead to bad decisions and suboptimal results. Even the most intelligent, analytical, accomplished people are vulnerable to the influencers discussed in the coming pages.

YOU ARE HERE

HIJACKINGS, BIASES, AND HEURISTICS; WHY WE KEEP GETTING IT WRONG

You see an advertisement on television for a candidate running for President of the United States. Let's assume you are a rare case and are truly open-minded about the candidates. From the moment you see the first ad supporting one candidate or attacking another, you start to form an opinion.

You are already leaning toward one of the candidates after this first commercial but tell your friends you haven't formed an opinion yet. After seeing a few more commercials, you do form an opinion, and it becomes a strong one.

What drove you to like your candidate better? What were the buzz words used in the commercials that won you over? Did the television pundits proclaim that one of the candidates had more intellectual gravitas or sounded or acted more presidential?

Once you have decided which candidate is best, your position hardens. Consciously or not, you begin treating your opinion as a fact; Your candidate is better than the other one. When the two main candidates engage in a televised debate, you are rooting for your chosen candidate to do well, and you take pleasure in any missteps by her opponent. Perhaps you even defend your candidate when one of your friends says something negative about her. Your reaction and defense of your candidate becomes even stronger if the candidate is from your preferred political party. This is a classic example of how we form an initial reaction, confirm in our own minds that we are right, and then become emotional in defending our choices.

Biological Design

Many of our initial reactions come from the fact that we are still physically designed to hunt and gather food and have not been biologically designed to sit around and think deeply about matters. If you have ever seen a documentary about animals in Africa, you may have noticed that all of the antelope graze together. They use their eyes, ears, and keen sense of smell to monitor their surroundings and are constantly on alert for signs of danger. If an animal that is not an antelope approaches them but they recognize the intruder as a fellow grazer, they put their heads back down and continue eating. If an animal wanders near them and they recognize it as a predator, they speed away. If two predators face each other, they literally try to size each other up. The predator that is noticeably larger than his competitors is usually given greater deference.

While we have more intellectual capacity than these animals, we are still part of the animal kingdom, and many times we react just like those animals we saw in the documentary. Like in the jungle, at first sight, we immediately decide if someone is a threat or if, for reasons we can't explain, we like him.

Historically, both men and women prefer taller men. Women instinctively feel that the taller man can provide greater physical security, while men look upon taller men with greater esteem. That is why taller men have historically made more money during their careers than shorter men and a taller male candidate generally has an advantage in an election. These heuristics, or small psychological tendencies, make sense if we are relying on physical prowess for security and putting food on the table. In modern countries, unless you are a professional athlete, size should make little, if any, difference.

While we may have physically moved on from being hunters and gatherers, our brains have not evolved. We still have the mental processes in place to make very quick decisions (gut reactions) because that is what was needed when we were hunting and gathering. Based on our experiences, especially in areas in which we develop expertise, we come to very quick conclusions that are often correct.

So, if our gut reactions are usually correct, what's the problem? Gut reactions are fine when the cost of being wrong is minor, but when the stakes are much higher, the risk of being wrong can be quite significant. Research has demonstrated that when we come to an initial conclusion, we resist changing that conclusion. When we have a serious matter at hand, these initial hardwired reactions push us in the direction of our final decision. We can only fight these powerful impulses if we make a concerted effort to do so.

Instinct *is* important, but highly impactful decisions should also be measured against a more analytical and thoughtful approach. To be clear, I am not suggesting that you should ignore your instincts. Your instincts are most often right, but when the stakes are high or the subject matter is outside your realm of expertise, you should not rely on only your gut instinct.

Each year, hundreds of billions of dollars are spent by people driven by their emotional reaction to some stimulus. Entire industries are devoted to mining metadata in order to determine the purchasing patterns of groups of people and individuals. Commercial websites use NSA-type software to sell you things that might interest you based on your prior purchases or keywords or phrases used in e-mails you send. Sophisticated retailers are now installing cameras in the eyes of mannequins to record what customers are drawn to in the window and store displays. When large television marketers like QVC or the Home Shopping Network pick their on-camera spokespeople, they test them for their Q score, which is a measurement of likeability rated by a sample of typical viewers. High Q ratings reflect high appeal for the spokesperson, product, and network that will ultimately result in higher sales.

Heuristics

While we react to all sorts of stimuli numerous times every day, we often aren't conscious about what we are reacting to or why. Psychologists refer to these as "heuristics." Heuristics are rules of thumb or experience-based assumptions/shortcuts we use in everyday problem solving and include biases, tendencies, and other influences that cause our minds to jump to a conclusion quickly.

Heuristics are powerful forces. They are so strong that psychologists often refer to them as being hardwired into our brains, but this insinuates that these tendencies cannot be changed. It is true that unless we make a very strong, conscious effort to overcome our initial reactions, they can taint the entire decision-making process.

Like any source of influence, if heuristics pull us in the right direction, they are helpful. If they pull us in the wrong direction, they are a force of destruction. We are aware of all physical sources of power—we can see, feel, and try to manage them. We can feel the pull of the ocean's undertow or see and feel fire. Heuristics are silent forces and often affect us without us realizing it. Have you ever heard a sound bite on the news or seen a headline in a newspaper that made you emotional before you heard the whole story or read the full article? The headline or sound bite caused you to have a reaction, which was exactly the editor's goal.

Lessons from Ron Burgundy

The movie *Anchorman* centered on a dimwitted but funny anchorman named Ron Burgundy, who was played by actor-comedian Will Ferrell. As part of a tie-in to the sequel, *Anchorman 2*, Dodge (a division of Chrysler) hired Will Ferrell to star in television ads discussing the Dodge Durango, while staying in character as Ron Burgundy. In one of several tongue-in-cheek ads, Ron extols the vast space of the glove compartment.

On *Conan,* the popular late-night talk show hosted by Conan O'Brien, Will Ferrell, again in character as Ron Burgundy, calls the Dodge Durango a "terrible car." Dodge reported an incredible 59% surge in the sales of the

Dodge Durango during the first month of the new advertising campaign. The CEO of AutoNation, a major car dealership conglomerate, was interviewed on CNBC and said that there was nothing aside from the Ron Burgundy ads that contributed to the increased sales of the Durango during that period.

I found these advertisements to be very funny, but should I let this campaign alone guide my decision to purchase this vehicle? If I like the ads and am looking to buy a new car, I might be predisposed to look at the Dodge Durango thanks to Ron Burgundy, which puts it in the "pole position" as the early favorite. I should then look at similar vehicles to determine which one is best for me. If I start out set on the Durango, unless something in the other vehicles is clearly superior, my sale is Dodge's to lose. Even if I don't fall completely victim to confirmation bias, I start out leaning toward the Dodge Durango, which means that in the case of a virtual tie, the winner is the Dodge Durango due to my initial impression and the likable ad campaign. In this case, buying a Dodge Durango may or may not be a good decision, but I should be aware of what pushed me in that direction. The same is true for many other purchases. It isn't a matter of right or wrong but is about understanding our decision process.

Ego in the Driver's Seat

Mercedes-Benz and BMW are both high-performance automobile manufacturers. Each brand has higher-end lines with even more power and acceleration than their base models. BMW's premium line is the M series. Let's compare the basic BMW 5 series to the M5, the M-series version of the basic 5 model. The standard BMW 528i has a list price of $49,500. The M5 has a list price of $92,900. What do you get for this price difference of 88%? The standard 528i can go from 0 to 60 miles per hour in 6.4 seconds, while the M5 can accomplish that goal in only 4.3 seconds. The acceleration in the M5 is much faster than the 528i, but 0 to 60 in 6.4 seconds in the 528i is still fast.

While the owner of the M5 has purchased the ability to get a speeding ticket on I-95 faster than the driver of the 528i (and has paid $43,400 more for this ability), what the M5 driver really bought is the ability to pull up to a fancy restaurant and demonstrate that he can afford to spend the extra money.

If you are shopping for a car, once you have decided based on various heuristics that you want the M5, you will look at all of the specific details, like greater acceleration, simply to convince yourself that it is the right decision. Does the price difference mean the purchase of the M5 is wrong? No. If you can afford it and it makes you happy, go ahead and buy it, empowered with a better understanding of what drove your decision.

These powerful and mostly very subtle forces don't just affect the weak-minded. It doesn't matter where you went to school or how high your IQ is; a strong-willed, educated person is subject to being influenced by biases and heuristics, as well. Being able to recognize your emotional triggers and subconscious biases will allow you to challenge assumptions that may otherwise lead you in the wrong direction.

Modern developments have dramatically changed our lifestyles and sped up the process of communication. Our faster, more complex lives demand many more decisions and a need for effective, timely decision making. Society has evolved from primitive hunting and gathering, but our thinking processes have not kept up with the speed of our technological advancements.

Even though we make dozens of decisions every day, most of us have never been properly trained on how to make a decision. The result of this is that we don't really know how to make a truly thoughtful decision and can rarely describe in detail how we came to our initial conclusion. Before you learn an effective framework for making good decisions, it's important to understand how you are prone to make decisions now, because nothing can totally inoculate you from all of your emotions, biases, and heuristics.

The Four Levels of Decision Making

Vast research has gone into determining what commonly influences our decisions, and all of us, no matter what age, sex, demographic, or economic group we belong to, approach every decision in one of four ways:

1. Non-thinking crisis response—Fight or Flight
2. Non-thinking gut reaction—How we make almost all of our daily decisions
3. Thinking Lightly—Replaying pre-existing thoughts or opinions rather than truly analyzing and thinking
4. Thinking Deeply—When the stakes are high, where you should be; the natural home and highest benefit of a structured decision-making process

Each of these approaches, which will be covered more in depth later in this section, is important and useful for the appropriate circumstance. However, the wrong approach at the wrong time can lead to suboptimal results, if not complete disaster. A crisis response to a non-crisis can actually create a crisis, and a simple gut reaction to a complex situation is a big gamble where risks could potentially be reduced with a more thoughtful approach.

While most people operate from one of the first three levels, real thinking happens at the fourth level. When Thinking Deeply, our emotional drivers, preconceptions, belief systems, and prejudices are acknowledged and met with logic, relevant data, and apt analysis. This is where a framework for decision making guides our analysis and optimizes our chances for the best result.

NON-THINKING CRISIS RESPONSE

FIGHT OR FLIGHT & THE AMYGDALA HIJACK

The amygdala is an almond-shaped gland in our brain that purposely shuts down our processing capability when we need to react to an emergency situation. An instinctive response to an emergency situation is as important a part of survival to humans as it is to other species. If our well-being is suddenly in jeopardy, we need to react immediately. In these situations, taking time to think through our actions is not a viable option, so instinct takes over to prevent us from harm. We respond to defend ourselves or attempt to escape the situation. While this is the "fight or flight" trigger that is hardwired into us, the actual trigger point for this response varies from person to person. The amygdala drives your instantaneous decision to run into a raging fire to save your child.

While there are times when the non-thinking fight or flight response is useful, these times are limited to real crises and emergencies. We rarely operate in this mode. More accurately, we should rarely operate in this mode. Unfortunately, crisis-response behavior happens much more than necessary, and often it happens when there is no real threat to our well-being.

Author and psychologist Daniel Goleman, in his 1996 book *Emotional Intelligence*, coined the phrase "amygdala hijack" to describe an irrational crisis response to a non-emergency situation—in other words, when the amygdala hijacks our rational, thinking minds. The amygdala hijack is what causes road rage. This irrational overreaction to stimuli such as being cut off or stuck in a traffic jam is out of balance with the actual situation. Road rage is the epitome of a crisis response to a non-crisis situation. Despite the absence of a real emergency, rational thinking is overtaken by emotion, and an inconvenience is responded to as if it were a life or death situation.

What about people who are often in emergency situations, like military personnel, police, firefighters, or emergency room staff? People in professions that are likely to encounter real crises are trained how to respond swiftly. Their reaction is not an amygdala hijack. People in these professions can't sit around and engage in really deep thinking when a crisis arises, so they are trained how to react quickly and appropriately to a crisis situation. Even if a police officer never has to use his weapon during a real-life encounter, he is trained when and how to do so.

When our emotions allow our amygdala to kick into action, by definition we are biologically forced into a non-thinking mode. Sometimes, without us being aware, the amygdala hijack creeps up on us as a slow burn that builds into a full-blown outburst. If you have ever found yourself in an emotional state in which you just start screaming at someone, realize that your brain is shutting down. Count to ten and then try to regroup and think clearly. You are never at your best when you don't allow yourself to use your brain in a non-emergency situation.

NON-THINKING GUT REACTIONS

THE POWER OF SUBCONSCIOUS FORCES

Research has long shown that, in decision making, people tend to be most led by their initial or "gut" instinct. Non-thinking gut reactions are a combination of powerful subconscious forces and past experiences. While they provide a convenient shortcut at times, they can also derail good decision making. This is why it is important to know how we form these initial gut-level, non-thinking conclusions.

First Impressions

When a person walks into the room, we immediately establish an opinion of him. With one glance, we decide whether he is trustworthy, likeable, or relatable. These instant judgments are based on instincts that we have retained from the primal days of hunting and gathering, and we need to use them. Using them is not wrong, but when these instincts are coupled with other tendencies that will be addressed in this chapter, we could already be on the road to an incorrect initial conclusion.

Through normal developmental experiences, we learn to judge feelings and moods. We learn to recognize facial expressions that tell us when someone is happy or sad. We are sometimes attracted to or have an immediate connection with someone for reasons that we can't explain. Our state of mind also plays a part in our judgment: Are we hungry or tired? Which moods can significantly influence our choices either positively or negatively?

All of these variables impact our first impressions of people and events, and most of these influences stem from our energy levels, emotions, and prejudices. When we form our first impressions, we are judging—or perhaps, more accurately, prejudging people and events, usually in the space of a few seconds or less. While it may seem unfair, we do it because we have to. We simply do not have time to fully examine everything that comes our way or have deeply probing, time-consuming conversations with every single person we meet.

Common Types of Influences

Countless academic articles, published treatises, and commercially available books cover these common psychological influences in great detail, so what follows here is a digestible overview of the most important points. These mental pitfalls are so common and unexpectedly powerful that it is probably worth your time to occasionally refresh your memory and train your mind. For quick reference, near the end of this chapter there will be a brief checklist of the most common habits that pull us in one direction or another.

Framing

Framing is the use of words to influence others. There are some great research studies on how framing can lead to vastly different results. These studies have found that the way information or a question is phrased directly influences the way people respond to it.

For example, the person who gets to name a law has a potentially huge advantage in getting it passed. Great thought was given to calling race-based admissions "affirmative action" rather than "reverse discrimination." Regardless of the merits of the policy, "affirmative" connotes something positive and "action" is viewed in a positive manner. "Reverse" means going backward and "discrimination" is never viewed in a positive light. The underlying theory and intellectual appeal is the same: "Affirmative action" has two positive words and "reverse discrimination" has two negative words. The people who strongly support or disagree with the fundamental aspect of the policy probably wouldn't be swayed by the nomenclature, but a large number of people who can relate to both sides of the issue might be impacted by the framing. The same is true of "pro-choice." "Pro" is in favor of something and "choice" is a word cherished by all Americans. "Pro-choice," again not an accidental phrasing, is very powerful in getting us to side with that view.

If I frame a question about whether the top 2% of income earners should pay their "fair share" of taxes, I have already increased the odds of getting agreement from the other 98% and put that 2% of income earners on the defensive. "Fair" is a term we all agree with; no one likes to be in a situation that is unfair. The typical emotional reaction to this framing is that, of course, people should pay their fair share. This is a great example of successfully framing a political question, because it suggests that the top 2% are currently not paying their fair share.

Sometime in the near future, a law will be passed that contains an enormous amount of wasteful "pork barrel" spending but will also include some positive things. If the proposed law is named "Congressional Wasteful Spending and Nothing Changing Act," it will be dead on arrival. If it has a name like "Full Employment and Fairness Act for Working and Middle Class Families," its chance of passing is greatly increased. As a member of Congress, would you want to be on record as voting against "employment and fairness" for "working and middle class families?" The framing of the title of the proposed law is brilliant.

Be aware of the way information is being framed when you are asked to make a decision or form an opinion. Is the question leading you or forcing you to be on the defensive? If it is, rephrase the question to qualify or eliminate the framing. For example, if someone asks you if you believe that we should do something that is "fair," ask them their definition of fairness and why they think it doesn't exist today. This doesn't assert whether the existing situation is fair or not, but it does challenge the framing and move the conversation to more neutral ground.

Priming

Priming is a powerful and subtle force that can shape our initial reaction to something and, ultimately, our final decision. This force is so subtle that even with a full understanding of the concept, we aren't likely to be aware of it happening. Priming does not involve words (like framing does), but instead encompasses nonverbal influences.

One scientific experiment on priming involved two separate groups of people who were outfitted with headphones playing the same exact content. One group was instructed to shake their heads from side to side, mimicking the physical reaction of saying no while listening to the recorded messages. The other group was instructed to shake their heads up and down, the nonverbal way of indicating agreement or saying yes. Even though both groups listened to the same content, the group who listened while nodding tended to agree with the message, while those who shook their heads were predisposed to disagree with the message.

Priming is a common strategy in negotiating. By reviewing points that have already been agreed upon before approaching the point of disagreement, one person primes the other person into a state of agreement in the same fashion as the experiment with the headphones. This literally gets people nodding their heads when you mention the agreed points.

As priming devices, music and colors have a similar impact. For instance, you probably wouldn't feel relaxed while waiting for a massage if heavy metal music was blasting through the sound system. Sophisticated marketers are intently aware of the impact of colors and packaging on the consumer's decision to buy. Certain colors are associated with hunger and, as such, are often used in advertisements for a restaurant.

Once, at a fundraising event, I was able to meet and talk with the featured speaker and have my picture taken with him. I admire this person a lot. I noticed that he was clear about where he would stand and where I would stand while the photographer took the picture of us shaking hands. Although I did not know why he insisted on this stance at the time, I knew there was a reason he wanted this position in the photo, so I researched it.

In countries where people shake hands, we generally use the right hand, even if the handshaking is taking place between two left-handed people. My hero knew this and placed himself on my right side (putting me to the left of him). Why? By being to my right and extending his right hand, he limited my ability to extend my right hand, which would let the photographer memorialize the fact that he appeared to be the dominant person in the photograph.

Framing + Priming = A Powerful Combination

There is a study of voting patterns showing that people have a tendency to vote in support of increased educational funding when the polling location is inside a school. Apparently, merely being present in the school while voting tends to influence people to be in favor of supporting the educational system.

Let's say there is a need for a budget increase, but the research shows that almost all of it is due to excessive golfing off-sites by members of the board of education. If signs saying "On July 1, Vote for the Children" are posted (framing), and the voting is held in a school (priming), unless we are very aware of all details included in the budget, we are likely to vote "for the children." What kind of person would vote against the children? What would the impact be on the electorate if, instead, the signs said, "On July 1, Vote to Continue to Fund Golf Outings for Board Members" and the voting took place at city hall?

The previous examples are not about whether school budgets should be increased or whether any particular law should be passed. It is about the enormous impact of framing and priming on many aspects of our lives.

Halo Effect

When you have a very positive first impression of someone, you are more prone to view everything you learn about him or her in a positive light. This is the "halo effect," and it happens commonly with people we admire, like movie stars or certain politicians, as well as in both business and personal relationships. When a star executive is brought into a company, it is not uncommon for it to take years before higher-ups recognize his flaws. His reputation for past success is established as their first impression, and then the halo effect lessens the impact of his poor decisions or mistakes until he makes one too many or one that is too costly. In personal relationships, we may be attracted to a charming person and fail to see major issues that are clear to others. Both of these are common halo effect distortions.

The influence of the "likeability" factor cannot be overemphasized. Earlier I cited an example in which the sales of the Dodge Durango shot up based on the likeability of Will Ferrell in character as Ron Burgundy, and the same thing happens with every government and large corporation, probably far more than you realize.

A great example of the halo effect can be seen in the various polling numbers throughout Barack Obama's presidency. I have never met him, but based on his numerous appearances on television, he seems like a likeable and relatable person. Both during and after his re-election campaign, polls showed that most Americans held him in high regard personally, but that they disagreed with the future direction of the country. Think about that. He is the leader of the country, and the majority of people don't like the direction the country is going. Still, the polls were flipped when people rated him as an individual. This is not an anti-Obama observation. The same can be observed about Ronald Reagan, the Republican president who was considered the first modern day "Teflon President," nicknamed after the nonstick cookware because the scandals and criticism that surrounded his presidency didn't seem to affect his individual popularity with the public.

I grudgingly admit that I am a beleaguered fan of the New York Jets although they have become a bit hapless in the past couple of seasons. Their former head coach, Rex Ryan, comes across as an affable, straight-forward person that the press usually adores. In the brutal world of the National Football League, where your job is rarely secure, did he remain on the job because he was the most qualified and the New York Jets were a great team or because he was well-liked?

While the halo effect is usually associated with positive traits and characteristics, it can have negative connotations as well. If you dislike a particular political candidate, you have a greater tendency to dislike all of his decisions and positions. If you didn't vote for Obama or didn't like him, you probably decided early on that Obamacare was not good for you or the country, even at a point in time in which you were uninformed about the details of the new law. To support your view, you would have a tendency to underrate the benefits of the bill and amplify the detriments. The exact opposite is true for strong supporters of President Obama. Many enthusiastically supported Obamacare although they neither understood nor read the law.

Extreme cases of halo effect can cause people to blindly follow what they are told without question or critical thinking. This can be harmless in many cases, like rooting for your school or company. The danger is when we follow people, ideologies, or political parties without being intellectually critical or honest.

Familiarity

It is well documented that we tend to favor the types of people and things with which we are familiar. Our basic animal instinct is to immediately assess potential threats of any kind. Beyond physical threats, we may perceive threats to our relationships, job security, reputation, and so on, which all ties into Abraham Maslow's hierarchy of needs. First, we need food and shelter to survive. Then, we need the feeling of security regarding those basic needs. If we see something that looks familiar and, in our own past experience, hasn't been a threat, we gain comfort and relax.

This is why Ponzi schemes are almost always perpetuated by someone of the same ethnic, racial, or religious background as the targeted victims. The term "Ponzi scheme" is named after Charles Ponzi, who preyed on fellow Italian immigrants in the New England area. Other major frauds of this type have historically targeted people from the same ethnic, racial, or religious background as the scheme's mastermind. People who look or act like us seem familiar and nonthreatening, so we let our guard down. We don't use the same amount of caution we would if someone very different and unfamiliar approached us.

There is a natural tendency to look for ourselves in other people. We like people who are like us. That means we have an inherent bias to be around, and to hire, people with our type of personality, educational background, and so on. What's wrong with that? This could leave out someone who could be wildly successful on the team but has a different educational pedigree or set of life experiences.

A few years ago, retired Supreme Court Justice Sandra Day O'Connor gave a speech that I attended. An audience member questioned her about her view on continuing diversity on the Supreme Court. Justice O'Connor shared that of course she believed in continuing diversity, as she was subject to harsh gender-based discrimination. When she graduated from Stanford University Law School, she was unable to get a legal job simply because she was a woman. This wasn't the case of a glass ceiling; it was the case of a steel-reinforced concrete door that prevented her from entering the building.

Interestingly, she then added that she felt the Supreme Court needed to also have diversity of thought and experiences. If all of the very talented and intellectual Supreme Court justices were to come solely from academia, even though they would be of different genders or have varying ethnic, racial, and religious backgrounds, they would all be academics with very similar experiences during their adult lives. There would be surface-level differences, but not necessarily meaningful experiential differences.

Name Recognition

Name recognition is a type of familiarity, but it requires a brief description of its own. If a name is familiar to us, we are more comfortable with it. When we know a name, whether it is a brand of toothpaste, a fast food chain, or a political candidate, we have a preconceived notion of whether or not that brand or name is a sound choice.

Name recognition is a powerful force in politics, even among educated people. Jon Huntsman ran for the Republican Party's presidential nomination in 2012. Although he was highly regarded and thought of as one of the brightest and most thoughtful candidates, he did not do well in the primaries and dropped out of the race. Despite being the most recent United States ambassador to China and a former governor of the state of Utah, he didn't have the same name recognition that other candidates had.

People tend to choose the candidate whose name they recognize. There is a natural tendency to choose something familiar over the unknown. Name recognition is another version of the earlier example of antelope grazing in the field being comfortable with a fellow grazer they have seen before. We believe the name we recognize is already "known" to us, which gives us a greater degree of comfort over something or someone unknown. In Daniel Kahneman's book *Thinking, Fast and Slow*, this type of bias is referred to as "pastness."

In the case of political candidates, we trick ourselves into thinking that the person whose name seems familiar must be a better candidate. After all, how can you vote for someone totally unfamiliar to you? Unless you are aware of where the candidates stand on issues that are important to you, either candidate would be a blind choice.

Consider how many celebrities may have been voted into office based upon the name recognition advantage: Ronald Reagan, Arnold Schwarzenegger, Al Franken, Jesse Ventura, and John Glenn, to name a few. It is safe to assume, based on the way we think, that many people voted for them simply because they knew the candidate by name.

Branding

America excels at marketing, and marketing is based on consumer psychology. We take great pains to create, polish, and defend our brands. The whole purpose of branding is to get people to associate the brand with quality, value, and other factors like popularity or affluence. Getting people to trust the brand is key.

The American car industry has had a branding problem in recent years. Many Americans who would otherwise prefer to buy a car from an American company buy foreign cars, mostly Japanese and German, mainly based on the perception that the German and Japanese cars are better engineered and manufactured. That is why the current advertisements for Volkswagen all stress the benefits of German engineering, even going so far as to refer to the car as "das auto." Your reaction to these ads might be that German or Japanese cars *are* better engineered, so the plight of American car manufacturers is unfortunate, but true. What if it wasn't always true?

Chrysler Corporation and Mitsubishi Motors Corporation entered into a 50/50 joint venture to produce cars some years ago. In 1989, they had a plant in Illinois that produced the Mitsubishi Eclipse and the Chrysler Eagle Talon. While there were minor differences in the colors and shape of the two car exteriors, they were almost identical cars that were produced in the same manufacturing facility by the same workers. If you were an American looking to buy that type of car in 1989 and you would prefer to buy from an American company, why would you even consider buying the Mitsubishi Eclipse when you could have purchased the Eagle Talon? The only logical reason is that you had a prior perception that Japanese cars were always superior to American cars.

Branding on Steroids—Politics

The single most common subject in which I have seen branding influence smart people to make decisions without thinking is politics. When we register to vote, we are asked which party we want to join. While a voter may not completely agree with either major party, there is still a tendency to register as either a Democrat or a Republican. In most states, a voter must be a registered member of a party to vote in that party's primary election; that alone is a powerful incentive to join one of the two parties. Once you choose your party affiliation, you have labeled yourself.

When you choose and publicly share your political party, you associate yourself with that party. While there is nothing wrong with sharing your enthusiasm, there is a reason people avoid bringing up politics at cocktail parties. It can become a very emotional topic. If you are a strong supporter of your particular political party, how seriously do you consider the other party's candidate? Do you approach the issue with a complete lack of bias, using only your analytical, thinking mind? Can you recognize branding at work in your decisions?

The season leading up to the 2012 United States presidential election became highly politicized and nasty. There were around a dozen possible swing states, and only a fraction of those were deemed particularly important due to the number of electoral votes they represented. Of note is that the opinions of the voters in these swing states didn't change much over the course of several months. Polls consistently show that almost all voting Americans make up their minds about which party to vote for nearly a year before the election is held. Is this open-minded and analytical or emotional? In starker terms, in 38 of the 50 states comprising the entire nation (76%), the election is all but over before the first high-dollar political ad hits primetime television. All of the various publicly available polls have determined that, outside of a bombshell pertaining to news that would be extraordinarily helpful or harmful to one of the two major candidates, we can predict with statistical certainty how most of the states will vote.

My wife and I were at a dinner party when the topic of politics came up. We were discussing an upcoming election for a US Senate position in another state. I lamented that neither of the two major parties had a candidate who was remotely close to being qualified to serve in any leadership role, much less the US Senate. One woman responded that the choice would be easy for her; she only votes for candidates from one party. This woman is smart and very accomplished, but is this a smart approach to decision making?

Anchoring

Anchoring is simple. If you start out somewhat "stuck" to a point, you don't vary far from that point. Like a boat that is anchored, you may move around a bit, but you won't move far from the anchor. All animals, including humans, try to avoid loss and thus are naturally risk-averse. Anchoring is part of our instinctive behavior. It drives decision-making outcomes in a very subtle way and is particularly notable in decisions involving numbers.

Anchoring is taught as an effective technique in advanced negotiating classes but limits us when it comes to thinking of a brand new approach to something. We think of improving on something, but we do not want to do something radically different. We are anchored to the original concept, even if our fundamental assumptions about that concept have changed. It can also skew our perception of value and drive us to take larger risks or assume greater costs than we would have without the anchoring. Retail sales, stock market prices, and real estate sales are perfect examples of anchoring that drives behavior.

Most retailers mark up goods they sell by 100% or more over wholesale cost. When the sign in the window advertises a 30% discount, we slow down to look for bargains we might find. The typical consumer feels like he is getting a great deal at a 30% discount, and he is if his thought process is anchored by the original retail price. A 100% markup discounted 30% is still marked up way over cost, which, without anchoring, doesn't seem like such a great deal.

In a transparent market like the US stock exchange, real-time stock prices are readily accessible via the internet. If Apple stock was as high as $700 within the past year and traded frequently between $550 and $600 for several months, I may think that its fair value of $600 per share is about right.[7] My opinion would be anchored by the fact that Apple was valued at $700 and then spent significant time trading around $600. Now, however, it is trading at around $450. Is Apple really a $400 stock, a $500 stock, a $600 stock, or a $700 stock? What if Apple had never traded above $500 per share? This might color my view, but it shouldn't. The reason it traded at $700 and the reason it is now trading in the mid $400s are both very important considerations, but if you are anchored to the fact that it once traded as high as $700, you might automatically see the stock as a steal at $450.

---

[7] Apple subsequently had a stock split. While the specific numbers would be different now, the point is exactly the same.

What if you are dealing in an opaque market where the exact value isn't that transparent and may just be the opinion of a chosen few? If you have ever bought or sold real estate, you've seen a classic example of anchoring in an opaque market. Anchoring can come into play in real estate in a couple of ways. First, despite a recent soft housing market, the sellers may feel that their house is special. Perhaps it was worth quite a bit before the market downturn, so the price they are willing to sell it for is above the current market value. The seller is anchored by the home's former value. Second, and most important, is the list price, which usually serves as the key anchor in negotiations.

Here is a real example that shows how anchoring can kill a deal: A seller had a lovely home in a great area with tremendous views of the surrounding woods and lake. The house was first listed on the market for $4.9 million. An all-cash offer (not contingent on the buyer getting a mortgage) came in at $4.4 million. Although this offer was 90% of the asking price, the seller held firm and refused to sell. Her conclusion was that they did not have to sell immediately and that this offer was too low. The seller felt the house was worth $4.9 million or very close to that. The buyer disagreed and chose to buy another house instead.

Many months later, after no other offers came in, the selling price was reduced to $4.2 million. The next offer was for $3.8 million from a buyer who could also pay for it without financing. The inspection process revealed a very small defect that would take about $20,000 to fix, and the buyer insisted that the seller remedy this before the sale closed. The seller, still seething over the prospect of selling the house for so much less than the already-reduced selling price, refused to do so. The second buyer also moved on and purchased a home in another area.

The house continued to sit on the market. The selling price was reduced further until the house finally sold for $2.8 million. What was the house really worth? The only thing we can say with certainty is that house has a market value of $2.8 million based on its selling price.

Let's look at the anchoring during various points in time before the sale. The first anchoring point was the asking price of $4.9 million. Whether or not $4.9 million was a reasonable price, it anchored the first offer. The first offer was only 10% less than the asking price, which means that if the seller had agreed, the house would have sold for $4.4 million, which would have become its market value. When the house didn't sell and no other offers came in, the asking price was reduced to $4.2 million, which became the next anchoring point for potential buyers. Unfortunately, the seller was still emotionally anchored to the original $4.9 million asking price. If the first offer of $4.4 million had been accepted, the buyer would have had a deal that was only 10% off the asking price. The second offer was for $3.8 million, which was just about 10% less than the new asking price of $4.2 million. If the second buyer's offer for $3.8 million had been accepted, the first potential buyer would have been glad that their offer of $4.4 million was rejected because, in retrospect, they would have almost overpaid for the house by $600,000.

The last person seems to have gotten a good deal. If you were the person who actually bought this house, how would you describe this deal to your friends? Would you tell them that it was a steal? You got a house that had originally listed for $4.9 million for $2.8 million, a more than 40% discount from the original asking price.

The seller could have sold it to the first buyer for $4.4 million, but because she was emotionally anchored to the original asking price of $4.9 million, she cost herself a lot of money when she eventually sold the house for $2.8 million ($1.6 million less than the original offer).

Anchoring in Negotiations

In 2013, professional baseball player Alex Rodriquez, better known as "A-Rod," was suspended for 162 games for allegedly taking performance-enhancing drugs (PEDs). Everyone has a view on A-Rod, whether they think he did something wrong or whether the suspension was just. It is worthwhile to examine the initial suspension offered by the commissioner and its likely impact on the final judgment.

Under the Collective Bargaining Agreement between the Major League Baseball organization (the MLB) and the players' union, this case was required to go to arbitration. That means an independent arbitrator would rule on the merits of the case and then decide the appropriate punishment. Before arbitration began, the Commissioner of Baseball wanted to suspend A-Rod for 211 games.

Ryan Braun, a star player with the Milwaukee Brewers, first denied, then admitted to using PEDs and received a 65-game suspension. Through an agreement with the MLB, all other first time offenders would receive a 50-game suspension. A-Rod denied everything and said that he shouldn't be suspended at all.

Without knowing any more facts, here are the realistic outcomes for the number of games A-Rod could expect to be suspended: 0, 50, 211, or somewhere between 50 and 211. The most important thing for the Commissioner of Baseball was to convince the arbitrator that A-Rod had used PEDs and that he deserved more than the 65-game suspension that was meted out to Ryan Braun. The commissioner needed to establish that his initial suspension of 211 games was not arbitrary but instead was justified in some manner. If he could establish that justification and if A-Rod's culpability could be established, the 211-game suspension would serve as an anchor. In the end, the arbitrator ruled that A-Rod violated the rules against using PEDs and suspended him for 162 games.

What if the arbitrator thought that A-Rod was twice as bad as Ryan Braun, who admitted he used PEDs? In that case, A-Rod would receive twice as much punishment as Braun, or 130 games. The commissioner either took the 50-game suspension given to first time offenders and added 161 games to it to get to his total of 211 games, or he took the biggest suspension on record, 105 games, and made it slightly more than twice that. I don't know exactly how his office came up with 211 games, but I am confident about why that number wasn't 212. An entire baseball season is 162 games. A 212-game suspension would have punished A-Rod with the first offender's standard 50-game suspension plus one entire season, which would have appeared to be excessive. Once the arbitrator found that A-Rod had violated the rules, he could reduce the commissioner's suspension from 211 games to 162 games to appear fair and still wipe out an entire season for A-Rod. A 100-game suspension would have allowed A-Rod to come back for part of the season to help his team win a championship.

Why is this "anchoring?" If we view the 211-game suspension as not being wildly arbitrary, it anchors the amount of games A-Rod could be suspended. If the commissioner's agenda was to get A-Rod out for an unprecedented entire season, this opening offer was brilliant.

Anchoring—Inertia and Status Quo

There is an emotional inertia to keep things the way they are, unless there is a clear need to change. We are anchored to the current state and assume that it is the best choice. We are also psychologically anchored to the status quo. If we suggest a break from the current state, especially if it is a substantial change, the decision maker is at risk both emotionally and organizationally. Since we are hardwired to avoid risk, there is a strong emotional pull to stay with the current state unless there is an emergency, which was probably created because we ignored all prior signs that the current state would not last. *Who Moved My Cheese?* by Spencer Johnson is a great book that cleverly illustrates our common attachment to the status quo.

A smart move in decision making is to consider all alternatives and assume that the status quo does not exist. If you were to design a new educational system in your state, would you assume that the schools should be closed during the summer months because that is the way it has always been done? That is anchoring. The only way to avoid anchoring when something needs to change is to craft a new solution from scratch and question all existing assumptions. The current way of doing things may not be entirely wrong, but in order to start with a clean mental slate and analyze the situation without bias, we have to ignore the prior system.

Sunk Cost Fallacy

Sunk cost fallacy is a further investment of monetary or emotional resources into a situation that already has suboptimal results. Sunk cost fallacy is easiest to see when money is involved, although it can also apply to personal relationships. In the investment world, sunk cost fallacy is often referred to as "throwing good money after bad." It creates an emotionally-driven decision that is usually motivated by our instinctive aversion to loss coupled with a fair dose of ego that prevents us from objectively acknowledging the current state of affairs.

It is well documented by reams of research that people hate losing more than they enjoy winning. In fact, research has shown that a common motivation among "winners," whether in business or sports, is abhorrence to losing. We like to win, but we hate to lose. Because we don't want to settle for the loss, we invest further in the situation in hopes that things will turn around. This almost always results in a poor decision.

While past events are relevant in that we should learn from the past and use it to help us understand how we can improve future results, all decisions should be forward looking. The past cannot be changed.

Let's say you are self-employed and are just finishing a large consulting project. You have a few proposals out for your next project but no signed deals. You determine that this would be a great time to take that well-earned vacation, so you pick your vacation spot and find a good deal on airfare. Suddenly, you are awarded a new consulting project that will bring in significant income, which you definitely need. Unfortunately, the client wants you to start the project when you are planning to be on vacation.

The trip is planned and the airfare is nonrefundable. What do you do? How much will the nonrefundable airfare weigh on your decision process? Let's say the airfare is $500 and the cost of the hotel stay is $2,000; the profit from the new project is $5,000. From a mathematical perspective, the $500 is fixed. Assuming that there is no cancellation fee, the hotel will cost the same now or later if you take the same vacation. What are you focusing on in your decision-making process?

You need the vacation and are looking forward to it, and you have already paid for your flight, but monetarily, the balance is in favor of forfeiting the $500 nonrefundable airfare. After the consulting project, you can plan another trip and will have more money to spend on your enjoyment and relaxation. Unless you are so stressed that you can't wait another month to go on vacation, you should accept the new project and change your vacation plans. Whatever you decide, the $500 is a sunk cost. You cannot get it back, so it should not be a factor in your decision.

In the corporate world and in government, sunk cost fallacy runs rampant. A corporate executive or high-ranking official pours extra money into a failing project that he launched because investing more money may seem like the only way to save his career and reputation. Unfortunately, it almost never works out well.

If you bought shares of a stock at $100 and then the price dropped to $80, what would you do? The only thing to focus on is what the stock will do from there. Your broker may advise you to buy more stock at $80, so that your average cost per share is $90, but beware! The psychology behind this seemingly attractive idea is powerful, but misguided. The idea is that if you buy more, you are only losing $10 per share ($90 average price, less $80 at the current value), whereas if you don't buy, you are losing $20 a share ($100 cost, less the $80 value). The only questions you should ask yourself are forward looking. What do you think the stock price will do from this day forward over the period of time you are willing to hold it? You may be "averaging down" to a cost of $90 per share, but if you follow your broker's advice, you have also doubled your risk and now own twice as many shares of the stock than you previously had. Are you comfortable with the additional risk?

If I write ten pages that my editor determines are not going to be useful or relevant, do I accept her criticism and advice objectively, or is my judgment colored by the fact that it took real effort to write those pages (sunk cost)? Do I insist on including them anyway? If I am a general in the US Army, do I invest more troops and machinery into a war because 500 hundred soldiers have already died and I want their sacrifice to be for good reason? Do I stay in a dysfunctional relationship with someone because I have already invested five years of my life with this person?

Sunk cost fallacy is prevalent in many important decisions, but it is very easy to fix. Remember that all decisions should be forward looking.

You can learn from the past, but you cannot change it. Don't let sunk costs drive your future choices.

Prejudice

Prejudice is another subconscious outlook based on generalizations rather than fact. We have a tendency to prejudge just about everything, and these judgments are influenced in many ways by our past experiences and personal or societal beliefs. We need to be aware that prejudging someone or something is commonplace, but we shouldn't automatically make our initial impression our final judgment.

Let's say you are in charge of casting roles for an upcoming Hollywood movie in which the main characters are athletes from different sports and different walks of life who are stranded together in a dire situation. The director wants you to cast two athletes from each of three different sports: basketball, football, and golf. In each sport, one athlete is from a poor background and the other athlete is from a wealthy background. What types of people will you call in to audition? You may think that you don't have a prejudiced bone in your body, but you are probably not going into these casting calls without some idea of what type of person would best fit each role.

At the end of the movie, the athletes have escaped to safety and captured the nation's attention. They get to meet the President of the United States. Who will you cast as the president? What makes someone presidential in your mind? What type of demeanor would they have? Would Hollywood have cast the same kind of actor to play the president fifty years ago?

Almost everyone has unconscious prejudices. Some are based on gender, ethnicity, race, or religion, and some are based on where you grew up and went to school or what you have been exposed to in life or on television. Did you choose women to portray 50% of the athletes? Did you choose a woman to portray at least one of the athletes? Without me raising this point, what was your thought process?

Prejudice Based on Generalizations (And They Are All Based on Generalizations)

You are hiring a new employee for your company. You are aware that there is a certain subgroup of the population, categorized by race, ethnic group, religion, or gender, that is perceived as being weaker than the general population in math and science and has historically not done as well in those types of careers. If a member of this subgroup interviews for the job with you, should you take the subgroup's statistical weakness into consideration? The answer should be a clear no, and not just due to political correctness.

The fact that this subgroup possibly hasn't performed as well in math and science does not mean that the individual you are interviewing is not exceptional in math and science. If math and science are relevant to the job, the candidate can be tested. As we will discuss later in the section on pattern recognition, data needs to be applied to your decisions appropriately. In this case, prejudice, even if it is based on some arguably reliable data, could lead you to not hire an outstanding candidate who could have been a valuable employee for your company.

What if there is another subgroup that has historically been more successful in business and reliable data purports to prove this fact? Will you favor applicants from this subgroup based on the presumption that everyone in the subgroup is superior to others in business? You shouldn't. All prejudice creates the same problem, and a positive prejudice toward one group is a negative prejudice toward other groups. When we brand one subgroup as superior, we are branding all other groups as inferior.

Prejudice by Educational Ranking

Staying with the job application scenario, let's examine something that most employers look at when hiring—education. Where you went to school and how you did is especially important when applying for your first job out of college, but after that, it doesn't really matter, right? Wrong.

As an attorney, I am acutely aware that certain schools have a reputation for producing the "best" lawyers, but what makes an attorney one of the best? How is "best" defined and by whom? *U.S. News and World Report*, a highly reputable magazine, is well known for its rankings of educational institutions by area of study, which includes law schools. The importance placed on these rankings in the current market cannot be overstated, as they become dispositive of the types and availability of jobs for graduates of the approximately150 ranked schools. Where you went to school almost always impacts your career and the way others perceive you even decades after graduation.

While lawyers, especially very successful ones, take pride in being smart and highly analytical, if you ask them where they would go to recruit future legal stars outside of their individual alma mater, most will list the same top-ranked schools. They are just following the advice of Claude Raines, who said in the movie *Casablanca*, "Round up the usual suspects." Despite all of their intellectual firepower and keen analytical prowess, these successful attorneys are as affected by branding and prejudice as any of us.

One could argue that the higher-ranked law schools must be better because they only take students with higher grade point averages and higher LSAT scores. While these are accepted metrics for deciding which undergraduate candidates will do better in graduate school, the underlying assumption there is that performance as an undergraduate is a direct indication of how well the student will perform as an actual lawyer both immediately after graduating and even five, ten, or twenty years later.

Energy

Those candy bar commercials you see on television are right; You really aren't your best self when you're hungry. There is a famous study that shows a parole board gave vastly different parolee reviews based on which part of the day the decisions were made. The parole board was aware of the gravity of their decisions. If they granted parole before the inmate was ready, they risked letting a potential criminal back into the general population. If they denied parole, they risked damaging the inmate's life more than necessary.

The pressure of these important decisions is energy depleting. As more mental effort is exerted, more physical energy is burned.

The influencing factor for the parole board didn't appear to be the specific time of day, but the time that had elapsed since the board's last food break. The average rate for approving parole requests over the course of a typical day was 35%. After having their appetites satisfied and their energy levels replenished, the approval rate was 65%. While it appears that there is a 30% difference, which is significant, the difference is actually 86% (30% increase in approvals, divided by the 35% average rate). However, as time elapsed since they last ate, the approval rate dropped. A couple of hours after a meal, the approval rate declined until there were almost 0% approvals right before the next meal. These judges didn't plan to have a differing level of approvals based on how much energy they had; it just happened, and that is a huge swing based on energy levels. If you are being judged by a panel (hopefully not a parole board), try to schedule your appearance right after the judges will have eaten!

Tony Schwartz, CEO of the Energy Project, was one of the lecturers during a three-day partners' event I attended a few years ago. Tony is an expert on mental and physical energy and has applied his research to the corporate arena. While he did not directly address the mental strain of thinking, he did address the mental and physical energy we lose during the average business day. One of his main ideas was that we spend a lot of effort managing time, but nearly no time managing our energy. His presentation was geared toward partners who spent most of their days dealing with client problems and meetings. Most of these professionals were tired and stressed both during the day and at the end of the day. If this happens to you almost every business day, you will not be happy either going to work or at home after work. Tony spoke about the need to recharge physically and mentally during the day. One of his suggestions was to take a non-smoking smoker's break. Smokers break every one to two hours and go outside to smoke. It takes five to ten minutes to smoke a cigarette, during which time your mind can wander. His suggestion was that you don't smoke, but take that mental break, step outside to get some fresh air and sunlight, and eat a small but healthy snack.

Heuristics Checklist

This list doesn't cover every possible heuristic that can impact your decision making, but instead is a brief review of the most common subconscious influencers mentioned previously.

INFLUENCE	EXAMPLE
Framing Uses words to influence an outcome	"Fair share"; "Affirmative Action"
Priming Nonverbal influences like colors, location, or physical action	Nodding your head up and down primes you to be more agreeable
Anchoring Attachment to one piece of information that may be irrelevant to the current circumstance; an emotionally charged resistance to change	The asking price in real estate
Sunk Cost Fallacy Further investment of resources into a situation that already has suboptimal results or is unfavorably imbalanced; throwing good money after bad	Buying more stock to average down your cost
Halo Effect An existing strong like or dislike of a person that colors our judgment of him by transferring the same feelings to unrelated attributes	A person that is likeable, with a prior positive reputation, gets to make many mistakes before being challenged
Familiarity / Name Recognition/ Branding Tendency to trust people and things that are known to us, even without cause or conscious reason	Ponzi schemes

Other Traps:

PREJUDICE	ENERGY
Prejudice goes far beyond race, religion, or social status. Remember prejudice by school ranking? Be aware of your subtle assumptions to reveal hidden prejudices that may be working against you.	Lack of energy, sleep, or other basic physical need depletes the brain's ability to function at peak capacity

THINKING LIGHTLY

THINKING WE ARE THINKING

Thinking Lightly is a higher level of focus than an instantaneous visceral reaction, but it is also a trap for the unwary, and almost all of us are unwary. Here, we are aware that we are using our brains to think, but the pitfall is that we think we are using the full power of our brains when we aren't. Using the full power of the brain requires us to operate at full energy, which we are designed to avoid and which can't be done all of the time, so we slide into an easier way of deciding something.

When we go into a room, we flip the switch to turn on the lights. We can see the room illuminate, so we know the lights are working. If a room has a dimmer switch, we can turn the lights on just enough to see. We have engaged the lighting system, but not at full capacity. Thinking is not an on-off switch; we are not either thinking 100% or not at all. Thinking Lightly is similar to using the dimmer switch to produce the minimal amount of light necessary to see.

Thinking Deeply requires that the dimmer switch be turned on to full capacity. It uses all of the power in our brains, but also requires commensurately more energy. When we use a lighting system, we can use our vision to see what the strength of the light is and whether we need to adjust it a bit. There isn't a clear visual indicator to discern how much we are really thinking. We most often delude ourselves into thinking we are using the full capacity of our mental abilities (Thinking Deeply), when we have only turned on our mental dimmer switch half way (Thinking Lightly).

Expertise

We can usually sense what the proper course of action is by using our years of prior experience or training. This is an efficient and normal way to make decisions. Something that doesn't seem right to a trained detective or a medical professional might be completely overlooked by a layperson. If we are not an expert on the subject at hand or the stakes are very high, even in our area of expertise, we need to rely on more than our gut reaction.

Here is the crux of the problem: We have a strong tendency to come to an initial conclusion on something even outside of our area of expertise either because we don't realize we are out of our area of competency or we think we are smart and naturally good at making decisions on all things. This happens frequently with successful people who view their academic pedigree or money-making ability as validation of their overall decision-making skills and is commonplace even when they are making decisions that are completely outside the sphere of their successful career.

US Soccer—Women: 15   Men: 0

The US women's national soccer team has won a total of fifteen World Cups, Olympic Gold Medals, and Algarve Cups (a significant international competition). The US men's national soccer team has never won a world championship. Same country. Same sport. Big difference. Why?

I have thought lightly about this. Let's first rule out that all of the women, but none of the men, have a hereditary gene that predisposes them to be exceptional soccer players. What about diet and exercise? I would assume that this is not a distinguishing factor, as both teams eat and train at top facilities. What about gender? The men's team doesn't play against women's teams in competition. The competitions are men against men and women against women, which should rule out gender as a factor. What could be the reason(s) that the women's national team is almost always highly ranked and the men's national team is not?

Here is my hypothesis: In the United States, football, basketball, and baseball are by far the most glamorous sports for men. They are the most televised, they have huge American fan bases, and their star players make a serious amount of money. This is not true for soccer. A lot of exceptional athletes play multiple sports when they are younger. When male athletes enter high school, they drop soccer and gravitate to the more popular sports that they see on television and that would bring them a higher social status among their classmates.

This is not so for women. Women don't have the same array of competing choices. They may play softball, lacrosse, basketball, or other sports, but these women's sports aren't glamorized like the popular men's sports. In other words, if you are a young woman who is skilled at soccer, there is a much better chance that you will stick with it instead of dropping it to play another sport.

Have I thought about this? Yes, but only lightly. I have used my brain, but only enough to casually speculate. My theory makes sense and seems "about right" to me. Should I be put in charge of a project to ensure that the US men's national team will win the next World Cup? Obviously I should not—at least not based on this thinking light "analysis."

My theory includes a couple of key assumptions that I have not verified. Did most of the bigger, stronger, faster male athletes actually drop soccer for other sports? If they did, have I interviewed enough people to determine why, sort the reasons into similar categories, and spot predictive trends in behavior? I haven't.

I also compared US men to US women. Did I compare US men to men's teams from other countries to see why the other countries are more successful in soccer? Did I compare the US women's team to women's teams from other countries? Did I take into consideration that talented players from other countries frequently drop out of school at an early age to concentrate solely on soccer, while most US soccer players do not? Did I approach this problem with the assumption that I am wrong? The answer is no to all of the above.

Regardless of whether my hypothesis turns out to be correct, my analysis was limited. I was Thinking Lightly, not Thinking Deeply. If I really thought deeply about this by using more than assumptions and a little data,

I would likely come up with many more possible factors than mentioned previously, but this assumptive Thinking Lightly approach happens every day, even with decisions of great importance, and especially by people who are intelligent and accomplished.

Most often, we are really *not* thinking as much as we think we are, meaning that we are using our brains, but not in an intensive, fully engaged way. We are not unconscious; we are aware that we are about to make a choice but are not concentrating on that choice. There has been a lot of research in this area, and all of the research makes it clear that while our minds are whirring, we are usually stuck in a mental loop of replaying biases and Thinking Lightly. I have heard this referred to as, "We think we are thinking when we really aren't thinking," but a more accurate description is that we think we are Thinking Deeply when we are really Thinking Lightly. It is the same difference between intense exercise and moving at a light jog. Both involve physical activity and are not to be confused with being a couch potato, but everyone knows that a light jog is a warm up and an advanced cycling class is a much more intensive workout.

The Path of Least Resistance

All animals are hardwired to conserve energy. Lions in the jungle will sprint to catch prey. If they are successful, they eat heartily and then rest. Even if they don't catch their prey, they rest before they plan their next hunt. A lion with too many unsuccessful hunts will become more tired with each burst of energy and less likely to be a successful hunter. Humans are no different. Remember the story about the energy level of the parole board? There is a natural, biological aversion to excessive use of energy. We don't operate as well when we are tired. Real thinking isn't trying to remember the name of that actor you saw in the movie last week or watching an episode of *Jeopardy* and trying to play the game at home. That's short-term memory recall, not Thinking Deeply. Thinking Deeply requires a lot of physical energy, primarily from glucose, and we are physically unable to exert that much physical energy too often.

Based on this natural tendency to conserve energy, we subconsciously search for the easiest way to accomplish a task. This doesn't mean a person is mentally or physically lazy, just a normal human being. To make the task easy, we search our memory for recent experiences to confirm or refute our initial reaction. At least two things normally occur at this point: First, we are subconsciously seeking confirming data and only confirming data. Second, we rely on memories of recent experiences more than memories of things that happened a long time ago. A headline about something you read yesterday will carry much more weight than a headline from a year ago.

A Lot of Thinking Lightly Does Not Equal Thinking Deeply

The average practicing doctor sees numerous patients in a single day. As she sees the patients and reviews their charts, she is viewing symptoms and the person's medical history and assessing the probable problem and likely solution based on her years of training and experience. She is drawing upon her expertise or "thin slicing," in the parlance of Malcolm Gladwell's book *Blink*.

As described in *Blink*, the term "thin slicing" is used by psychologists to describe how people are capable of formulating a conclusion "based on the thinnest slices of experience." It is the process by which we can come to the right answer in the blink of an eye. In the case of our doctor, she is basing her reactions on years of highly intensive training. She is thin slicing. She can't be engaged in Thinking Deeply, because there is a waiting room full of people and she doesn't have the time or the energy to think deeply about each of them. The real test for her, and all professionals, is to spot the cases in which she needs to think deeply about the issue confronting her in order to diagnose it or call in an expert that has seen the same problem before *and* has already thought deeply about it. Getting another point of view and experiential learning from a colleague is always the right choice when needed, but two or three professionals Thinking Lightly do not equal one person Thinking Deeply. As pointed out in *Blink,* conclusions based on thin slicing are often erroneous.

"Facts"

I have never spent even one minute trying to memorize the words to a song or lines from a movie, but I know some of them quite well. How did I come to be able to repeat them word for word without even trying? Simple repetition. If we hear things often enough, it becomes easy to recall them. This is not just true about music or movies but many things. When you repeatedly hear something on television that appears to be true, the narrative becomes a "fact" that everyone "knows," even if it's not true.

In this fast-paced world, which requires us to make more decisions more quickly than our predecessors, the factual basis for our initial reactions is often built on preconceived notions or the conditioning of information presented as facts. This is a natural conditioning and saves us a lot of energy analyzing whether facts are actually facts or not, especially when they seem "about right." While unwittingly memorizing song lyrics is generally harmless, constant bombardment of "facts" asserted by television and other news sources can be quite damaging.

I drink almond milk instead of dairy milk most days. I also take a few vitamins that I think will help me, including Omega 3 (fish oil) pills and red yeast rice to reduce cholesterol. I have heard and read many times that almond milk is better for you later in life when you need calcium and that you should reduce your consumption of dairy products. I've also heard beneficial things about Omega 3 and red yeast rice. Do I think my habits are reasonable? Yes. Do I know as absolute fact that these are the best choices for me? No. I don't have the time or the skills to do the scientific research myself to determine whether the almond milk or the supplements are the right choices for me. Instead, I am following some level of accepted knowledge. If you and I met at a cocktail party and you told me that you thought that my habits were all wrong, I couldn't argue with you because

I don't know for a fact that my choices are right, but I would ask how you came to your conclusion.

How do you get most of your facts? Is it from various news sources? I read the *New York Times* and *Wall Street Journal* just about every day. Do I think these are well-written, reliable sources of facts? Yes. Do I believe everything written in them must absolutely be true and not tainted with the hidden biases of the reporters? No. When I was in law school, my professor in ethics class brought in outside speakers to discuss various aspects of ethics. One speaker was a senior reporter for a very prestigious and well-known newspaper who told us that he made up things that were then reported as facts on the front page. His rationale for doing so was that many media outlets were mistakenly (and sometimes deliberately) distorting facts in *their* reporting of the same global events. He felt his actions were ethical because his "facts" would counter those other "facts," thereby giving the reading public a more balanced view.

If you start out with the assumption that something is a fact when it isn't, you are building your decision-making process on a shaky foundation. If you are Thinking Lightly, you won't go back to challenge that assumption and will base your decision on false information. This frequently happens in group settings, especially in large corporate meetings. A person (often one in a position of authority) states a "fact" that may have been reported in the newspaper or on television recently, and while it might apply to some situations, the speaker asserts that it applies to all situations, which is not true. Others nod in agreement rather than politely challenging this speaker. The group then tries to solve a problem based on an incorrect assumption. If you are trying to solve a problem based on bad facts, your solution will be a bad one.

When we hear a narrative that sounds about right, we have the tendency to take the information at face value. Remember the headlines about a lady who spilled coffee on herself and sued McDonald's because the hot coffee burned her? When I heard this on television, I was outraged at how wrong our legal system has become. I was glad I made the choice to practice corporate tax law and not personal injury cases. I thought this case showed that we don't seem responsible for our own actions anymore, instead blaming someone else for our mistakes and picking up some free money along the way.

What if the facts that were presented to the jury were not the same as the headlines claimed they were? What if the reporters conveniently omitted some facts that might change your mind and your initial reaction? As told in the documentary film *Hot Coffee*, seventy-nine-year-old Stella Liebeck went to McDonald's for breakfast with another person. The other person was driving, she was in the passenger seat, and they picked up their food at the drive-thru. He pulled into a parking space so that they could get themselves ready to eat and drink before they started their drive. While the car was parked, Ms. Liebeck used her knees to hold the cup so she could remove the lid. In the process, she spilled the coffee on her groin area.

Did she cause the coffee to spill? Absolutely. Was the coffee hot? Of course. Unless you order iced coffee, you expect your coffee to be hot. This coffee, however, was much too hot.

As the documentary shows, Ms. Liebeck received severe burns (with blackened, charred skin) and had to undergo several skin grafts. According to the documentary, there had been more than 700 prior complaints to McDonald's about burns from hot beverages. Before I knew the actual case presented to the jury, I initially concluded that this was a ridiculous lawsuit based only on the headlines. I had a gut reaction and did a little bit of Thinking Lightly. There was nothing triggering me to think that a jury, who had the real facts, actually got it right. Even as a lawyer, I didn't have any inclination to find out what the exact facts were. I don't know how you feel about this case, but being aware of more evidence certainly changed my view. I don't personally know what actually happened, but I now have a clearer picture of what was presented to the jury. When you are Thinking Lightly and start out with the wrong facts, you get going in the wrong direction; then, with confirmation bias, you will likely arrive at the wrong conclusion.

Occupy Calabasas

The cause of the recent recession has been debated and discussed ad nauseam for the past few years. I was part of a panel discussing the current regulatory environment and what changes Congress might insist on to prevent its reoccurrence. The audience was comprised of very senior lawyers who have practiced law in New York for years. My observation was that in order for us to design laws to prevent something bad from happening again, we should first agree on what caused the problem in the first place.

According to the very educated audience, it was a "fact" that the excessive risk taking by Wall Street was the sole cause of the financial crisis. The politicians were quick to point to Wall Street as the only reason the economy was in a tailspin. It was a politically brilliant position because no one outside of Wall Street likes the people or compensation packages they receive. For every problem, we seek a solution. We have a desire to understand, and if someone comes up with a believable narrative, we accept it. So began the Occupy Wall Street protest movement against social and economic inequality. All fingers pointed at the financial sector as the main cause of the injustice. Not only did the story resonate with most people (who have no idea how the economy or Wall Street works), but with a clear geographic location to point to, it was perfect politics. My opinion is that while Wall Street was clearly part of the problem, it was not the only problem, but you decide for yourself.

First, let's review some actual data. The catalyst for the problems in the United States was an overheated housing market and mortgage loans that should not have been made. Whether it was due to banks and mortgage companies that tricked unwitting consumers into taking out loans they couldn't repay or it was due to consumers who knew they were taking a risk but hoping the house would continue to appreciate, without these loans being made, there would not have been an excessive volume of bad loans in the housing market. The increase in mortgage defaults was the primary catalyst of the Great Recession. As I reminded the audience, the large Wall Street firms don't make mortgage loans to individual homeowners. It takes too long and they can't make big money sitting down with you to review your loan application. I challenged the audience to a geography test of sorts.

Countrywide Financial, based in Calabasas, California (near Los Angeles), made a lot of mortgage loans. IndyMac Bank, which conducted basic banking, went bankrupt and had to be bailed out by the FDIC. It also was based in Southern California. Washington Mutual (WaMu) was a bank whose main line of business was making mortgage loans. It also was going under and had to be acquired by JPMorgan. WaMu was based in Seattle, Washington. Wachovia had huge losses and, with some clever backdoor assistance from the US Treasury, was acquired by Wells Fargo. Wachovia was based in Charlotte, North Carolina. The largest players in the mortgage market by far were the two quasi-governmental agencies Fannie Mae and Freddie Mac. They are based in the Washington, DC area.

Now we finally get to New York. The mortgage loans were put together into large groups and rated by S&P and Moody's, which are both headquartered in New York and not owned by any Wall Street firms. Many of these loans had the backing of the two quasi-government agencies. If the ratings had been appropriate for the increased risks of defaults, none of this mess would have occurred. Why not? Wall Street would not have been able to sell these securitized loans to investors around the globe as "AAA rated" (the safest type of investment) if the large rating agencies didn't rate these assets as high as they did.

Wall Street is a very sophisticated casino where large bets are made without the statistical certainty of the odds of roulette or black jack. The firms of Wall Street make large bets, most often with each other and then with large customers. Thus, all of the large Wall Street firms and some other large firms were interconnected with each other. It was this interconnectivity that threatened to bring down the entire financial system—not just Wall Street, but "Main Street."

In my opinion, the crisis was caused by three things:

1. Bad mortgage loans

2. Bad ratings by the rating agencies
3. The interconnectivity of the Wall Street trading houses

If you are Thinking Lightly, you will conclude that the above analysis must be wrong because you have consistently heard on television that Wall Street was the sole cause of the Great Recession; that posit has become a fact in your mind. I am not lionizing everyone who works on Wall Street or saying that the typical Wall Streeter has a stronger moral fiber than the rest of the population, but if you have repeatedly heard the narrative that excessive risk taking and greed on Wall Street was the sole cause of the Great Recession and it seemed about right to you, you probably accepted it as fact—just as I accepted as fact that the jury verdict in the McDonald's coffee spill case was ridiculous when I first heard the snippet on the news. The newscasters had a brief sound bite, which presented the wrong facts (although I didn't realize it at the time). Based on my pre-existing bias against frivolous lawsuits, their comments seemed about right.

Learning from Past Success and Failure

As a post-script to this Wall Street story, it is important to note that this whole mortgage mess could have been avoided if we had better decision makers in charge just a few years earlier. An analogous scenario had played out before, and not that long ago.

In 1998, a hedge fund known as LTCM lost a lot of money. Almost all of the big banks and investment banks had done huge deals with LTCM before this, and LTCM owed them a lot of money that they then couldn't repay. Wall Street had the same interconnectivity then as it did in 2007, so the whole industry had a problem. The amounts of money at stake in 1998 were large, but nowhere near as large as the sums in 2007-2008 that triggered the demise of Lehman Brothers and others. The regulators gently, and not so gently, leaned on all of the firms to allow LTCM to recapitalize (not pay all the money it owed) so that no one bank would be overwhelmed.

The Wall Street firms generally suffered equally so that no single institution would be seriously damaged.

The system survived, so nothing was really changed after that. This is a classic example of not learning from past mistakes. The LTCM crisis happened less than ten years before the housing market started to unravel in the summer of 2007. We didn't learn anything then because the pain wasn't great enough. The lesson here is simple: If we have a serious problem but the outcome is not painful enough, we fail to analyze it, learn from it, and take action to avoid that problem in the future.

Research supports that we don't usually learn from our mistakes; rather, we look for excuses. This is incredibly common when it comes to investing. If the value of your portfolio decreased during the crisis in the Euro zone, it would be easy to blame the people and governments of a few countries in southern Europe. It may be true that if problems did not exist in Greece, Cyprus, and a few other countries, your investments might have done well, but did you understand the global, macro-level risk you were taking when you made your decision?

When we recall our investment decisions from the past, we tend to remember the outstanding results and can explain why we "knew" that the outcome would happen, which reinforces our confidence in our decision-making ability. When our investments do not work out well, we have a tendency to blame that on an event we couldn't control and no one could foresee. Here is the question to always ask yourself in investments and other areas in which you can look back at past decisions for lessons. If the bad outcome is the result of bad luck, doesn't it mean that the good outcome was the result of good luck?

Instead of only learning from past mistakes, make an effort to learn from past successes. Look at what went right and why, as well as what could have gone wrong but didn't. Was your decision a good one, or were you just lucky?

When we get the outcome we want, we assume we made a great decision. If the decision was important, it's great to be happy about the result, but we need to review the process even when we're successful. Although the result was what you wanted, were all your assumptions correct? Where did luck play a part? By "luck," I don't mean things that were beyond your control that you had considered and were willing to risk, but things that went your way that you forgot to consider.

The Problem With Being Smart

The people who defend their initial reactions the most are highly-confident, educated people. If a smart person has a strong initial reaction to something, it is very difficult for him to change his mind. Why? He feels that he is smart, which gives him confidence in his choices. Instead of doubting himself, he will defend his position, possibly with a compelling argument. A person who is not as confident in his intellectual ability will not have the same confidence level and will keep more of an open mind. The person with less confidence thinks he has something to learn, whereas the person with hubris thinks he has something to teach.

There is a valuable psychological need to have a certain level of confidence. In his book *Psycho-Cybernetics*, author Maxwell Maltz points out that we are designed to remember how to do things correctly and to forget all the things we did wrong before we figured out how to do it right. He uses the example of a baby learning to feed itself. After several attempts, the baby successfully gets the spoonful of food into her mouth. The baby has now perfected one of her first actions without thinking. After a while, she doesn't think about what to do; she just does it. She doesn't dwell on what she did wrong, just the neural muscle reaction to get it right. If the baby thought about all of the mistakes she had previously made and what could go wrong, she might not try to feed herself due to a lack of confidence in her ability to put the spoon in the jar and get a spoonful of food cleanly into her mouth. In this case, it is unnecessary to focus on the trials and errors we make. We just concentrate on how to do it correctly.

For things like neural linguistic behavior or "muscle memory" for sports, we are hardwired not to think about the activities, just the results. If we think too much about a physical activity just before we perform it, we have a tendency to tense our muscles, which can often get us a result we don't want. A classic example is the golfer who takes too long standing over an important putt.

What happens when we *should* be thinking about something, like an important decision? If we reflexively do what we've done before and there are meaningful factual differences or assumptions, it may not work again. You need to have confidence in your mental ability, just as a high-performing athlete needs confidence in her ability. It is healthy to hold your confidence slightly above where your ability is, but not too much. The reality is that you are not a natural-born decision maker outside of your area of expertise.

Overconfidence

Unfortunately, while confidence is a good thing to have, overconfidence is not good. It has been well documented that when it comes to predicting future events, smart people will inaccurately predict with a great deal of confidence (or overconfidence) what the business, economy, or world affairs will look like five to ten years hence. Why do they get it wrong? They get it wrong because they are overconfident in their ability to accurately predict the long-term future.

When you are predicting the future, you can only base it on past events. You have to assume there will be no radical new events that can change your prediction—I don't mean incremental changes, but radical new advances in technology or world events.

If you are a clothing merchandiser, you may have data showing that men's business attire has become more casual. With this information, you may forecast that men will only need to own two formal business suits and will need to buy more business-casual attire. If you own a dry cleaning store, you can use this information to plan on an increase or decrease in the amount of garments that will need dry cleaning, but can you predict the invention of an inexpensive and high-quality new fiber that can be tossed in the typical household washer and dryer and come out looking perfectly clean and pressed? Short-term predictions can be accurate because you don't have to foresee as many potential impactful events or developments. The change may come in the next twelve months, but the chances of radical change are much greater the further out on the time line you go.

How can you know which new radical events will or will not happen? There is an old truism: "You don't know what you don't know." Here, the person with less confidence in his assumptions has an advantage because he is aware of his limitations to predict the future. As a result, he is more open-minded. The smart person who is overconfident lets himself believe that he knows what will happen in the future.

If you were a senior executive in the car industry before the creation of Tesla, would you have predicted the impact and huge success of Tesla cars? You might have imagined an electric car that some people would purchase for environmental reasons, but did you predict a high-end, powerful car that has the highest safety ratings and that people would line up to buy at a price point of $75,000–$100,000? Did you predict it would come from an American company and not a Japanese or German one? If you were the CEO of a major record label, would you have anticipated iTunes? If you were a high-ranking executive at Apple years ago, would you have predicted the creation of Pandora or Spotify? Could you, as a consumer or business owner, predict the existence of digital currencies? What is your prediction for the future of Bitcoin or other digital currencies, and on what is your prediction based? Regardless of your prediction, are you being honest in your assessment of the chances that you will be wrong? You don't need to assume you will be put out of business by inventions such as these, but you should assume that some key assumption of yours, whether business or personal, will change over the course of time.

Intelligence Is Not an Area of Expertise

If you are smarter than someone else, you have the ability to grasp ideas more quickly or better than that person. This is an ability, but it is not an area of expertise. LeBron James stands 6'8" and weighs about 250 pounds.

He is an exceptionally skillful basketball player who has the physique of a Hall of Fame NFL linebacker. While his size is an advantage, size alone doesn't make him great at hitting three-point shots, dribbling adroitly with both hands, and being a great defensive player. That takes skill.

Every team would love to find the next LeBron James. If I find a person who is 6'8" and weighs 250 pounds, should I assume that he will be as good a basketball player as LeBron James? If I represent this person and want to get him an NBA contract, I could call a team's general manager and say that I have a person who is the same size and weight as LeBron, but the general manager would want to know about the player's skills. If my only response is that he is 6'8" and weighs 250 pounds, the general manager would probably (and correctly) assume that the player I represent is not skillful; he's just big. Perhaps he is really only qualified to be a 6'8", 250-pound spectator sitting in the stands.

Likewise, people who are smart, or think they are, confuse their intelligence with skill. You might actually be as smart as you think you are, but that doesn't make you an expert at everything you do. I might have been the world's best currency trader if I had started my career in that area, but I didn't, so don't hire me to trade currencies for you—even if you give me an IQ test during the interview process and I have a great score. The same applies to decision making. Being smart is an advantage, but it doesn't mean that smart people are naturally skilled at always making the right choice.

Confirmation Bias

Confirmation bias is a slippery slope of self-validation in which we look for and believe information that confirms our current opinions while ignoring or downplaying contradictory information. It is precarious because it often comes disguised as thinking when it is simply affirmation of a prior initial conclusion. The combination of overconfidence and a natural aversion to Thinking Deeply usually results in confirmation bias. While it is helpful to give our thoughts or decisions another look, using the same set of information (or lack thereof) to confirm the original, emotionally-driven choice offers no real value. Due to confirmation bias, which has been over-whelmingly demonstrated by various researchers, you rarely vary from your initial reaction. You are just replaying your non-thinking initial reaction.

An easy way to avoid confirmation bias when faced with an important decision is to assume you are wrong. Instead of making a bad decision and doing a postmortem, do a premortem. The classic postmortem examina-tion is done by doctors in the morgue who are trying to assess the cause of death. Don't wait until your deal goes south. Before you are about to embark on a major decision, even when your analysis indicates that your choice is the likely the best one, do a premortem.[8] Use the assumption that your deal will fail and figure out the most likely reasons why. Even if you stay with your original choice after your premortem, you may be able to button down a few loose ends, which will decrease the risk of the outcome not being the one you desired.

Confirmation bias is the poster child for Thinking Lightly, and it happens to all of us on a much too frequent basis—even when we are educated about it and aware of its pull. When there is emotion involved, which happens all too frequently when we have stated our initial conclu-sion in front of a group of people, we feel a strong need to defend our position. This is confirmation bias on steroids. Look for it at your next cocktail party or business meeting.

Our initial reaction, when supported by confirmation bias, becomes our final reaction. It's a simple formula:

INITIAL REACTION + CONFIRMATION BIAS = FINAL DECISION

If we assume that confirmation bias adds no value, it becomes a zero factor. In that case, the simple formula becomes even simpler:

INITIAL REACTION = FINAL DECISION

Thinking Lightly is not wrong. In fact, it is the appropriate way for us to make most decisions and use our brains in an energy-efficient way.

---

[8] Klein, Gary. "Performing a Project Premortem." *Harvard Business Review*, September 2007.

An athlete knows what level of energy he needs to expend. Is he going for a jog in the park with friends, or is he in a competitive race? In decision making, people are often confused about their situation. Is it okay to merely jog along (Think Lightly), or is it time to expend some real energy (Think Deeply)? In real life, there is no starting gun to abruptly remind us to ratchet up the brain power. Thinking Lightly is the correct decision-making approach when we are in our true zone of expertise and the stakes aren't that high. The problem is when we stick with Thinking Lightly when we need to put our mind into a higher gear and Think Deeply.

THINKING DEEPLY

IF IT'S IMPORTANT, DIG DEEP

At this point it should be clear that we have a natural aversion to Thinking Deeply because it drains a lot of energy from our system. If you know when you have to think deeply and have a structured plan on how to do so, the process becomes much more energy-efficient and the quality of your decisions improves.

Thinking Deeply involves objectively analyzing data and thinking about the problem in a programmatic way well before reaching a final or even a tentative conclusion. It isn't only about analyzing the data you have, but also about realizing what inputs you don't have. You need to challenge the underlying assumptions of everything. Thinking Deeply is not spotting the first indication of a possible conclusion and then assuming that you have already solved the problem. That is Thinking Lightly, which puts you back into the closed-end loop of confirmation bias. In Thinking Deeply, it is important to be open-minded and aware of any biases or heuristics that can pull you astray. You must begin with no view on the outcome. Like a trained detective, you must let the evidence lead you to the right answer.

Brain Drain

If you are an educated person who thinks you are particularly smart, your belief may be that you really do think deeply almost all of the time. The truth is, it doesn't matter how much schooling you have or where you went to school; you can't think deeply very often. It is hard science based on biology that we use up a lot of energy when we operate our brains at full capacity, especially under stress. It may be that you are better at Thinking Deeply than the average person, and it may be that you think deeply more frequently, but you don't think deeply very often. In fact, even the most intellectual person doesn't think deeply most days. The laws of biology, like the law of gravity, apply to all, regardless of IQ and educational training.

Have you ever seen a world-class athlete perform? Regardless of whether it's in the Super Bowl, the Olympics, or Wimbledon, even the best-trained athletes cannot compete at a high level for an extended period of time. A marathon runner can't successfully compete every day in a new marathon against a fresh field of marathon competitors. Regardless of these athletes' training, they are tired, don't perform as well at the end of the competition, and need to rest afterward. This is the same result we have when we think deeply. It just can't be done all day, every day.

In sports, it is relatively obvious when we need to expend great energy. It isn't clear in the rest of life, with a few exceptions: When you studied for the SAT, you knew you had to take the test, which would be administered on a certain day at a specific time. It was clear when you would need to focus.

In the book *Thinking, Fast and Slow*, the authors observe that we only shift from Thinking Lightly ("System 1" in their parlance) to Thinking Deeply ("System 2" in their book) when something triggers us to do so. This signal, or trigger, needs to be strong enough to challenge our initial gut reaction. If it isn't, and our first impression seems about right, then nothing triggers the need to spend time Thinking Deeply about the conclusion. If your reaction is that something doesn't seem right about the situation, such as "it seems too good to be true," you might start searching for the reason that your gut instinct tells you something is wrong.

When to Think Deeply

Here is the good news: You don't need to engage in Thinking Deeply very often. Most of the decisions we make don't require our full mental power. The trick is to know when we need to do so and how to go about it. A catalyst may or may not trigger us to think deeply at the right time, but in hindsight it may be clear that we should have. We can't rely on our gut-level reaction or Thinking Lightly apparatus to always correctly inform us that it is time to move to a higher mental level.

Instead of hoping that your Thinking Deeply system will be alerted when it should come into play, there is a simple, systematic way to recognize when you need to dig deeper. If you are in either of the following two circumstances, it's time for Thinking Deeply:

1. When you are out of your area of expertise in an important decision
2. When the stakes are high, meaning the result of the decision is of substantial consequence (even when you are *in* your area of expertise)

Expertise is Specific

I have had various roles in the business arena, but my original core competency is tax law. In addition to being a lawyer, I have an advanced law degree (LL.M) that focuses solely on tax law. If someone asks for my opinion on a complex matter involving taxes and financial institutions or financial products, I can research the law, deeply analyze the facts, and come to a very clear and precise conclusion. If my client asks for my opinion and the amount at stake is $1 million, I will send them my opinion. If the amount at stake is $1 billion, I make sure I get a detailed second or third partner review. Why? Very simply, the stakes are much higher, even though it is in my area of expertise. There is too much risk to my client and myself to not ask a fellow expert or two to give me thoughtful critiques.

If I am asked to render an opinion on an area of law other than tax—for example, real estate law—I will ask for a second partner review when the amount is $15 million or more. While I know a good deal about real estate law, it is not my academic specialty, so my threshold for Thinking Deeply about it is lower than it is in my area of expertise. In the example from the previous paragraph, I have done two things. First, I have looked at the absolute amount at stake. Second, I have narrowly drawn my sphere of expertise. The most common mistake that causes people to Think Lightly when they should be Thinking Deeply is convincing themselves that their area of expertise is broader than it really is.

Say that you are the CEO of a manufacturing company. You know your products well, are respected by your competitors, and know this industry as well as anyone. Your investment bankers convince you that it would be extremely advantageous for you to acquire a significant competitor. Are you an expert in mergers and acquisitions? Do you understand the difficulties in pulling off a successful merger? How do you define success? What do you and your advisors predict the outcome will be five to ten years from now? If the deal makes sense overall, have you considered the appropriate pricing? At what price point will you walk away from an otherwise attractive transaction?

The failure rate for large mergers and acquisitions is quite high because the typical CEO does not realize that he or she is not an expert in large mergers. You need to narrowly define your area of expertise. Yes, I am an attorney, but my expertise is tax law, not family law, bankruptcy law, or employment law. It doesn't mean I know nothing about those areas, just that I am not an expert in them. Make your own case as to why you are NOT an expert, and I mean a world-class expert, within the area you are about to make a decision. Put your ego aside and ask yourself whether you are truly an expert in that field. Unfortunately, most people think they are experts at life and then make very important life decisions solely by instinct. With a divorce rate hovering around fifty percent, we might want to re-think our true areas of expertise in life.

Even though I mentioned this before, it is worth repeating:

Being smart and well educated or having a high IQ can be
an advantage, but these are not zones of competency.

Common Decision-Making "Strategies"

When a critical situation arises that demands real thought, you need a specific plan for how to think. How do you make decisions currently? The most common response I hear from people is that they make a list of "pros" and "cons" by writing down all of the positive and negative attributes of the situation or action they are considering. Is this helpful? Sure it is, but let's examine this approach further. A list of pros and cons is really just a list of your prior thoughts categorized as positive or negative attributes. How do you know you captured all of the pros and cons? Did you give equal value to each of them? If not, how did you address all of the nuances besides staring at the list and going with your gut instinct? The pro vs. con list is beneficial to a degree, mainly when the answer you are looking for is a simple yes or no, but the list doesn't challenge you to consider alternatives.

In the organizational setting, people don't usually use pro vs. con lists, but they may use a SWOT analysis, which lists strengths, weaknesses, opportunities, and threats. While the SWOT analysis is a useful tool, it is roughly equivalent to the pro vs. con list in that it doesn't provide a systematic way to come up with all of the inputs for SWOT. While we can use SWOT to start an analytical approach, by itself, it does not require a deep, thoughtful analysis.

The somewhat standard, more sophisticated response to "how does your company make a decision" is that the organization makes sure that the problem gets the appropriate focus of the right people. These people consider all of the options and then pick the best one. As made clear earlier in the book, that is not really a method of decision making; it is a definition of a hoped-for result. The questions to ask those people are HOW did they ensure they considered all of the available options, and HOW did they then determine that they chose the right one?

Imagine that you are President of the United States and are contemplating a military action. You need to decide whether to engage in a military maneuver and, if so, how to do it. You have the best generals, all of whom have been trained in military history. If you use a general from each military branch—the Army, Air Force, Navy, and Marines—you have four advisors. Let's add the Secretary of Defense to make it five experts. What do you do if your five advisors don't agree? What if there is an informal vote where three vote for military action and two don't? Does majority rule? Of course not! (At least, it should not.) How do you decide? How do you dig deeper into how they decided? Getting top-notch experts in the room is absolutely the right move, but without a plan or structure for analyzing the decision, how do you know who is right?

With a framework for thinking in place, you are able to make better decisions with less stress for you and your organization and, most importantly, greatly improve your chances of obtaining your desired outcome. Having an established methodology also allows for a more efficient use of your mental and physical energy. Thinking Deeply with a plan allows you to focus your thoughts and reach better decisions more efficiently. It also reduces stress, as there is a plan for how to proceed and a confidence level in that plan.

How We Decide Now Recap

All people approach every decision in one of four ways:

1. Non-thinking crisis response: "Fight or Flight"
2. Non-thinking gut reaction: How we make almost all of our daily decisions
3. Thinking Lightly: Where we are guilty of "confirmation bias" and are not using the full power of our brains, though we may believe we are
4. Thinking Deeply: The natural home and highest benefit of a decision-making framework

During this past year, you spent almost all of your time in categories two and three. You probably did not spend enough time, if any, in category four.

How We Decide Now Checklist

- Everyone uses heuristics (shortcuts) to make decisions. We have no choice when it comes to everyday mundane matters, but unfortunately, we usually rely on them for important decisions as well.
- Emotions are a powerful force in decision making. These can control us whether we are extroverts or introverts.
- There is a strong biological tendency to avoid real thinking. It takes too much energy and can cause stress, which we try to avoid. This is normal, regardless of your educational background or IQ.
- We can avoid all of the common pitfalls in decision making by being aware of internal and external forces and using a structured framework for making meaningful decisions.
- There is strong tendency to have confirmation bias of our initial decision. While we believe we are analyzing our first impression, what we are really doing is searching for confirming data points and experiences. We are thinking, but we are thinking at a relatively shallow level, in other words, Thinking Lightly.
- Thinking Deeply about a decision rarely happens, even for smart, well-educated people. It is biological. If you enter this zone, you are unlikely to have a plan for how to think about the problem, which leads to a greater aversion to Thinking Deeply.

The purpose of this book is to help you make better decisions faster and with less stress. The way we achieve this is by utilizing the four-point framework detailed in the following pages. We are not sacrificing quality for speed; we are making better decisions more efficiently.

THE FOUR-POINT FRAMEWORK FOR MAKING BETTER DECISIONS

There are four sides to our decision framework: Timing, Balance, Probabilities, and Pattern Recognition. If you are making a decision that has important consequences, you need to engage in Thinking Deeply by using the entire four-point framework. While all four factors work together to make a cohesive whole, Timing must be the first consideration. The other three factors can be applied in any order, as long as you don't gloss over any of the points.

TIMING

While the concept of timing is not as intellectually challenging as some other aspects of decision making, it is both a critical step in the process and the most overlooked. There is, in fact, much more to timing than you might initially think based on its simple name.

In this chapter, you will learn

- How to prioritize decisions
- How to give yourself the right amount of time to make the best decision without wasting time
- How to set and achieve realistic deadlines, leaving ample time to engage in Thinking Deeply
- How to challenge existing longstanding practices and reassess their continued viability
- How to avoid self-inflicted stress caused by allowing non-emergency situations to reach crisis mode

It is not mere chance that timing is the first of the four cornerstones that make up the decision-making framework. If you miss the optimal time for deciding on a course of action, the decision will be suboptimal. Failure to make a timely decision can make a late decision less valuable, worthless, or worse, harmful.

The Case of Battling Aphorisms

We have all heard the saying "haste makes waste," which warns us that rushing into action can lead to suboptimal consequences. It is true that not spending the time required to reflect upon our appropriate choices can lead to a poor decision.

The opposite aphorism of "haste makes waste" is "a stitch in time saves nine," which means that a quick decision can stop a small predicament from growing into a much larger problem. Which philosophy is correct? The answer is that both can apply, but not simultaneously. Figure out what time constriction or allowance you have by first identifying when the decision has to be final, and then take all the time you need within your time frame to engage in Thinking Deeply about the decision.

People generally fall into one of two types of decision makers. The first is the quick decision maker who feels that he is wasting time reflecting on decisions that, at first glance, are quite clear in his own mind. He feels that he is smart and that his ability to think quickly and come to a conclusion quickly is a reflection on his overall intelligence. His common thought process goes something like, "A good solution was sacrificed because of the other group's search for the perfect answer," or, "A little progress is better than no progress." These thoughts can be correct in the right circumstances, but they could also reflect our natural aversion to taking the time to really think. These are the "stitch in time saves nine" types.

The other type of decision maker is more deliberate and doesn't want to rush into a decision. These people also think they are smart but believe that the more deliberative approach is intellectually superior to the quick reactionary style of the other group. This type of decision maker seeks a well-reasoned approach, which is a good goal, but the reality is that the time they spend on the decision is usually spent Thinking Lightly, rather than engaging in real, deep thinking. As covered earlier, confirmation bias comes into play, and then Thinking Lightly replaces Thinking Deeply as existing biases or opinions are cemented, often past the optimal deadline.

Unnecessary Stress Does Not Make for Better Decisions

Some people claim that they work best under stress. They are confusing their own inability to focus timely on matters of great importance with the best time to think deeply about an upcoming decision. Of course, there is a natural tendency to put off important decisions because real thinking takes focus and energy.

We have to make a conscious effort to engage in physical exercise; the same is true for rigorous mental work. There may also be a fear of being wrong and hoping the problem will go away or solve itself, but neither of these are good reasons for postponing important decisions.

What gets accomplished by putting off important decisions? Nothing but the creation of additional stress. Stress caused by our own lack of timely action is completely unnecessary and avoidable. Any delay simply reduces the amount of time we have to consider the other three aspects of decision making—Balance, Probabilities, and Pattern Recognition.

Giving yourself ample time to think about the solution to your problem not only maximizes your chances for better results, but also reduces unnecessary stress caused by waiting until the last minute to decide or by having second thoughts about your decision because you didn't think things through earlier.

Deadlines

When faced with an important decision, the first thing to do is ask yourself when you have to make this decision. Is it tomorrow? Next week? Next month? Six months from now? Does the decision have any deadline at all? Without a deadline, important decisions can be unnecessarily deferred—sometimes at length, sometimes forever.

The deadline to decide is not the deadline to start thinking.

It's very common to get the timing part of decision making wrong by focusing only on the decision's deadline and overlooking what leads to that deadline. Whether the deadline is set for you or you set it yourself, you need to plan time to really think about your decision. Don't mistake the deadline for the time you should start thinking about the decision. If there is a decision that must be made two weeks from now, start thinking about it now. Allow yourself ample time to consider the decision.

Timing When There is a Set Deadline

There are many things ranging from the relatively mundane to the very important that have a set deadline, such as filing taxes, applying to schools, and submitting financial statements. We can put those due dates on a calendar and set an alarm. Let's say that you have to get applications in to schools, and they are due no later than December 31. In the beginning of September, you are concerned about the various applications and which schools you should apply to but feel no need to set aside time to focus on them because you have four months before your deadline, right? Not exactly. More realistically, you would have three months to decide. Such an important decision should be given an allowance of one month to calmly reflect; decide to add or drop a school; fine tune essays, applications, and recommendations; or decide to change nothing at all.

Timing When There is No Set Deadline

It is extremely common for important decisions (switching jobs, getting married or divorced, buying a house, etc.) to lack a deadline. When there is no deadline, there is a fundamental flaw in the decision-making process. Even companies with the deepest pockets and funding to implement all kinds of initiatives suffer from poor timing in their decision processes. A common complaint among the boards of directors of companies I have met with is that the decision-making process takes too long and is a waste of time.

When I interviewed high-ranking business executives, there wasn't one that focused on timing when they described their decision-making process. The typical response was a somewhat automatic, "Of course we get decisions done on a timely basis." If it isn't a focus and you are just assuming you will get it right, you will get it wrong.

When there isn't a structured process for decision making that incorporates timing, the process gets slowed down—not just a little bit, but to the point that things are decided too late, if at all. There is no corporate culture that is immune to this problem. The articles mentioned earlier on Shell Oil and Google focused on each company's lack of discipline regarding timely decision making. The only cure is to have management be accountable for timely decisions.

Deadlines need to be realistic. Unrealistic deadlines undermine good decision making. In the corporate world, a sense of urgency is all too common with most decisions. You often hear, "We needed it yesterday!" Another common request is, "We need it whenever you get to it, but sooner is better than later." Again, no consideration is put into the process. Instead, you have a sense of urgency that may or may not be necessary. Unfortunately, it is rare to hear, "After using a thoughtful, appropriate decision-making framework, when can you have a proper decision made?" The goal of decision making is to reach the best decision in a timely fashion, not to just make quick decisions.

The lack of an appropriate deadline is not just a corporate issue. It happens with incredible frequency in important personal decisions. Almost anything to do with our general mental or physical health can be put off for too long. There isn't a smoker out there who isn't aware of the harmful consequences of smoking, but he finds a reason not to quit today while maintaining that he knows he has to quit "someday." The typical smoker is waiting for the "right" moment. Unfortunately, the motivation that finally forces him to quit may be a spot on his lung that his doctor finds during a routine check-up.

Setting A Deadline Is Not A Rush To Judgment

The board was facing an important decision by anyone's definition of the word "important." Not only could the decision at hand dramatically impact the next few years of the company's future, but failure to achieve the best result could decide the entire fate of the organization. As the board was contemplating its next steps, I simply asked, "When do we have to decide on this?" Immediately, one of my fellow board members shouted, "I will not be rushed into a decision!"

I knew this man to be a very thoughtful, cerebral person, yet his reaction suggested that he misunderstood my question and interpreted it as an attempt to force a quick, non-thinking decision on this serious matter. What my question was meant to address was the optimal time for making the decision. The board needed to determine a deadline. Due to the circumstances at hand, we concluded that the appropriate timing of the decision should be the next two to three months. A thoughtful decision reached in six or nine months would be too late and put the organization in jeopardy.

I was trying to avoid a deliberative process without any target deadline. With no target deadline, the process would just meander along until the group was faced with some external impending deadline, which would force us to make the decision under pressure. This pressure, which would definitely constitute a self-imposed crisis, would only result in a decision that would be inferior to one not made under duress.

By setting a deadline, we are avoiding a rushed judgment. We are setting a realistic timeline for when we should be prepared to act. While most self-imposed deadlines can be moved, if you find yourself continually moving your deadline back, be honest with yourself and admit that you don't have a real deadline.

Targets, Delays, and Deliberations

Let's say you set a target deadline for your decision at the first day of the next month. As the day approaches, you feel pressured, so you move the target deadline back two weeks. Will doing so cause you to make a suboptimal decision? Perhaps, but not necessarily.

A target deadline is just that—a target. Think of the classic target used with a bow and arrow. In the center is the bull's-eye, which is surrounded by a number of circular bands that make up the entire target. The vast majority of decisions will not have to be made by the exact date (the bull's-eye), but every subsequent day we miss may make the problem worse and worse. For things that don't have a set deadline, most often we are looking at the overall target. We aim for the center, but if we miss, we still hit the larger target, which should suffice.

Let's take the target example further. We decide to delay the decision until six months after our original bull's-eye. What is our conclusion now? We have to be objective in determining whether the delay is based on good reason and whether we are still capable of hitting the larger target. The more we delay, the better the reasons need to be. Every time we delay, we need to honestly reassess whether we can still hit the target area. When very high-end corporate decisions have received the appropriate amount of energy, focus, and real thinking, it is rare that an excellent decision cannot be made within six months to a year, regardless of the complexity involved. The execution of that decision may need to go beyond a year, but the decision itself should not take more than a year.

If you can't meet the original deadline, ask yourself why. When the reason is beyond your control—for example, you are awaiting critical forthcoming information—reset the deadline to allow yourself reasonable time to get and analyze the data. If you miss a deadline simply because you are too busy, what are you prioritizing ahead of that decision? Take a hard look at what you are spending your time on and whether those things are really more important than the decision you need to make.

Failing to take timely action on something that is important should only be acceptable if there is an intervening crisis or if something more important takes priority. Over time, you will realize that these two exceptions do not happen nearly as often as you might think they do.

There are two common reasons that people either never set deadlines or postpone important decisions: fear of making bad decisions and no framework in place for making good decisions. Without any real foundation or structure for analysis, our minds will whir rapidly through various aspects of the problem at hand, often leaving us feeling that we might be missing something—and we probably are.

As noted in the section "How We Decide Now," there is an inertia that leads us to avoid diverting from what we are already doing. In large organizations, people are punished much more harshly for making a bad decision than for making no decision. For this reason, people will often shirk decision-making responsibility before risking the repercussions of making a decision with less than optimal results. If you make a decision and the results are poor, everyone knows who to blame. Organizations need to have a clear structure for decision making and empower people to make optimal, focused, well-thought out decisions. If the actual corporate culture (not the one in the company handbook or brochure) punishes bad outcomes and does not equally reward good outcomes, the equation is against the employee and rewards inaction.

Urgent versus Important

We always seem to be operating at full tilt, whether in work, school, or social activities. People often complain that they have no time for themselves, and many times, that is exactly the case. We are constantly putting out fires and rarely have time to relax and reflect. The result of this is that we make poor decisions about the really important things because we are too busy dealing with daily life. These important decisions also affect our lives. When we make the wrong decisions, we create more stress.

Combining the widely taught concepts of well-known management gurus Steven Covey and Ken Blanchard, I can tell you that we focus too much on urgent tasks, even if they are not important, and avoid things that we should be doing but don't like to do. This tendency to put off making decisions on important matters becomes a habit. As we subconsciously avoid the energy-depleting and stressful act of thoughtful decision making, we create self-inflicted crises. Then, under duress, we are forced into Thinking Lightly about important decisions.

There is no need to rush into a decision right away if we have the opportunity to reflect on it for another two weeks. This important window gives you time to really contemplate your options. By allowing yourself time for reflection, you optimize your decision process and avoid last-minute or knee-jerk reactions. All of us, regardless of how smart we are, can see alternative solutions and outcomes when we have the opportunity to think things through without the added pressure or stress of an urgent deadline.

If You Aren't Taking Time to be Strategic, Who Is?

While in office, a recent President of The United States reportedly adopted a very effective management practice. He tried to block off most Thursdays to review strategy. He knew that being fully engaged in the endless daily responsibilities placed upon him would not give him the time necessary to reflect on the direction of the country and all of the important issues confronting the nation, so Thursdays were reserved for this important task. While we may not face the same issues and challenges as the President of the United States, setting aside time for consideration and thinking will help us make better decisions. When you are always busy handling your daily duties, you don't have the time you need to think about your ultimate goals and the direction and strategies it will take to accomplish these goals. If you set aside time to really think about the important items on your list, you will gain a sense of control about the choices impacting your professional and personal life.

The President of the United States is in charge of setting the strategic direction of the country. If he isn't thinking about strategy, who is? If you aren't making time to reflect on the strategy and direction of your professional and personal life, who is? The fact is that if you aren't doing it, it's not getting done.

On any given day, it seems okay to postpone a longer-term important decision, but what about the next day and the day after that? At some point, the decision needs to go to the top of the list. If it doesn't, you very likely will have dramatically reduced your chances for a good outcome.

Write down a short list of things that must get decided next week. This should not be a wish list of everything you would like to handle. This is a list of the priorities. Now write a separate list of the most important things you need to decide on in the next two or three months, or even longer.

Scheduling time to think about these long-term important items needs to be added to your short list; otherwise, the deadline for the decision will arrive when you are unprepared.

Be aware of upcoming important decisions and actually schedule time in your calendar to think about them. Treat these calendar appointments with the same importance as high-level business meetings. The same is true for decisions impacting your personal life. Make the time you need to think things through, even when you think you don't have the time.

Creating Crises—What Abraham Lincoln Can Teach You about E-mail

Abraham Lincoln has long been considered one of the greatest leaders in history. Dale Carnegie, author of the famed business book *How to Win Friends and Influence People*, also wrote a book about Abraham Lincoln titled *Lincoln the Unknown*. In this book, Carnegie tells a story about Abraham Lincoln that provides a great example of the importance of thinking through our communications before sharing our thoughts.

According to Carnegie, Lincoln was known for a time to have a particularly vitriolic manner and a rapier wit, the effect of which was amplified by the fact that he often criticized people publicly. In fact, he once so annoyed a fellow politician that he was challenged to a fight to the death. As he and his opponent prepared for the duel, their colleagues intervened and prevented the pair from fighting. This was a turning point for Lincoln, and he began making extraordinary efforts not to publicly criticize others.

There most likely wasn't a period of more stress in Lincoln's life than during the Civil War. The Union Army exasperated Lincoln with their repeated mistakes and failure to defeat the famed Confederate General Robert E. Lee. During the Battle of Gettysburg, the Union Army apparently had the Confederate forces trapped while a flooded river closed the Confederates' avenue of escape. Lincoln both telegraphed and sent a special messenger to Union General Meade with very specific instructions to act decisively and quickly. Apparently, General Meade defied Lincoln's direct orders, constantly finding excuses for a delay. As General Meade sat passively by, the flooded river subsided and allowed the Confederates to escape. Lincoln was livid. He wrote a scathing letter to Meade emphasizing his disappointment in the general's unforgivably grievous blunder. We will never know if this letter would have changed General Meade's behavior or altered the course of the war because, according to Carnegie, the letter was found in Lincoln's papers after his death, and thus, was never sent.

What if Lincoln had e-mail? Would he have hammered out the letter in his fit of rage and immediately hit the send button, which happens all too often when emotions take control? While it is unknown why Lincoln did not send the letter, Carnegie, who was a Lincoln expert, surmised that writing it allowed the commander in chief to vent, but upon reflection, Lincoln knew that his harsh words would not help Meade be a better general and might also undermine his confidence and future actions. Perhaps Lincoln had the foresight that so many of us could use in times of heightened emotion. While his was a matter of grave importance and involved protecting the country in time of war, he managed to maintain perspective while his temper flared. The situation was important, but not urgent. The damage was done. The troops had already escaped. Operating from emotion rather than thinking through the communication could have created a crisis when one didn't exist.

This happens all of the time in our technologically advanced society, where communications take a fraction of a second to be transmitted around the globe. We need to ask ourselves if we are responding right away because it needs to be addressed instantly, or if our emotions are taking control.

Writing can be great therapy. Often we jot down our innermost thoughts and true feelings; however, just because we wrote it, doesn't mean we should share it. One of the most common mistakes, not just in business but made by everyone in all walks of life, is the decision to write something electronically and then impulsively hit the send button. Once you hit send, your words, and perhaps your emotions, are permanent and easily sharable with a lot more people than you may intend. As many people involved in litigation find out, a document in writing, including e-mail, can be used as evidence. How many people have had to publicly retract or apologize for e-mails, tweets, and text messages they have sent? Don't create a crisis. Think before you communicate, especially in matters of importance or when the repercussions could be significant.

Reevaluating Previous Decisions

Failure to make a decision to change something is a decision to continue doing it the same way. On an important matter, that choice should be an affirmative decision, not one of neglect.

It's long been rumored that the size of the US space shuttle engines was decided using the girth of a horse's rear end. Clearly, no horse is involved in the operation of the space shuttles, so why would the width of a horse's behind impact the design of one of our country's most advanced innovations? Because long ago, a decision was made.

Follow this anecdote. The standard US railroad gauge (distance between rails) is 4'8.5". English expatriates designed the US railroads to follow the English model, and the English rail lines were designed after the pre-railroad tramways using the same tools that were used to build wagons. Wagons were designed for the long-distance roads in England. The roads had deep ruts into which the wagon wheels had to fit; otherwise, the wheels would break. Imperial Rome originally built these roads for their legions, and the ruts were caused by Roman war chariots. Roman war chariots were designed to accommodate the width of two war horses' rear ends.

Now, fast forward a couple thousand years. There are two large solid rocket boosters (SRBs) attached to the US space shuttle. These SRBs were made in Utah and transported to the space shuttle launch site via railway. The engineers who designed the SRBs would have preferred them to be larger, but the boosters had to fit through railway tunnels, which are only slightly wider than railroad tracks. The width of the railroad tracks, as mentioned, can be traced back to the Roman war chariots, which were designed to be pulled by two horses.

This is a great illustration of past decisions and habits driving future decisions without further analysis or thought. If we were to design a new high-speed rail to run between San Francisco and Los Angeles, should we assume it should be the same track width as all the previous train tracks that have been around for hundreds of years? Maybe; maybe not. Don't be anchored by the decisions of the past.

We need to adapt to changing circumstances and be aware of when change is needed. What does this have to do with decision making? Everything. Regardless of how brilliant (or not) our decision was years ago, it may not be as brilliant today. In fact, it could be detrimental. Those major decisions and the underlying assumptions need to be revalidated in our current circumstances.

But We Have Always Done It that Way

In corporations, it's common practice to do things as they have always been done, even when it's more likely that efficiencies could be found by reevaluating long-standing operations. I was once hired to lead and manage a large group of professionals, so I met with each of them to try and understand what each person typically did on a daily basis. While there was a bit of unintentional stress because I was the new boss and no one knew whether or not to trust me, the interviews gave me valuable insight into the business operations and revealed some startling discoveries.

I found out that people were spending an exorbitant amount of time capturing data that wasn't necessary. While sifting through mounds of documents to extract information was necessary in the past, it was no longer needed, nor was the information gathered in this process relevant to current operations. To be clear, this inefficiency wasn't the fault of the hardworking employees, but the failure of management to rethink decisions made long ago. People continued wasting time by looking for useless information and ignoring data points that could have been helpful because no one thought to reexamine existing operations. They did it that way because they had always done it that way.

My favorite story about challenging the status quo involves Kevin

Kelley, a successful high school football coach in Arkansas.[9] Without explaining the intricacies of football, the team in possession of the ball gets four downs (tries) to advance the ball at least ten yards. If they make it, they get another four chances to advance the ball until they score or fail to make the ten yards in the allotted downs. It is conventional wisdom that if your team can't advance the ball ten yards after three tries, you use your fourth down to punt (kick) the ball far across the field, forcing the opposing team to start its march toward the goal line from much further away than where your offense stalled.

Kelley never lets his team punt the ball. He saw a video that was produced by a Harvard professor who examined 2,000 football games over a 3-year period and concluded that football teams should rarely, if ever, punt. This professor examined the statistics and, based on purely mathematical evidence, decided that the traditional method of punting on the fourth down reduced the chances of winning. Kelley also rarely goes for a traditional kickoff, instead opting for the on-side kick. Based on the professor's data, in a typical kickoff, your opponent will receive the ball on their own 30-yard line. If you try an on-side kick and it fails, your opponents would usually end up on their own 47-yard line, a difference of 17 yards from the kickoff. If your on-side kick is successful, your offense gets the ball on your opponent's 47-yard line. One of the keys to winning in football is getting turnovers, which is when one team, through a fumble, interception, or recovering an on-side kick, gets the ball from the opponent. Here, Coach Kelley is trading 17 yards for the turnover opportunity.

This coach wasn't being radical just to be radical. His method was successful. His non-punting teams won the Arkansas high school championship three times, and over a ten-year time-frame his record was 124 wins and 22 losses.

What I like about Kelley's decision is not just that his approach is different, but that he used some evidenced-based data to think about the "why" behind punting the ball. Based on statistics that might only work at

---

[9] Grantland, "The Coach Who Never Punts," YouTube video, 6:31, November 13, 2013, https://www.youtube.com/watch?v=AGDaOJAYHfo.

the high-school level, he decided to approach things very differently and got notable results. He didn't blindly accept conventional wisdom and the adage that "it's always been done that way." If he didn't question a key assumption, he probably wouldn't have won as many games.

How Do You Choose Which Decisions to Reevaluate?

You can't spend time reviewing every decision you or your predecessors have ever made, but you can and should revisit the important ones. How can you possibly make time to revisit old decisions? Like Coach Kevin Kelley, you can do this by recognizing how important the impact is. If your department has been doing something the same way for ten years and a new CEO is brought on board, that CEO will probably want to know how things are done and why they are done that way. You need to be able to explain both, especially the why. If you were the new CEO and the operation in question is not in your area of expertise, what questions would you ask? Think like an intelligent outsider and be prepared to answer the questions you would ask.

The concepts behind the process improvement techniques of Six Sigma can help. Without getting into the details of Six Sigma, let me provide a simple summary that applies to decision making. Six Sigma is a management tool used by many large organizations to improve operational efficiencies. The creators of this tool don't maintain that using it will completely eliminate any risk of mistakes in your processes, but Six Sigma focuses on areas in which the largest number of mistakes are made and areas in which the greatest risk exists for highly impactful (read: costly) mistakes. Identifying these areas provides a great guide to help determine which prior decisions should be revisited.

What activities in your department have the greatest impact, positive or negative, on your department's contribution to the company? In what area do most people in your department spend the majority of their time? Is there a better way to redeploy exceptional human capital to achieve the best results?

When you start a new executive job, look at the areas you are responsible for and ask the same questions that a good CEO would ask. Be careful not to assess blame or insinuate that you are a better executive than the prior person, which could be both a political minefield and counterproductive. Ask questions about the most important areas, listen to the explanations, and engage in real thinking. Apply the framework as if the activities and operations were brand new challenges that no one at the company had previously faced.

On a personal level, you may also wish to review the decisions of your past year or couple of years to identify areas in which you made the most mistakes, suffered the most from poor decisions, or currently risk the most consequences. Just like Six Sigma at a corporate level, recognize and reconsider decisions that impact daily activities and reexamine any areas of major importance. Remember, decisions are forward moving, so have the mental discipline to use the framework to treat these decisions as new. Whether you decide to make the same decision or make a different decision, it will be a new decision.

A former colleague of mine was a high-level executive at a large multinational firm. She was the consummate professional, extremely competent and well liked, and her career at the company was on a steep upward trajectory. On a joint trip to review some of the company's European operations, she shocked me when she revealed that she was interviewing for a position with another company. I asked her why she was unhappy in her current job, and her reply was that she wasn't unhappy. She really liked her current job and position with the company, but she needed to "make sure." I was intrigued and impressed that someone in her position, who was juggling many large responsibilities and seemingly always busy, would take the time to reevaluate her past decisions.

She confided that every few years she interviewed for positions at other companies. She did not feel that she was being disloyal or unappreciative of her current company, but that interviewing with other companies gave her perspective. She wanted to work wherever she could best apply her capabilities, and finding out where that was meant comparing her current position with other opportunities. She continued to find that potential jobs were less desirable than her current position, and interviewing with other companies made her come back to her current job with renewed enthusiasm and energy.

Stewing versus Jumping Ship

There is an old anecdote about the reaction of two frogs placed into two different pots of water. The first frog is placed into a cold pot of water that is slowly heated so that the water gets gradually warmer. The frog continually acclimates to the ever-warming water and stays in the pot as it is heated. Eventually the frog is boiled to death. The second frog is dropped into a pot of water that is already boiling and immediately jumps out to stay alive.

The frog story is a great analogy for decision making in certain situations and an illustrative case for reevaluating past decisions and current circumstances. We've all known people who were unhappy in their jobs or personal relationships. They may complain about their situation, but they don't do anything to change things. Like the first frog, they find themselves in increasingly uncomfortable situations but stay put as they adjust to the discomfort. They may assume that when things get bad enough they will jump, but they fail to notice when things reach the critical boiling point. If you start working at a great company and over the course of several years, see the company or your job going downhill, at what point do you say it's time to move on? Periodically evaluate your surroundings. The case of the frog dropped into boiling water is the extreme; it's the rare instance in which the need for change is obvious.

When there is something that needs improvement in your personal or professional life, which frog are you? Determine what your personal boiling point would be in that situation and then reevaluate often. Don't wait until you hit the boiling point to start thinking about your decision. Plan ahead and choose the action you will take if or when you reach your limit. Most of us can recall past occasions when we knew a situation was bad, but we held on, hoping it would get better. Hope can be a powerful emotion when used properly, but hope is not a strategy for problem solving. Remember the cool pot of water you first entered. Is it warmer now? How much warmer? If it's too warm, fix the temperature in the pot or make the choice to get out.

Undoing a Previous Decision

It is rare, if not impossible, to completely undo a prior decision because decisions are always forward moving. Once you make a decision and act on it, it is done. You can't change it, and you can't go back in time, so move forward. Let's say you work at Company A. You leave and join Company B because you think you will make more money and have a better job. Unfortunately, your stint at Company B does not work out as envisioned. If Company A replaced you when you left, going back to Company A is not an option; even if it was, the decision to rejoin Company A would be a new decision. You then decide to explore a job with Company C. Again, this is not the undoing of your first or second decision, but a new decision.

Many people become unhappy with a prior investment decision and try to undo the decision with a subsequent action. Let's say you bought stock at $100 a share, and five days later, it's trading at $80 a share. You're not happy when you look at your portfolio, so you decide to sell the stock at $80, take your loss, and move on to the next investment. You haven't undone your prior decision to buy the stock at $100; you have made a subsequent decision to sell the stock at $80 to avoid further loss.

Selling the stock is of course related to the decision to buy, but selling it is a separate decision. Lamenting over the stock value dropping 20% shouldn't be your focus. Your analysis should instead be focused on what to do from here. If you think it is unlikely to reach $100 a share again anytime soon but speculate that it is likely to drop to $60 or $70, selling it at $80 is an optimal decision. If you hang onto the stock without analysis solely to try and regain your loss of $20, this is classic sunk cost fallacy and is emotional, not thoughtful, decision making.

Recap

Timing can be your friend or your enemy in decision making. By prioritizing the important things, whether they are personal or professional, you can avoid unnecessary stress and allow yourself the time you need to engage in Thinking Deeply. You can't undo a prior decision, but you can make new decisions going forward. Reevaluate on occasion, and always set a deadline.

Timing Checklist

- Any time you are confronted with a meaningful choice, your first thought should be **when do I have to make this decision?**
- **If there is no deadline, make one.** If there is no clear due date for your decision but what you are deciding or acting upon is important to you, then your first step is to set an appropriate deadline.
- **Don't confuse the decision deadline with when to start thinking about the decision.** Do not wait until it is time to make the decision to think about it.
- **While everything may seem urgent, it isn't.** Be aware of whether your situation is urgent or important and decide to act accordingly.
- **Don't create a crisis where there isn't one.** Emotional decisions and actions can create crisis situations. Think through your choices before reacting. If you don't set an achievable target deadline, you can create an unnecessary emergency.
- **Force yourself to set aside time to strategically think things through, even when you think you don't have the time.**
- **Reevaluate long-standing habits and decisions made long ago.** Check the temperature of your situation and reexamine important decisions to be sure they are still serving you well.

BALANCE

What is your risk tolerance? How far outside of your comfort zone will you go for a meaningful benefit? Are you overvaluing the benefit of a decision because you are emotionally attached to the desired result? These are the questions we ask to determine balance in a decision.

In this chapter, you will learn

- How to discover hidden risks
- How to balance your initial reaction with a more thoughtful process
- How to determine acceptable risk and unacceptable risk
- How to avoid "creeping risk," a variation of sunk cost fallacy
- How to view balance in human relationships

Balance focuses on the risk-to-reward ratio, what value you are placing on your perceived payoff, and what monetary or non-monetary costs you are willing to absorb in order to achieve your desired result.

Let's begin by positing a general rule: Almost all decisions are in balance, which means that if you accurately estimate the potential benefits of your proposed decision, there will be an equal and offsetting amount of risk. If you begin by assuming that your decision is balanced, you will be forced to account for *all* of the risks that exist and not just the first one or two that pop into your mind. Most people are positive and can readily envision the benefits of the decision but don't spend as much time looking at all of the risks. You don't want to gloss over very real risks that might lie beneath the surface of your initial reaction.

While there are situations where the risk-to-reward ratio is out of balance in your favor, this rarely happens and is the exception to the general rule. In your exuberance to move forward with a decision, you might think the exception applies and that your upside dwarfs the risk you are taking, but remember that these exceptions are rare. A common example of seeking favorable balance is a financial investment in which the investor seeks to maximize his return while minimizing risks. The reality is that in almost all cases, despite what you or your financial advisors hope, risks are usually directly proportional to rewards. The holy grail of the financial markets is to find those areas in which the potential reward is disproportionately high compared to the risk, in other words, an unbalanced situation where the lack of balance works in your favor.

When a decision is not in balance, most of the time that lack of balance works against you. When a decision is imbalanced against you, like the man who put his life savings on one spin of the roulette wheel, it is a bad decision. If we are predisposed to decide one way or another prior to any analysis, we become attached to this decision, creating a halo effect and causing us to overrate the reward and underestimate the risk. Beginning with the general rule that all decisions are in balance forces you to consider ways that you might have underestimated the amount of risk involved.

Data versus Instinct

Should you be led more by your gut instinct or trust impartial data? During my research, the vast majority of people I talked to had a tendency to put themselves in one of the following two camps: the "go with your gut" camp and the "evidenced-based" camp.

In the book *Judgment*, which focuses on key calls made by business executives, authors Noel M. Tichy and Warren G. Bennis make an observation that is fully consistent with my own experiences and interviews. They polled hundreds of people about their good and bad decisions, and a sizable number said that many of their bad decisions occurred because they hadn't followed their gut instincts. While the authors don't cite exact numbers, they also say that many other business leaders said exactly the opposite—that they made mistakes because they relied too much on their gut reactions and did not employ a more thoughtful, logical approach.[10]

So, which one is it? Not enough gut instinct or too much? The answer is neither; both approaches are wrong. A high percentage of the executives got important decisions wrong because they didn't balance their gut reactions with a more thoughtful analysis. The mistakes made by most of these high-ranking executives apparently stemmed from a lack of a personal and organizational decision-making framework. If there had been a decision-making structure in place, there would not have been a conflict between too much or too little gut instinct.

STATISTICIANS 10, POETS 0

An article in the *New York Times* titled "Statisticians 10, Poets 0" pointed out myriad ways that individuals use and sometimes obsess over data, whether it is related to lifestyle, sports, social media, etc. The conclusion of the article is that the "nerds" have won; we have become the "United States of Metrics."[11] Some people lament that the constant desire for more data has reduced our sensory connection with things and people, but the easy access and availability of vast data shouldn't be viewed as one side having won out over the other.

With the continuing growth of the internet, there is no shortage of available data. If you are involved in sports, the financial markets, marketing, or any area with metadata, you may be used to trolling for relevant information. As we will discuss in the chapter on pattern recognition, the most important thing is to be able to focus on key data that is relevant. It is a complete waste of time to study all 800 pages of information that people

---

[10] Tichy, Noel M. and Warren G. Bennis. *Judgment*, 218-219.

[11] Feiler, Bruce. "Statisticians 10, Poets 0." *New York Times*, May 18, 2014.

have proffered in their attempt to demonstrate that they have done a thorough analysis.

First, identify relative data that helps you gauge the true risks and true rewards. Data can tell a story, but it can also be misleading when taken out of context or interpreted through a filter of existing biases. People and numbers can both paint a distortive picture. Always question the underlying assumptions that support the data you are using. Analyzing data serves as a check and balance against the emotions that run our instinctive decision process. Measure your instinct against hard numbers or real evidence. They should lead you to the same conclusion. If they don't, investigate further.

Moneyball

There isn't a story about data versus instinct that I like better than *Moneyball: The Art of Winning an Unfair Game*. The book, written by Michael Lewis, is about Billy Beane, general manager of the Oakland Athletics baseball team, and the innovative way that the team began evaluating players in order to assemble a competitive team.

The entire baseball community historically picked players solely on gut instinct. The Oakland A's no longer had the vast sums of money needed to buy the top players, and with star athletes demanding more than they could afford, the team needed a better method for predicting how players would contribute. Through extensive statistics and computer analytics, the Oakland A's revolutionized the selection process for baseball talent. This eventually led to the team reaching the playoffs and competing against teams that spent three times Oakland's budget to acquire talent. While the book paints a picture of team management overwhelmingly dominated by numbers, a closer examination also reveals that relying solely on numbers was not the perfect solution either. If you see the movie or read the book after reading this book, notice the resistance that Beane faced from the team's scouts and coaches due to the fact that they had "always done it that way." Total dependence on either data or instinct alone does not guarantee success.

Calculating Value

Balance tests the value you are placing on an intangible reward and provides perspective on the risk you are considering. Colleges are a great example of this perceived value. Say your son or daughter is deciding which college to attend. As we know, there are state schools and private institutions. At the writing of this book, the average cost to attend a private institution is around $50,000 per year, including tuition, room, board, and miscellaneous items. The state universities in New York currently estimate a total annual cost of $20,000 for New York State residents and $30,000 for non-residents. A balanced decision would estimate the intangible value of attending a private university at $20,000 or $30,000 per year over the state school. Multiply this by four years for the total difference of $80,000 to $120,000. This should be the basis by which you and your teenager analyze a school's value. Is the real or perceived value of the private school worth the price difference? Will the private university diploma be worth $80,000 to $120,000 more than the public university diploma?

The same analysis applies when you receive financial aid. Let's assume that one college offers your student an annual $25,000 financial grant, totaling $100,000 over the course of four years. The only way that it makes sense to ignore this offer is to conclude that the value of attending a different school is worth at least $100,000 more than the school that offered your student the large financial incentive.

High Stakes Imbalance

Many people think that athletes and Wall Street traders are over-paid, but you would have a hard time convincing a trader who just made $100 million for her company that she shouldn't get at least $10 million in compensation. Let's say this particular trader was paid $10 million for making the company $100 million in one year. Despite her acumen, she loses $90 million for the company the next year. During the 2-year period, the company would have made $10 million off her trading strategies and paid her a $10 million bonus. Clearly, she should not be paid $10 million for making the company $10 million. This compensation system is out of balance in how and when it is calculated. This is exactly how most of Wall Street operated its compensation model prior to the Great Recession.

The imbalance here is the risk-to-reward ratio—namely, the risk to the institution and the reward paid to employees. The issue is not about compensating good traders for good work. The issue is a lack of balance that could be solved with a clawback provision, for example, reducing the trader's compensation commensurate to any monies lost for the company over the subsequent three years. If our star trader made the company another $20 million in her third year, the total company profits resulting from her trades would be $30 million. With a 10% bonus rate, she would earn $3 million, not $10 million for the first year and nothing for the second year. Year three would be determined by what she did in years four and five. This would even the balance between the company's risk and the trader's reward. While it is glaringly clear in these terms, the calamitous imbalance should have been recognized before the financial crisis of 2008.

"Rough Justice" for a Large Potential Payoff

Greater risk should lead to greater rewards. Sometimes it makes sense to assume greater risk, but only when the potential reward is greater as well. Very few National Football League contracts have substantial guaranteed payments. While it is true that New England Patriots quarterback Tom Brady signed a contract extension for a reported guaranteed $57 million, most headlines touting the massive sums offered to sign pro athletes are illusory. Athletes who get injured and can't perform on the field only get the amount of money they are guaranteed in their contract, nothing more. This is out of balance for these players, who are expected to perform at peak intensity in a very physical game and constantly risk career-ending injuries. A player could be a true role model off the field, stay out of trouble, eat well, and train hard, but if his 325-pound teammate accidentally falls on him the wrong way during practice, he could be out for the season, if not forever.

With such a dramatic imbalance in the risk-to-reward ratio, why not guarantee the entire contract? Completely guaranteed contracts are out of balance against the owner. If a player with a guaranteed contract is injured, the owner ends up paying two people to play the same position—a substitute and the injured player. The simple truth is that professional sports contracts are not designed to be balanced in a perfect way, but they are in balance in a "rough justice" manner. There is a lot of risk on both sides. For the owners, the risk is poor performance or injury. For players, the risk is the same. The owner would like to pay less, and the player would like more guaranteed.

Let's say a player signs a contract with a total potential value of $10 million over five years. The contract is structured so that the athlete only gets $1 million guaranteed. The other $9 million is not guaranteed, and is paid over the next five years if he remains on the team and meets certain performance standards. If the player is a star performer for the next five years, the owner will have paid him the full $10 million. If the owner could see into the future and knew at the time of signing that his player would become a top performer and stay healthy, he would have gladly granted the player a contract worth only $6 million, but all of it guaranteed. This is $5 million more than the original guaranteed amount of $1 million but less than the potential $10 million. The player cannot see into the future either and has no idea whether he will be a good performer and stay healthy for the next five years. With that lack of clarity, he would be more than willing to sign for a guaranteed $6 million instead of a possible $10 million. Because the owner cannot see into the future, he is willing to possibly pay an extra $4 million to compensate for the risk he takes if the player doesn't perform well. The player also requires an extra $4 million for the risk he is taking.

Determining Acceptable and Unacceptable Risk

Everyone has his own risk-tolerance level. There is no right or wrong, but you have to be honest with the amount of risk you are willing to take.

Big decisions always carry some level of risk. If you have ever applied for a mortgage, you know that it is common practice for mortgage lenders to require borrowers to purchase homeowner's insurance, which typically covers damage due to fire, hurricanes, and other events. The insurance gives the lender the comfort of knowing the homeowner can repair the asset until the loan is paid off, and the insurance protects the asset in the meantime. The bank is willing to risk that you will continue to pay your bills on time, but it wants to eliminate all other risks to the asset. The bank is reducing its risk in loaning you money by requiring you to carry insurance on your house until the loan is paid off.

What if the lender did not require you to buy homeowner's insurance? You would have to decide whether to carry it on your own. While you would think through all four factors of the framework outlined in this book, the most important element to consider here is balance. You would need to weigh your risk-to-reward balance, or in real terms, you'd need to weigh the cost of the premiums against the cost of a catastrophe.

Let's say you buy a house for $300,000 with a $60,000 down payment and a loan for $240,000. If you choose not to carry insurance, your financial risk is your $60,000 equity plus the $240,000 loan you are carrying. If a major catastrophe happens, could you afford the risk? You are balancing the economic damage if the catastrophe happens against the insurance premiums being saved over a period of time.

As in every decision, you think about timing, balance, probabilities, and pattern recognition. Let's assume that after you do some research, you find out that while fires happen every day to someone somewhere, the chance of a fire destroying your entire house is very remote—much less than 1%. That 1% is your analysis of the probabilities. Insurance companies are in the business of making money, so let's assume that your insurance company will charge you at least a 2% premium on a 1% risk. Timing is relevant because you can buy insurance policies on an annual basis, so you could change your mind from year to year, but the key factor to consider here is balance.

In this case, you are paying premiums for a risk that is extremely unlikely to happen. If it does happen, however, the economic pain could be substantial. From a mathematical basis, the premiums cost more than the risk of a major catastrophe, which is why insurance companies make money. Even if the catastrophe happens and completely destroys your house, the land would remain yours. Depending on its location, your lot would then be worth less than, equal to, or more than the $60,000 you paid as a down payment. If it's worth at least $60,000, your equity would not be at risk, but you would still be on the hook for the $240,000 debt you assumed in taking out the mortgage loan.

Most people faced with the same dilemma would buy the insurance rather than assume the risk, however remote. This would be their primary residence, and they would not have the financial wherewithal to absorb a loss of such magnitude. As a result, they would be unable to buy another home and likely have to compromise their lifestyle as a result of the substantial financial hit.

In the insurance world, you pay premiums toward something that is highly unlikely to occur, but when you balance the costs of the premiums against even a remote risk of catastrophe, the risk is usually unacceptable. Here, the insurance premiums you pay protect your financial well-being and provide peace of mind, an intangible but important variable on your personal balance sheet. The key here with any personal or professional decision is to determine whether you are willing to accept catastrophic risk.

Risk of Inaction

While risk most often involves an investment you make or an action you take, sometimes risk is assumed by choosing not to do something. In this case, the risk is related to the reward that could have been achieved by choosing to act instead.

William was a hardworking guy. He applied himself in his job and spent quality time with his family. He taught his children to be kind and honest and to study hard in school so that they would reap the benefits inherent in learning and thinking. William's son did very well in school and got accepted to a top-ranked university, Harvard. In America, ratings rule.

While there are hundreds of great colleges and universities in the United States, a school's rankings drive the perceived value of its educational offering and, as a result, the perceived value of its graduates as potential employees. Of course William felt incredibly proud to tell people that his son would be going to Harvard University. Harvard deservedly has international brand-name value. William knew that people would always be impressed with the fact that his son went to Harvard and that being a Harvard graduate would open elite doors of opportunity for his son.

Then, after attending Harvard for two years, young Bill made the unexpected and unwelcome announcement that he would be dropping out of Harvard to pursue a business venture.

I don't know how you would react if this was your son, but given the same situation, I would be dumbfounded, among other things. After regaining my composure, I might first try to appeal to his logic, listing all of the risks he is taking in dropping out—including the possibility of never graduating, never getting the Harvard degree that could open so many doors to success in life, forfeiting association with one of the best brand names ever, and discarding all of the hard work he did in high school to get to where he is.

The risks, or potential costs of dropping out of Harvard, would be significant, albeit unknown. Perhaps he could mitigate his risk by committing to return and finish his degree at Harvard if the business venture was not successful within two years. With that agreement, would the risk be acceptable? The business was totally innovative, in a completely new industry. There was nothing quite like it in the marketplace. The venture was extremely risky with huge obstacles but tremendous potential for great financial success.

How did the scenario play out in real life? You would have to ask William and Mary Gates whether or not they supported young Bill's choice to leave Harvard. What if they had convinced their son that dropping out of Harvard was a foolish idea? Would Bill Gates have gone on to be as successful? Would Bill Gates be a household name today if he had stayed on the more traditional path and graduated from Harvard? There is simply no way to know. While there are often calculable risks in doing something, there is often an incalculable risk in choosing not to do something, as well. With Bill Gates, his risk wasn't just monetary; he may have been successful anyway. His risk was missing out on the business opportunity, not following his passion, and, as a result, never making the substantial impact on the world that he did make by following his dream.

Balance in Relationships

Any successful long-term relationship needs to be in balance (mutually beneficial) over the course of time. Regardless of whether it is romantic, platonic, or business related, you can view that relationship using a "balance sheet" approach. You can also think of it as a savings account. Building up the savings account allows you to draw down that savings account when you need it.

In real life, if your savings account or balance sheet is at zero and something causes you to have a cash shortfall, you have nothing to fall back on and dire consequences could result. The same concept applies in relationships. You need to build up all of that personal goodwill with each other so that when something happens in the relationship that is less than perfect, there is an emotional savings account from which to draw. Most relationships do not fail because of a single identifiable event. There may be one event that stands out, such as infidelity in a marriage or a major mistake that irreparably damages a client relationship, but most erode over time. If you have a strong relationship with your spouse and he comes home one evening and lashes out, you will see that as out of character for him. If he comes home day after day and does the same thing, it starts to draw on the emotional balance sheet until one day you no longer love him. The balance sheet drops to zero until there is nothing left. Business relationships operate the same way. If a client feels that they are paying for services that have been declining in quality over some period of time, you are vulnerable to losing that client to a competitor.

If you focus on building up the balance sheet of goodwill in all relationships, you will have a strong income statement. If you only focus on the short-term income statement—what is good for you and only you—there won't be anything to draw upon when something goes wrong, and something *will* go wrong at some point in any relationship.

Responsibility = Authority

Whether you are dealing with your teenage child or with your boss, you need to make sure that responsibility and authority are equal. If your teenager wants the authority to drive your car, she needs to demonstrate a level of maturity and responsibility equal to the authority you grant her with the privilege.

If you are in a corporate environment and are given an important project, make sure that your responsibility and authority are equal. If you are responsible for the outcome, you need the authority to make the important decisions. If you don't have the authority but will still be held responsible, this equation is working against you and is a recipe for disaster.

Determining and Sticking to Your Risk Parameters

When making any important decision, it is important to know how much risk you are willing to accept. What is your comfort level? If the level of the risk is known upfront, like the example of homeowner's insurance, you can make your decision based on that known amount of risk. If the risk is unknown, you need to look more closely at the other factors, namely probabilities and pattern recognition, to help predict the most likely outcomes and define your risks better.

Risks are not always static. Often times we experience "risk creep," which is when the amount of risk increases, sometimes through a series of small increments, and you end up with a very different risk than you originally signed up for. As mentioned in the section "How We Decide Now," psychologists use the term sunk cost fallacy to describe the phenomenon of dumping more time, effort, or money into something that has already used up more resources than it is likely to be worth. The tendency to pour more money into an investment because we already have a lot invested in it is emotionally driven—we don't like loss, so we try to avoid it. When you find yourself facing risk creep, step back and analyze your situation. All decisions are forward looking. Decide if it's still wise to invest more resources or cut your losses.

Creeping risk and sunk cost fallacy happen all the time for small business owners. Let's say you are a fabulous baker and have developed a strong customer base that is willing to pay well for your gourmet cakes and pastries. With your solid reputation and established customers, you have less risk than an unknown startup, so you decide to open a small retail shop and estimate that you will need to invest $50,000 in order to get started with the proper equipment and location. Based on your conservative assumptions, the bakery will turn a $30,000 profit in its first year. While some of the after-tax profits need to be put back into the business each year, based on your calculations, you should be able to repay the original loan and 5% annual interest within three years. What is your risk? Your risk is that you will not earn your target profit.

The bakery gets off to a very fast start, far better than you imagined. A large corporate client wants to contract you to be the single bakery vendor for several local hotel properties they manage, but the client wants a guarantee that the bakery is capable of handling the volume. To get this large and influential client, you will need to buy extra equipment, hire help, and rent additional space adjacent to the space you already have. This requires another investment of $50,000, which seems quite reasonable based on the potential business it will bring. Now your risk has doubled since your original investment.

You assess this to be a sound financial investment in a small yet potentially thriving new business venture, but what other risks do you have? You are the key employee, and you have the skill set that has created your reputation. What if something happens to you and you are unable to work for several weeks? How will the bakery fill orders and operate at the level you need to keep customers happy and your reputation strong? What kind of investment in staff, training, or other resources will you need to make to protect your investment? If there is a disruption in service, the hotels could select another service provider, and you may never get the business back. What if the hotels close or change ownership?

If the corporate client was unwilling to guarantee a certain volume or a reasonable term for the contract, you would need to assess your risk differently. At what point would you limit further investment? Make that decision ahead of time and be disciplined about it. Otherwise, your risk may grow beyond the point that you can afford and you may end up much deeper into an investment than you ever intended or would have consciously decided.

This is the dilemma of small businesses around the globe—the success rate is slim, risks can creep upward, and emotions are hard to ignore. It's important to keep your eye on the rate of return to compensate for the risk involved. Look ahead with hope for success, but prepare for possible failure by knowing in advance how much loss you can absorb. Be aware of creeping risk and be careful to make your decisions based on real facts.

Risk Unbalanced in Your Favor

The only thing better than balanced risk is risk that is unbalanced in your favor. Again, remember that this is the exception to the rule. When investing, unbalanced risk does not mean that you are guaranteed to make money. You will still be taking a risk, but if you win, the reward will greatly exceed the risk you have taken. When the risk and reward are out of balance in favor of the investor, it's rare but good news.

In the book *The Big Short*, author Michael Lewis chronicles the housing bubble of the early 2000's, along with some interesting stories about how people profited from the housing market crisis. Part of the book tells the story of a small group of investors who discovered an anomaly between binary events and the Black-Scholes formula for pricing options.

The Black-Scholes option-pricing model used widely within the area of finance is a mathematical model used to set the price for options to buy or sell financial assets. The value of an option on a stock is determined by how much the strike price (the price at which the option allows you to buy the stock) varies from the historic prices of the stock in the recent past and the length of time of the option coverage. For example, if the stock has traded in the range of $40 to $60 for the past twelve months, we would expect the stock to stay in that range or very close to it.

The concept is that if stock prices have historically moved in a methodical way, without high spikes or dramatic dips, future prices should behave in the same manner. The foundation for this is really quite rational—if a stock has not behaved in a volatile manner in the past, it should not behave in a volatile manner in the future.

Lewis tells the tale of Cornwall Capital Management (CCM), a money management firm that was started with a little over $100,000 by two people operating out of a shed behind a friend's house.[12] These two people, and later a third, were smart but had very little experience investing in the markets. These backyard investors realized that the market determines pricing for options by assuming there will only be normal movements in that particular stock, not abnormal movements.

Cornwall Capital Management looked for opportunities in which a stock was likely to have a price movement that was vastly out of its normal trading range. They scoured the markets to find a situation that was likely to occur in the near future and that would have a large impact on a company's stock. While they didn't know whether the impact would be positive or negative, they knew that options pricing would continue to be premised on normal price movements, which were more subdued.

They found such a binary event involving the stock of the financial company Capital One. Capital One's stock had been battered after management disclosed that it was under some specific inquiries by its regulators, which never indicates anything good. No one knew whether the regulators would or would not find problems in the company. The stock was trading around $30 a share, but the people at Cornwall Capital felt that this was definitely not the right number. They speculated that it could go down to

[12] Lewis, Michael. *The Big Short: Inside the Doomsday Machine* (New York: W. W. Norton & Company, 2010) 293.

$10 if there were real issues, or it could reach $60 if the regulators had no valid concerns about the company's treatment of certain items. They didn't have the money to buy a large amount of actual stock, but since the price for an option to buy a stock is always less expensive than the stock itself, they decided to buy options.

So, what did the people working out of a shed in the back of someone's house do? They bought 8,000 options to buy Capital One stock for a total cost of $26,000, betting that the stock would go up. With a total war chest of investable cash slightly over $100,000, their total possible capital loss of 26% was a significant bet for Cornwall Capital. What happened? The binary event occurred in the direction they anticipated. They made a profit of $500,000—an almost 20-fold increase over their $26,000 investment. The investing balance in this case was out of whack with almost $20 reward for every dollar at risk.

The Cornwall Capital Management anecdote illustrates a very good point about unbalanced risk. An asymmetrical bet in your favor doesn't guarantee a win. CCM could have lost the entire 26% of their working capital. Instead, a highly unbalanced risk-to-reward ratio on a relatively manageable bet set the stage for a huge payoff.

These young men decided that the regulators would come to a conclusion, but they weren't sure when or what they would conclude. In order to account for the timing part of the process, they bought a long-dated option on the stock that enabled them to exercise the option any time over a two-year period. This, they figured, would likely be enough time for regulators to come to a conclusion.

With the risk-to-reward ratio in mind, let's look at the odds. There was a very good chance that the regulators would resolve any issues within two years, so let's estimate this chance for resolution during the two-year period at an 85% probability. Let's further assume there was a 50% chance that the result would be what Cornwall Capital Management thought it would be. This would give CCM only a 42.5% chance of success (85% multiplied by 50%). However, if they were successful, the bet would pay off at almost

20:1 (the $500,000 they profited to the $26,000 they invested). This is a case where the reward was greatly in excess of the risk.

Opportunities in which the financial rewards greatly outweigh the risks are rare but make for great stories. Unbalanced risk in your favor isn't a sure payoff, but it is a good bet. Cornwall Capital bet a lot of their total capital, but it was a tolerable risk. They made great money and could have made even more if they had made a larger bet, but a larger bet would have risked more than they had deemed acceptable. Remember, while this was a smart bet, they could have lost. Losing $26,000 would still leave them enough money to make more investments. If you are operating out of a shed in someone's backyard and lose all of your capital, you may be serving shakes and fries at your next job.

High Stakes Risk

Long-Term Capital Management (LTCM) was a well-known hedge fund started in the 1990s by an elite group of academic math whizzes and traders from Salomon Brothers. In the world of finance, there are many such groups who are smart and effective and often make lots of money for their institutions and themselves. However, investment groups like this usually make money in spurts, earning great sums of money for one to three years before suffering losses and eventually fading from Wall Street stardom.

This group was like that, except for one notable difference: Their trades almost always worked. When they didn't, LTCM would confidently stay with the trade or double down, knowing that eventually the market would act in a logical way.

When Wall Street trading profits grew large enough to become a critical piece of an institution's income, the industry eschewed hiring local people who started out as runners and worked their way up to the trading floor. Instead, a greater value was given to people who traded less from gut instinct and opted to use sophisticated mathematical models to explore asymmetries in the marketplace. They would explore the global marketplace and look for occasions that the price of an asset was illogical and wrong. Based on the very logical premise that these imbalances in the global market would eventually be discovered and corrected, the traders would decide which bonds to buy using various algorithms. When they were right, they profited, but in order to make a mind-boggling amount of money, they had to trade in size—and by "size," I mean extremely large amounts even by Wall Street standards.

Because LTCM traded in size, they needed investment banks to clear their trades and sometimes act as counterparties. The people of Long-Term Capital Management had truly impressive academic credentials and included two Nobel Prize winners. The large institutions on Wall Street were enamored and allowed LTCM to engage in large, highly leveraged trades (borrowing heavily to make these investments.) Highly leveraged investments can be likened to going all-in at poker. When you win, you win big, but when you lose, you risk losing it all. Long-Term Capital Management had loads of data and the expertise to analyze that data, so it makes sense that their investment decisions would always be accurate, right? Not exactly.

Remember, you should always seek a balance between instinct and data. Some people use computers to find correlations in the data that might help guide them through certain decisions, while others steadfastly maintain that number-crunching nerds don't have any feel for things and don't realize the limitations of mathematical models. If there is a lot of reliable data available and you ignore it, you might still make a good decision, but you're not using the tools you have at hand to facilitate the most optimal result.

Long-Term Capital Management had great models and brilliant minds to analyze the data, but the firm's over-reliance on computer models eventually led to its downfall because one thing that the mathematical formulae of LTCM did not take into account was human behavior in times of economic stress.

Was the economic stress predictable? Absolutely! When markets are severely disrupted (as they were in 1999 and again in 2007 through 2008), there is usually a flight to quality phenomenon that occurs. "Flight to quality" means that in times of great uncertainty, people look for the safest investments rather than the riskier ones that could make them more money. In recent decades, this has led global investors to flock to the security of bonds issued by the United States government. They buy US Treasury bonds because they know that the United States will not default on its bonds and that the market for US bonds is extremely deep.

LTCM's logarithms did not take into account that in a global crisis, investors would look to invest in and hold United States bonds, ignoring other ways to explore inefficiencies. Any of the old-fashioned traders on Wall Street would have known this and immediately closed out all other trading positions to the extent that they could. They would expect flight-to-quality behavior regardless of the absence of supporting data. That was LTCM's oversight and, ultimately, its fatal flaw. The firm relied on their computer models to the exclusion of trading knowledge that was not anchored in a mathematical formula. Because LTCM was so highly leveraged, it did not have enough equity to absorb losses on its positions.

Both Cornwell Capital and LTCM were searching for and finding inefficiencies in the marketplace that presented opportunities to make money, but there was a major difference in their decision-making approach. The guys operating out of a backyard shed were smart, but not experienced, so they were careful with their risk-to-reward balance. They were willing to assume significant risk, but not enough to jeopardize their entire company. The folks at LTCM were bright, experienced, and overly confident in their data and ability, so they borrowed to bet big with little equity at stake. They either never considered the possibility that they could be wrong or ignored what would happen if they were. As a result, LTCM went bankrupt and almost took down the entire financial system in 1999.

Perhaps if regulators were using a process for thinking through decisions, they would have recognized a pattern and installed measures to prevent the similar but more severe financial crisis that would occur less than a decade later.

Black Swan Events and Human Nature

LTCM suffered from overconfidence in their algorithms and disregarded the possibility of a Black Swan event. In his book *The Black Swan*, author Nassim Nicholas Taleb defines a Black Swan event as one that is highly improbable and has three principal characteristics: the event is unexpected, has a significant impact, and is rationalized by hindsight. Natural disasters like earthquakes, tsunamis, and hurricanes can be considered Black Swan events in that we know that these will happen, but we don't know where, when, or what the magnitude will be.

LTCM should have accounted for the possibility of a Black Swan event in light of the Russian bond crisis. We often forget about economic crises that reoccur every few years because they pale in comparison to the current Great Recession, but they do happen on a recurring basis. The Silicon Valley dot-com bubble was a Black Swan event, as was Argentina and Brazil defaulting on their loans. The list of countries that have defaulted on their debts is long. Which one will default next and exactly when it will happen may be unknown, but the fact that something will go wrong in the global economy is quite predictable. LTCM, despite their impressive pedigree and status, failed to account for this and paid the ultimate price for their oversight and overconfidence.

Determining the Cost to Succeed

Risk versus reward is about cost compared to benefits. One of the things we need to do in any aspect of decision making is look to the future after the outcome is already known. Game theory experts refer to this as "backward reasoning."[13] I call it "backwardization." The term backwardization is more consistent with the overall framework and can be applied even when game theory is not applicable. We look to the future and then backtrack to determine the best path to achieve our goal. In this decision process, we apply the concept of backwardization by asking ourselves what we are

[13] Dixit, Avinash K. and Barry J. Nalebuff. *The Art of Strategy: A Game Theorist's Guide to Success in Business and Life.* (New York: W. W. Norton & Company, Inc., 2008) Chapter 2.

willing to do to succeed. At what cost will this still be worth it, assuming we succeed?

Some important decisions are not money-driven. It could be that in a fit of rage you decide to sue someone as a matter of principle, no matter what it costs. If you're a multibillionaire, perhaps you can afford to make this decision based on emotion, but the rest of us need to calmly calculate the cost of planned litigation and then reflect on whether our satisfaction in beating our opponent (assuming we are successful) is worth the cost.

One of the classic arenas of game theory is warfare. War is not a game, nor should it be taken lightly, but it is classic game theory. Game theory, in its simplest form, is the analysis and prediction of what your opponent will likely do based on the action you are considering taking. In applying game theory, we ask ourselves: What would result from our actions, or what is our opponent expected to do in response to our actions? Backwardization in game theory is about planning your approach based on both your opponent's predicted behavior and the subsequent outcome of that behavior.

"He who wishes to fight must first count the cost."
— Sun Tzu, *The Art of War*

There are no more important decisions than military decisions that involve addressing potential threats to our country, but these come with a dear price—human life, physical injuries, and mental stress. Former Defense Secretary Robert Gates had been involved with various areas of the US government for decades. Most of those years were spent in senior leadership roles with the Central Intelligence Agency and the Department of Defense. Based on his experience, Gates is probably the foremost expert at analyzing the various security risks presented to the United States and finding the most optimal solutions to those problems. Robert Gates is the only defense secretary to work for Presidents from two different political parties (George W. Bush and Barack Obama), an achievement that is nothing short of spectacular. To say that he is highly regarded is an understatement.

The *New York Times* interviewed Defense Secretary Gates as he was about to retire from his latest position and reported about it on Sunday,

June 19, 2011. The article stated, "Even as a trained historian, [Gates] said, he had learned over the last four and a half years that wars 'have taken longer and been more costly in lives and treasure' than anticipated."

Defense Secretary Gates's statement is alarming because it reveals that one of the key data points involved in the decision to go to war is unreliable. Clearly this is not a political party issue between Democrats and Republicans. It is an issue for any president, who, by definition, is the commander in chief of the United States Armed Forces. How can the chief decision maker of the United States and its military optimally decide any military action without an accurate sense of the expected costs? The costs of war are tremendous, both monetarily and non-monetarily. The most important of these costs is the cost of human lives. An accurate assessment of the most likely outcomes and worst-case scenarios is necessary for any decision to produce optimal results.

Most anyone who is planning to build a house, buy a car, or spend significant resources on anything would look at the estimated costs before deciding to proceed or not. How can the commander in chief of the Armed Forces not insist on having accurate data? Endless statistics exist for predicting baseball, basketball, football, and other sports outcomes, as well as the outcomes of fantasy leagues. Shouldn't we have a sense of the original estimate for the human and monetary cost of prior wars and how much the variance was when they were over? As the authors of *The Art of Strategy* assert, "The first rule of strategy: Look forward and reason backward."

In the case of war, you would need to determine the cost you are willing to accept. Would you support the military action if it cost 100 US soldiers' lives? What if it cost the lives of 1,000 US soldiers or 10,000 or 100,000? Ideally, the cost would be zero lives lost, but that ideal is usually irrelevant in war strategy. If the president is willing to risk the lives of 100 soldiers but not 1,000, perhaps the cause is not important enough to command action after all. Here we are engaging in Thinking Deeply and analyzing our risk-to-reward or cost-to-benefit ratio.

Let's assume a simple hypothetical that the lives of 100 US citizens are at stake now or in the near future. Military leaders meet with the president

and indicate that they can take action to save these 100 lives, and they estimate that they will probably lose ten soldiers. Although a multitude of other
factors must be considered, based on the numbers, the president might be
inclined to risk ten soldiers' lives so that 100 civilians could be saved. What
if the number of soldiers that would likely die was 200? That would be
a very costly mission to save 100 civilians. Unless there are compelling
reasons to the contrary, this might seem too high a cost for the benefit.

The backwardization concept is important for military action because
not every mission will go as smoothly as a perfectly orchestrated SEAL
Team operation. How many lives should we risk in any military conflict?
The answer should depend on the conflict and the concomitant risk to the
country.

Recap

Calculating balance forces us to focus on the risk-to-reward ratio and
helps us make more sound decisions by replacing simple biases or emotion
with a deeper awareness of the facts. When we take a look at the perceived
value we hope to receive, we need to balance it against the costs we are
willing to risk in order to achieve that success, and we should aim for a
balanced result or results that are out of balance in our favor. If our decision is in balance, the potential reward should be equal to, or in balance
with, the potential risk. When things seem out of balance, engage in real
thinking, look for relevant data, and check your biases.

Balance Checklist

- **Good decisions should lead to balanced results or results that are out of balance in your favor.**
- **Relevant data is a check and balance against the emotions that run our instinctive decision process.** Both gut instinct and real data should be factored into any decision.
- **Be aware of the value you are placing on an intangible reward** to gain perspective on the risk you are considering.
- **The risk of inaction is equal to the benefit or reward** you may have achieved by taking action.
- **Know and stick to your risk parameters.** Anticipate that your risk may increase over time (creeping risk) and have the discipline to walk away rather than invest further in a decision that is not working out well (sunk cost fallacy).
- **Use backwardization, or backward reasoning, to predict the cost of success** before you pursue it and determine whether the cost is equal to, less than, or greater than the benefit.
- **A decision with a risk-to-reward ratio imbalanced against you is a poor decision.**

PROBABILITIES

Probabilities define the likelihood of a particular event or result occurring. Our goal is to identify ways to increase the odds of getting what we want and avoiding what we don't want. Like all other factors in the framework, the term "probabilities" accurately describes the concept of this step but requires a deeper explanation in order to apply it.

In this chapter, you will learn

- How to use probabilities to stay focused on your goal
- How to use backwardization for planning actions to reach your goal
- How to assess the strength of your underlying assumptions
- How probabilities should be considered even when something is certain to happen
- How to best use expected values to predict results

If we know whether or not something is likely to happen, we can base our decision on that probability. We are very often confronted with situations in which no single option clearly has more than a 50% chance of being successful. This happens all of the time in personal, business, sports, and gambling decisions.

Even when you are going by instinct, you quickly estimate that the best chance of success lies in the decision you just made. One of the only exceptions to using probabilities is a decision to do something because you feel it is the morally responsible course of action. The other exception is an instance in which our amygdala appropriately kicks in—if our house catches fire, we run to save our children without calculating our chances of being successful. All other decisions, especially important decisions, must consider the probabilities of success and failure.

Establishing and Clearly Defining Targets

One of the benefits of focusing on probabilities is that it forces you to clearly define your goal. Probabilities won't determine your goals for you, but they pave the way to clarity and help you get specific about your goals. After all, you can't decide on the best way to reach a destination without first determining where you want to go.

The optimal path to achieving your goal begins with clearly defining your goal, so get specific. The more explicitly you can articulate your objective, the more able you are to see the best way to reach it. If you don't have a clear goal or set of goals, you can't choose the optimal method for obtaining your goal. How do you know if you've been successful if you haven't defined what success is?

Many people claim that they want to be their own boss, which is not a clearly defined goal. Do they want to own their own business? What kind of business? Maybe they want to be an attorney in their own firm, but what kind of attorney and in what size firm? Specializing in what? The more detailed your goal is, the more able you will be to determine the probability of reaching that goal and, in turn, to identify what you need to do to get there.

Success in itself is not a clear goal. You need to be able to define the kind of success you want. Is it monetary? Is it reputation and awards? How is timing involved? In other words, when do you want to achieve the milestones—in a year? Five years? Ten years? When you get specific, "I want to be my own boss," changes to, "I want to be a successful tax attorney in my own firm grossing $500,000 per year in revenues within the next five years." That is a specific goal!

Expected Happenings, Outcomes, and Values

An expected happening, or the outcome we expect to happen, is one of the basic concepts of probabilities and most relevant when significant data or a mathematical formula can be used to predict results. While the term is "expected happening," the result is binary—the event either will or won't happen.

When the meteorologist forecasts a 40% chance of rain, she is also saying that there is a 60% chance that it may not rain. Most people hearing such a forecast will grab an umbrella as they leave the house, because 40% is a great enough chance of rain to make the minimal effort required to be prepared. When you get home that evening, you will either be glad you brought the umbrella because it did rain or you will mumble something about weather forecasters because you had to lug that umbrella around all day for no reason. The actual occurrence of rain was binary—there were only two outcomes: rain or no rain.

The medical evidence is clear: If you smoke cigarettes, you greatly increase your chances of getting lung cancer or other diseases and dying prematurely. This is what professors call "expected outcome" when teaching about probabilities. Expected outcomes are about expected results. They drive probabilities and weigh heavily in decision making.

Not everyone who smokes cigarettes gets lung cancer. Not everyone who gets lung cancer smoked cigarettes. A person who smokes and then contracts lung cancer will never know which cigarette was the tipping point that caused the disease—was it the first cigarette, the hundredth, the ten thousandth, or the last cigarette? We don't know and will never know based on current medical technology, but we can say with statistical certainty that smoking cigarettes will increase a person's chances of developing lung cancer and that not smoking greatly decreases the risk of getting lung cancer. Sound decision making should seek to optimize our chances to avoid bad things as well as achieve good things.

A Hit or a Miss

If you're a fan of baseball, you have been dealing with expected outcomes your whole life. A baseball player who has a .400 batting average gets a hit 40% of the time. This is a very high percentage by baseball standards, and he is a very valuable player to have on your team. If your team is behind by one run in the bottom of the ninth inning with the bases loaded, a base hit will at least tie the game and could very well win the game. As manager, at this point you have a choice about whether to put in the hitter with a .400 batting average or another player whose batting average is .250 and gets a hit 25% of the time.

Ignoring on-base percentages, most people would agree that the right move is to use the player with the .400 batting average. Does this guarantee that the .400 player will get a hit and the .250 player won't? No. Based on their averages, there is more than a 50% chance that neither player will get a hit, but the batter with the higher average improves the team's chance to tie or win the game and would be the best choice. The actual result will again be binary; the batter will either get a hit or will miss.

Gambling

Gambling, at its core, centers on probabilities. Probabilities are key to gambling because one way or another, when you place a bet, you are laying a wager on what you believe will happen. Your view regarding the probabilities of whether you have the winning hand or not is critical to your decisions on whether or not to bet and how much to bet. Even when bluffing in poker, you are betting on the likelihood that you will pull off the bluff. While bluffing may be one of the more exciting ways to win, remember that you are only bluffing if you believe you have the weaker hand. If you think you have the strongest hand but do not, you aren't bluffing; you are just misjudging the probabilities.

Let's assume that you just want to spend some time in the casino to enjoy yourself and play a little at the roulette wheel. You are hoping to be lucky and certainly don't hope to be unlucky, but you are realistic and expect to lose some amount of money while you are there. If you plan to spend three hours at the roulette wheel being neither especially lucky nor unlucky, what are your expectations regarding how much you will lose? These probabilities can be found by looking at the odds and payoffs in roulette.

There are 38 separate numbers on an American roulette wheel: numbers one to 36, zero, and double zero. You can bet on individual numbers, groups of numbers, even or odd numbers, and so on. To illustrate how we determine the expected outcome of playing for three hours, which here is the expected loss, let's focus on betting on a single number. On the roulette wheel, your odds of winning are 1:38.

Expected outcomes based on odds would indicate that over the course of an evening in which you played roulette 38 times, betting $10 each time, you should reasonably expect to lose $20. With odds at 1:38, you would spend $380 in bets with a one-time win of $360. Of course, in reality you could either lose the entire $380 or make money if you won more than once, but based strictly on the odds, you would lose $20. The expected loss is determined by dividing the 38 total attempts by the expected loss of $20. For every $10 bet, your expected loss is 53 cents, based on the average of making 38 consecutive bets in the course of the evening. The expected loss of 53 cents per bet can never happen in reality if you only play once because, again, the result will be binary. You will either win $360 or lose the entire $10 each time you play.

How is the expected loss valuable information in this case? Expected values are only reliable when there is a treasure trove of reliable data, not in rare occurrences. Calculating how long it would take you to play the roulette wheel 38 times, you might reasonably assume the risk of losing $20 to enjoy free drinks in an exciting atmosphere. Because everyone thinks less when they drink more, you may begin to irrationally feel that you are "due" to get lucky and keep playing when you would have stopped the betting and cut your losses. The casino's revenue is built on true statistics and the law of large numbers. Casinos profit from people betting in volume and quantities. They are better off having you at the roulette wheel betting

$100 each time rather than $10, because then they will make $200 from you on average, not $20. Whether you bet $100 or $10 a time, though, the casino's odds remain tipped in their favor.

These are just a few examples of the most common ways we use expected outcomes to guide our behavior. Expected outcomes can be good or bad. Good outcomes create value, and bad outcomes create costs. In business, insurance companies, investment banks, and most other organizations use this fundamental concept as part of their core business analysis. The whole concept of a diversified, balanced investment portfolio is based on expected outcomes, not guarantees.

100% Probability, Variable: When

"On a long enough timeline, the survival rate for everyone drops to zero."
—Zerohedge.com

Situations requiring keen decision making come in all forms. Sometimes there is a 100% certainty that something will happen, but when it will happen is unknown. The simplest example of this is death. At the writing of this book, there is no known human being who has lived forever. Therefore, death is assumed to be a 100% probability for all of us. The variable in this case is timing, and the question then becomes how long will you live?

Many people are operating, perhaps unconsciously, under the assumption that they will live to a certain age. This presumption is evident in decisions they make about when to retire. At a glance, it seems perfectly reasonable to expect to work until age 60, if you think the probability is that you will live to be 75. If you actually thought that you would only live until 60, you may set a goal to retire at 55 or much earlier if you can afford it, rather than working right up until the day you die.

Researchers at the Max Planck Institute for Demographic Research in Rostock, Germany, have recently concluded that 72 is the new 30. The research is based on the fact that 30-year-old people in the year 1800 would have the same risk of dying as someone who is 72 today. While this dramatic increase in life expectancy may be partly influenced by increased awareness of the importance of diet and exercise, it is mostly due to incredible achievements in medical science. How many people do you know who take medication on a regular basis? Do you know anyone who has undergone physical therapy after an MRI helped his or her physician diagnose the problem? The list goes on and on. Scientific developments in medicine are vast and have dramatically increased our lifespan, which is almost all good news, except financially.

If you are a male who grew up in the United States and you live to be 65 years old, chances are you will continue to live to age 82. The assumption about your estimated life expectancy is not just wishful thinking; it is the current estimation used by the US Social Security Administration.[14] A woman who reaches the age of 65 can expect to live until she's 85. This life expectancy gets longer, not shorter, with each passing year and advances in medicine. Why does that matter? That reasonable assumption, based on the probability of it happening, drives your decisions on when to retire, how much money you will need, and more. Is there a guarantee that you will live to 85? Of course not, but to ignore the probability would not be prudent.

Let's say you estimate that you will probably reach age 85, but you actually live longer. That's good news, right? The problem with living past 85, in this case isn't life itself; it's making sure you have money to support you if you are fortunate enough to live that long.

There is a model in the investment business that financial advisors use to tailor your investment portfolio to dovetail with your desired retirement date. That makes some sense, but to do so without regard for reasonable life expectancy is not the best method. I would like to live until I'm 90, if I can afford it. Living until 90 as a destitute old man is less enticing. I don't want to be hobbling around at 92, gathering shopping carts and asking, "Paper or plastic?" While some people plan for the unfortunate event of early

[14] "Actuarial Life Table," Social Security Administration, accessed August 17, 2014, http://www.ssa.gov/oact/STATS/table4c6.html.

death by buying life insurance to care for their families in their absence, most people, and certainly most governments that provide pensions, don't plan for the unlikely event that we will live much longer than anticipated.

Considering probabilities is great for planning. When there is a 100% probability (certainty) of something happening, but when it will happen is unknown, the key is to determine the most likely (probable) time of the occurrence and then work backward to plan your actions or decisions for optimal results. This is another example of backwardization. In this case, the likelihood may be that you will live to be 85, but we don't know.

100% Probability; Variable: Who

Other circumstances come with a 100% probability that they will happen, but rather than the key variable being *when* it will happen, the key variable is *to whom* it will happen. Odds of winning the Powerball jackpot are remarkably slim, but it is statistically certain that someone or some group of people will eventually win that lottery. There are dozens of theories about how to predict the winning numbers, but none have been proven to work without fail. The only sure probability is that you can't win if you don't play. Despite the odds, we buy the tickets to increase our probability of being the one who wins.

There are unfortunate events that have a 100% certainty of happening, as well. With these events, we want to direct our decisions and actions to avoid being the one who suffers the misfortune. For instance, it is statistically safe to assume that someone will be in a car accident today. Unfortunately, it is statistically safe to assume that someone will die in a car accident today as well. We wear seatbelts, stay aware, and abide by traffic laws in order to decrease the probability that we become one of these statistics. When things are virtually certain to happen, but it is uncertain whether they will happen to you, take measures to avoid the bad things and maximize the chances of the good things coming your way.

The odds are against those who pursue the arts as a profession. Becoming a top music, television, movie, or stage star is highly remote, but if we only pursued goals that were more than 50% likely to happen, most of us would never chase our dreams. If your goal is something that is highly unlikely to happen, it is important to first be realistic about your possibility of achieving that goal. Using as unbiased a view of the situation as possible, you will be better equipped to assess the situation and determine which steps will increase your probability for success. A realistic view will also gauge your true desire and willingness to pursue your goal as you're faced with the expected challenges inherent in reaching for the stars, so to speak. Once you have assessed the situation, you can begin identifying ways to increase your probabilities.

Let's say you join a Fortune 500 company hoping to someday be the chief executive officer. The way most Fortune 500 companies work, a very small percentage of people will ever be given such a high level opportunity. While the odds are against you, the probability is nearly certain that someone will be given the position you seek. Likewise, we may have no idea who will be the biggest star in music five years from now, or even what genre of music will be the most popular, but it is certain that somebody will rise to fame and fortune in the music industry.

When you wish to achieve a lofty goal—one that is certain to happen but has very low probability of happening to you—you need to first understand how the people who have achieved this goal before you have done so. Pattern recognition, which will be covered in the next chapter, is excellent for identifying steps or variables necessary to reach your objective. Musicians don't get their start playing sold-out stadiums. Often they start by playing for free or for very little money to build a following and hone their skills. If you want to be an actor on Broadway, you probably need to live in New York City. If you dream of TV stardom, you may need to live in Los Angeles. Moving to L.A. or New York doesn't guarantee that you'll instantly become a sought-after actor, but it does increase your ability to participate in the industry or field you wish to pursue, thus increasing your chances of success.

If you want to be a high-level business executive for an established company, do you need to get a business degree? Will an undergraduate degree suffice or will you need an MBA to be considered for the executive track you seek? If you want to run a technology start-up, the path to CEO may be totally different. Rather than follow the traditional educational route, you may find that you can increase your chances for success by moving to Silicon Valley or other tech hubs, where you can network with other creative types and venture capitalists who might invest in your concept. Identify which things will get you the highest possibility of success in whatever you desire, and implement those things.

Less than 100% Probability

The "law of large numbers" is a phrase that means that larger samples of data provide more predictable results. If we conduct an experiment involving two people and the results are identical, we should not assume that the results would continue to be consistent if we extended our sample size to 20,000 people. When relying on our own personal experiences or even objective data that is based on a small sample size, we are not using strong enough data and are leaving ourselves open to be influenced by our biases.

Actuaries annually estimate how much money a government or company needs to infuse into a pension plan in order to make it solvent. There are two big assumptions here. The first significant assumption is how long the pensioners will live. The longer the pensioner lives, the more money has to be paid out. That is the outflow of cash. The second significant assumption is the rate of return the invested funds will earn over time, or the cash inflow. If the cash inflow from the investments is not great enough, the government or company has to contribute more money. If the investments are sufficient, there is no need for the government or company to contribute more money.

Let's say that the actuary has assumed that the funds will earn 8% annually. If 8% is incorrect, and the assumption should be a 5% return, the results are dramatically different. Let me clarify that the difference to the fund is not a simple 3%. Due to the compounding of earnings upon earnings, the difference could result in a pension plan being underfunded by billions of dollars. For those who aren't familiar with compounding, think about the trajectory of a golf ball that is improperly struck. A tee shot that is hit one quarter of an inch from where it should have been struck does not land only one quarter of an inch from its target. The ball will end up very far from its intended target due to the (seemingly minor) initial miscalculation. The same thing happens when you use the wrong interest rate assumption over a long period of time. This is what happened to the city of Detroit. By changing the assumption about the investment returns to a more realistic number, Detroit suffered an estimated $3.5 billion shortfall in its pensions and did not have enough cash to make the problem go away.[15]

Size Matters

Bill Gates went to Harvard and then dropped out to start Microsoft. At one point, it was estimated that Gates was worth over $100 billion. Mark Zuckerberg also went to Harvard and then dropped out to build Facebook. He is estimated to be worth more than $30 billion. Based on these two stories, should you do all you can to get your child into Harvard and then encourage her to drop out? I would think not. The sample size is too small. We are ignoring any information regarding people who dropped out of Harvard and never achieved any monetary success. Remember this when you realize that you are about to reach a conclusion regarding probabilities based on a small sample size.

What if only a small amount of data is available? If you have some reliable data, but it violates the law of large numbers, you should still consider it. It may not be perfect but if it is the only data you have, it should still be factored into your decision.

When using data for any analysis, remember two things:

1. Be aware of the strength or weakness of your sample size,

---

[15] Walsh, Mary Williams. "Detroit Gap Reveals Industry Dispute on Pension Math." *New York Times,* July 19, 2013.

AND

2. Always check the assumptions underlying the data, even with a large sample size.

Recap

Optimal decisions involve taking the path of the highest probability to achieve our specific goals. Expected happenings and expected values are often binary and will either happen or won't. Once you have decided what you want the result to be, you can begin to assess the chances of achieving what you desire. If you are avoiding a bad occurrence, you will look for ways to decrease your probabilities. If you are trying to increase the chances of a good occurrence, you will look for ways to increase your probabilities of that good fortune becoming yours.

Probabilities Checklist

- The optimal path to achieving your goal begins with clearly defining your goal. **In order to assess the probabilities, you must first know what your goal is.** Get specific.
- **Be aware of the law of large numbers** if you are relying on numerical data, and always make sure you **understand the underlying assumptions**.
- To identify the best choice in decision making, **look for the option that presents the highest odds of success.**
- **Expected happenings and expected values are most relevant when significant data can be used to predict results.**
- Some things are certain to happen, but whether they will happen to you and when is uncertain. **Probabilities will help you identify measures to avoid the bad things and maximize the chances of the good things happening to you.**

PATTERN RECOGNITION

Pattern recognition is about "connecting the dots" by reviewing all of the data you have in order to identify which elements or facts can influence or directly cause you to have the best chance of reaching your desired outcome. This is the most intellectually demanding part of decision making and what separates great decision makers from not-so-great decision makers.

In this chapter, you will learn

- How to train yourself to spot predictive patterns
- How to analyze the three separate categories of correlation, relevance, and causation
- How to best manage and simplify vast amounts of data

While all of the four analytical steps require Thinking Deeply, pattern recognition usually requires the deepest thinking of all. It is intellectually challenging and can also be physically demanding, as you will burn glucose by using your brain intensively. It is also the part of the decision-making thought process that can be unintentionally influenced by various biases the most. If you begin pattern recognition with the mission to find a pattern that supports your hoped-for conclusion, you will be easily misled into spotting one. Good decision making is not a debate; you don't aim to prove your case. Done correctly, it is objective analysis.

Pattern recognition involves sorting data into groups in an effort to spot predictive trends. We use the concepts of correlation, relevance, and causation to find a relationship between facts and outcomes. The key to successful pattern recognition is determining which factors correlate with the outcome, which of the correlative factors are relevant to the outcome, and which may be causative factors. High correlation does not necessarily equal causation, which means that a perfect correlation will not necessarily get you the result you want. Few things are causative, but the fact that something doesn't directly cause the result you want doesn't mean it should be dismissed. A fact may not be causative, but it can still be highly relevant. Assuming that things are only either causative or non-causative leaves out the very important category of relevance.

Pattern recognition is the most difficult of the four factors because most of us are trained to know specific information or perform specific tasks, not to see subtle trends at a glance outside of our narrow area of expertise. In our areas of expertise, we may instinctively spot patterns. For example, an experienced doctor can often recognize a certain disease based on various symptoms. Years of medical training and practice allow the doctor to identify the disease with a high degree of certainty. What happens, though, when this doctor has to spot a pattern that doesn't involve medicine?

You can train yourself to be good at recognizing patterns, especially outside of your area of expertise, even if it doesn't come naturally to you. As you train yourself to spot true patterns and recognize false patterns, you will dramatically increase your critical thinking, and the results of your decisions will dramatically improve.

Training Your Brain to Connect the Dots

Pattern recognition involves analyzing all of the tidbits of information we have access to in order to find greater meaning and be able to predict a future outcome. Once you have gathered your data, there are three steps to recognizing a pattern. These steps, which will be discussed in greater detail, are

1. To determine whether a **correlation** exists in your data

2. To look for **relevance** in the correlation
3. To consider whether one of the relevant factors can actually **cause** an event to happen or not

Knowledge versus Understanding

During most of our schooling and professional lives, we are rewarded for knowing specific information, not for our overall intellectual aptitude. Despite the rhetoric on how our schools, at any level, teach critical thinking and analysis, our institutions generally reward the regurgitation of specific facts rather than thoughtful evaluation. Our educational system puts a premium on knowledge that is easily measured and less subjective. In school, we are tested on very specific knowledge. For instance, we take courses in American history, European history, the history within a certain timeframe such as Medieval Europe, and so on. We are tested on dates, times, names of emperors, and noteworthy battles. We are not usually, unless in graduate school at Yale University, taught the history of histories, which illustrates how all histories from all eras and cultures relate to each other. Instead of simply memorizing data points, if we learned to recognize the connections and patterns in those data points, we would gain invaluable insight about why people and cultures behave the way they do, why conflicts happen, and how to prevent conflicts from escalating into wars.

I can teach a parrot to say, "You are beautiful," every time a woman walks into the room, but the parrot is not making a thoughtful judgment. It is only doing what it has been trained to do. Instead of high grades or a paycheck, the parrot is rewarded with its own currency—a cracker. There is an important difference between the ability to repeat a fact or data point and a deeper understanding of the data in relation to the circumstances that surround it.

As a tax attorney, I made a decent living by knowing a lot of data about specific financial products and institutions. Large international financial institutions paid me a relatively good fee because I was perceived as a leading expert on certain sections of the US Internal Revenue Code. I was not an expert in most sections of the Internal Revenue Code, nor was I an expert in law in general. Certainly, no one was going to pay me because of my IQ or my view of history and world affairs. I was rewarded for being very good in a few areas of tax law and for my ability to help clients keep their tax burden as low as legally possible.

This is the way our culture works. If you have an earache, you go to the doctor and probably to an ear, nose, and throat specialist. You don't go to a cardiologist. Your doctor may be the smartest person you know, but if your car has a problem, you don't ask him to fix it. From CPAs to shoe repair, professionals are paid only for their areas of expertise.

There is value in learning large quantities of specific knowledge, but without also learning the larger concepts related to these bodies of knowledge, we have spent a lot of time learning data points without a purpose. We spend all of our time learning the dots, and very little to no time learning to connect the dots. This is like pouring volumes of data into a computer to produce thick and impressive spreadsheets that no one can make any sense of.

The Importance of Analysis

In general, champions of the game show *Jeopardy* are well-read, well-educated people. I wish I had their encyclopedic knowledge of books, politics, religion, history, and other topics, but whether they are truly intellectuals or just very knowledgeable is unknown. They may be intellectual, or they may just possess an impressive array of specific knowledge.

Ken Jennings, one of the most famous champions in the history of *Jeopardy*, lost to Watson, a computer programmed with a vast array of data that was constantly updated and perfected by a team at IBM. Watson didn't get tired and could work 24/7 without stopping. It was inevitable that a sophisticated computer supported by a team of human programmers would defeat a sole human being in a test of specific knowledge in a contest where time is a constant factor. Does that mean that Watson is smarter than Ken Jennings? If you judge intelligence as the ability to regurgitate specific bits of information quickly, then yes, Watson is smarter. I think that Ken Jennings is smarter than Watson. Jennings can think and look for trends, patterns, and reason. Watson can look for high degrees of association between facts but not intellectually seek reason in the findings.

Do not equate volume of information with depth of intellectual analysis. I have heard many fellow lawyers say something like, "He is the expert in this area. He wrote an article on this topic that was 550 pages long!" While I may appreciate the thoroughness and work ethic of the author in question, the length of an article does not indicate that it reflects any great legal analysis. I can scour the internet and assemble an extensive compendium of articles devoid of any intellectual analysis or insight. True intellectual ability allows us to summarize complex issues into understandable components.

While most of us are not trained in school or in life to be experts at pattern recognition, learning how to analyze and identify correlation, relevance, and causation can dramatically increase critical thinking that leads to better decision making. While correlation, relevance, and causation all focus on the association between facts or data points, pattern recognition looks to identify which data points or factors correlate with the outcome, which of the correlative factors are relevant to the outcome, and which may be causative factors.

> *"There are two ways to do well in life. One is to go an inch wide and a mile deep and become an expert in something, and the other one is to be able to connect dots and go wide. There are times in your career where you need to go deep, you need to become an expert and get really good at it. The unique people are the ones that can connect those dots. The real game changers are people that are taking those verticals and connecting them horizontally."*
> —Seth Waugh, former CEO of the Americas, Deutsche Bank[16]

[16] Madkour, Abraham D. "Former CEO Seth Waugh on Leading, Learning, Golf and a 'No Assholes' Rule." *Sports Business Journal,* April 28, 2014.

Step 1: Finding Correlation

Correlation is a Relationship Between Data

The first thing to look for is correlation between certain factors and your desired goal. Correlation occurs when a connection exists between two or more separate things or events. With advances in computer technology and access to a treasure trove of widely accessible public data, it is much easier to spot correlation now than in the past. That's the good news. With some data and a computer, just about anything can be correlated. This is a trap for the unwary and can lead people to assume that a mere coincidental correlation has a deeper meaning.

Large organizations, from the National Security Administration to the internet giants Google and Facebook, recognize the value of being able to predict human behavior, and they spend tremendous resources analyzing mounds of metadata to find predictive trends. When there is a high degree of correlation between facts or between a fact and an outcome, we frequently mistake correlation for causation, convincing ourselves of a cause-and-effect scenario that does not actually exist between the correlating data and the outcome. In other words, our desire to identify what causes our desired outcome can push us into the trap of seeing a connection that isn't really there. Remember to slow down, use your brain, and don't let emotions cloud your judgment. Correlation doesn't necessarily reveal causation.

There are a few common pitfalls to watch out for during data analysis. In today's social media tsunami, every pundit and professor publishes at will. As a result, thought-provoking but sometimes deceiving articles are often published. The fact that it is published does not mean that it is unbiased or reliable. If you are getting results from media sources invested in catching your attention with headlines, ask yourself a couple of questions:

1. What are the assumptions that were made in the research?
2. What was the sample size?

While we are ideally looking for causative factors, helpful correlative factors that don't rise to the level of causation can still be relevant. As addressed in the chapter on probabilities, the larger the amount of reliable data (sample size), the more reliable the correlation may be.

Let's say that you review previous situations in which the desired outcome was obtained and you see that factor X was present 62% of the time. This is interesting to note and may be important, but 62% is only 12% more than half of the time. If that same factor was present 92% of the time, it would be an even greater correlation and may be quite meaningful. On the other end of the spectrum, if you examine similar historical situations and see that factor Z has never been present, this presents zero correlation and there is a presumption that factor Z is not relevant in your decision-making process.

Jumping to Conclusions

Don't let correlation automatically drive you into thinking that a factor must be a relevant or causative factor. Finding correlation is the beginning of finding causation, but be cognizant that correlation is only a relationship between data. There is not yet enough information from which to draw conclusions. If you automatically assume that one correlating data point reveals causation, you are Thinking Lightly or, more likely, being driven solely by a non-thinking gut reaction. Your initial impressions allow you to make snap judgments very efficiently, but stay open to the possibility that you are wrong. Pattern recognition demands more analysis.

On a professional football team, there is probably no position more important than that of quarterback. The National Football League is often referred to as the "quarterback's league," and elite quarterbacks command compensation packages in excess of $100 million. If you are the owner, general manager, or coach, your job is to build a winning football team. As such, your choice of quarterbacks is extremely important. Even if your area of expertise is football, this is a high-stakes decision. You should not rely solely on your gut instinct, regardless of how many years you have been involved in the professional football business. This high-stakes decision screams for the need to have a decision-making structure and some real, hard facts.

If your draft choice becomes an elite quarterback, your team will be successful. If your draft pick doesn't work out, you have incurred two costs: first, the monetary expense of signing a first-round draft choice, and second, a squandered opportunity incurred because your selected player did not deliver as expected. You otherwise could have traded away your first-round draft slot for an experienced proven player.

Three well-known experts were invited to appear on a popular television sports program to discuss which college quarterbacks should be chosen in an upcoming National Football League draft. This particular trio of experts had an enormous amount of aggregate football expertise, yet the only statistic they focused on was height. Two quarterbacks in the current draft had done very well at the collegiate level but were less than six feet tall. The college athletes being discussed were not 5'6" or 5'8". Both of them were at least 5'11", and one was 5' 11 ¾". The height statistic these experts used was based on the fact that in recent history, four quarterbacks who were less than six feet tall were selected in the early rounds of the drafts, and only one of them was successful. Based on this 75% failure rate alone, it would seem almost reckless to waste an important draft choice on a quarterback under six feet tall.

Remember the earlier discussion about how prejudice can lead you to an accurate but misleading statistic? The lone statistic is misleading because it doesn't tell the entire story. You need to fill in the other statistics to get the complete picture. Since the goal is to draft a quarterback who will be successful at the professional level, let's assume that "success" was a clearly defined term, which it wasn't. What are the other statistics you might want to know? What is the success rate for quarterbacks over six feet tall? If it's the same as the rate for quarterbacks under six feet tall, height is irrelevant. Notice that the experts anchored themselves to a six-foot height standard. What is the success rate for quarterbacks over 6'4"? If height is the determinative factor, maybe they shouldn't draft players under 6'4".

What we have here is a single factor (height) that seems to have a high correlation with failure in the NFL. They didn't compare the success rates of quarterbacks between 6 feet and 6'2", nor between 6'2" and 6'4". Was there ever a successful quarterback who was taller than 6'7"? Was the sample size of four quarterbacks large enough to be reliable? Were there other factors that could account for the 75% failure rate? You need to have all of the facts, not just a few arbitrarily selected facts, before you can determine correlation and a possible connection between success in the National Football League and the height of your quarterback.

The quarterback has to make extremely quick decisions that drive the outcome of the game. Were all of the quarterbacks in question properly trained and smart enough to do this? How fast could each of the quarterbacks run? How far and how hard could they throw a football? Did they have any off-field issues like crime or addiction that helped cause their failure? To determine that only one factor is important, you have to rule out other factors that may influence the outcome.

This trio of football experts agreed that they would be very hesitant to draft a quarterback that was not at least six feet tall. Am I questioning their experience and ultimate conclusion? Not necessarily, but if their conclusion was right, it was mere luck. If I was the owner of a team and they were spending my millions of dollars, I would not accept their (lack of) analysis. I would make them read the book *Moneyball* and tell me why they think its concept only applies to baseball players and not football players.

Apply All Data That Matters

Let's say you are hiring. You receive two resumes that contain the educational background for applicants who are both recent college graduates. One is from an Ivy League institution, and one is from a local state college. You have never met either one, but you might jump to the reasonable conclusion that the Ivy League graduate is going to be smarter than the local state-college applicant due to the common knowledge that Ivy League schools have much more rigorous standards for acceptance.

Now you interview both candidates. The Ivy League graduate interviews well enough, but she is nothing spectacular. The local state-college graduate is charming and smart and answers all of your questions to your complete satisfaction. She even handles the intellectually challenging questions superbly! Now what do you do? The interview is a second data point, but which element is more important? Do you hire the Ivy Leaguer because you are anchored to the preconception that she is smarter? There is no concrete right or wrong here, but this scenario happens all of the time.

Be honest with yourself. If your mindset is to hire an Ivy League graduate no matter what, save yourself time and don't even bother interviewing anyone who didn't graduate from an Ivy League school. If that is your choice, let's look at your conclusions. First, you are concluding that an Ivy League graduate is always going to be more intelligent than a non-Ivy League graduate. Second, you are concluding that higher intelligence is determinative to success in the position you are hoping to fill. Third, you are assuming that high intelligence will cause this person to become a great long-term employee.

While these assumptions may or may not be true, recognize them. If other factors can come into play, what are they? A highly intelligent person may have greater opportunities and could leave for a better offer shortly after taking the position. You may only need a person with above average intelligence, not someone with very high intelligence. What about social skills? If interpersonal skills matter, decide beforehand just how much the interview will count.

Assumptions and Statistics

Let's look at what happens when we involve statistics in pattern recognition. Statistics are hard data, which should eliminate mistaken interpretations, right? Not exactly. In fact, statistics can be more misleading if only selective data is being emphasized. This same thing happens every day in the news as editors strive for eye-catching headlines rather than a fair and thoughtful presentation of facts.

Let's hypothesize that 2% of the general population commits crimes. Let's also hypothesize that one particular subgroup of the general population with a shared background, religion, or skin color commits a higher rate of crime than the general population. We will call this community "Group X." Let's say that 4% of the people within Group X are criminals. That's a 100% increase in the rate of crimes committed compared to the general population. It would be accurate and make for a controversial headline to state that Group X commits twice as many crimes as the general population, but what does this statistic mean? (Let's not delve into why this statistic exists; let's just assume it is accurate.) It is only one piece of the puzzle. The other relevant statistic is that 96% of Group X is comprised of law-abiding citizens.

Sticking with our hypothetical situation, is there correlation? Absolutely. Assuming this is reliable factual data, there is a correlation between this group and increased crime. Does this correlation show relevance or causation? To answer this, we ask whether the group's distinguishing factor (religion, ethnic group, skin color, etc.) *causes* them to commit crime. Clearly it doesn't, because only 4% of them have committed crimes. If this factor caused them to commit crime, 100% of them would be criminals.

All prejudgments, whether they are based on substance or fiction, tell our brain that there is a possibility or even a high probability that our preconceived outcome will actually happen. When basing your decision solely on that possibility, be aware that you are going from an increased possibility or probability to an assumed certainty. Your preconceived biases may misguide you into falsely assuming a 100% probability that all people in Group X are no good.

What would your emotional reaction be if a news headline announced that the statistics for both the general population and Group X combined together showed that around 97% of people are law-abiding citizens? You would have no cause for alarm and would probably feel good about the society you are in because almost all of your fellow citizens are law abiding, just like you.

Step 2: Determining Whether Relevance Exists

While correlating data is the first thing we look for in pattern recognition, even data that correlates completely is not necessarily relevant.

100% Correlation ≠ Relevance

Drinking Milk Correlates with Drug Addiction

If we did an exhaustive study, we would likely find that all cocaine addicts drank milk at some point in their lives prior to using illicit drugs. This would mean that there is a 100% correlation between drinking milk and being a drug addict, but what do we do with this information? Does drinking milk cause drug addiction later in life? We can easily agree that it does not, inasmuch as most milk drinkers do not become drug addicts. In fact, if we assume that all people who never become drug addicts also drank milk, there is a 100% correlation between drinking milk and *not* being a drug addict. Therefore, the 100% correlation that addicts previously drank milk is not relevant to their status as drug addicts. This simple example is meant to illustrate the importance of thinking critically about a correlation and whether or not that correlation has any relevance to the decision in front of us.

Relevance Found in "WHY"

When correlation exists in similar outcomes, find out whether relevance exists by asking why. If there is no answer or reason found, you do not necessarily have relevance, no matter how coincidental your outcomes are.

A widely read business website published an article about the forthcoming earnings season and the impact on technology stocks. The article positions IBM as the bellwether for the stock market stating, "When IBM beats estimates, 80 percent of the time the S&P trades higher over the next five weeks and vice versa. When IBM goes down, the S&P goes down 75 percent of the time over the next five weeks."[17]

This recognition of a pattern asserts that if IBM goes up, the entire stock market will also go up 80% of the time during the next five weeks. What do we do with this information? If IBM goes up, should we immediately invest

---

[17] "Time for a Tech Sector Reboot, Wall Street Pros Say," CNBC, accessed October 30, 2014, http://www.cnbc.com/id/100634809.

more in stocks or buy S&P futures? After all, an 80% chance of success is pretty good. The probabilities are in our favor.

Assuming that the above data is correct, the next step would be to understand *why* it is correct. Why does IBM stock predict the movement of the entire stock market 80% of the time, and what happens the other 20% of the time? This article strongly implies that there is a connection between IBM's earnings being in excess of what the market had estimated and the rest of the stock market. If this is true, why isn't the IBM stock movement predictive 100% of the time? You have to examine the facts to find the differences between times when this correlation works and when it doesn't work. What if the statement was true but included data from the 1960s, 1970s, and 1980s, when IBM was a major bellwether of the overall economy? Would that data be relevant in today's prediction of how the market will perform?

You can't make an intelligent bet if you don't understand the "why" behind correlation and the assumptions underlying the numbers. If you understand why the market either went up or did not go up when IBM's stock went up, you can be comfortable predicting a pattern. If you can't predict the pattern because you cannot find clear relevant or causative factors, then investing based on this correlation is misguided. You would be assuming, without evidence, that the correlation *causes* the outcome or is directly *relevant* to the outcome.

Think of a young child who asks an adult why something works the way it does. The adult has to explain it in terms that the child can understand, which often prompts another "why" question. How the adult answers the next "why" will teach the child or make it clear that the adult either doesn't know the answer or doesn't understand it well enough to explain it clearly. The next time someone states that an outcome is caused by some correlative data, ask why it works that way. If a person cannot explain his reasoning plainly in terms that you can understand, don't assume that the correlation has relevance.

Step 3: Finding Causation

Finding causation is finding a factor or group of factors that directly causes the outcome. This is the "holy grail" of pattern recognition.

When Correlation + Relevance ≠ Causation
Sushi and Same-Sex Marriage

Correlation with relevance does not always equal causation. A brief article came out recently showing an almost perfect correlation between people who eat sushi and those who support same-sex marriage. The percentage of correlation varied among age groups, but within some age groups the correlation was nearly 100%. The statistic makes for entertaining cocktail party banter, but what does it mean? Does it have relevance? Is there causation?

Interestingly, the correlation highlighted in the article was not based on a single study but rather on two independent studies conducted by separate groups for different reasons. The first study, undertaken by Pew Research Center, examined the assorted views on same-sex marriage between varying age groups, religions, political party affiliations, and regions in the United States. The second study, undertaken by Public Policy Polling, explored the various cuisine preferences by gender and political party affiliation.

The article took the results of these two unrelated studies and combined them to find a surprising correlation between those who ate sushi and those who supported same-sex marriage. For example, 52% of people polled within Generation X, born between 1965 and 1980 said they don't eat sushi. In the second poll, 48% of people within Generation X did not support same-sex marriage. The correlation was equal or greater for all of the other three age brackets. In all four of the age brackets, the younger groups ate more sushi and more approved of same-sex marriage than the older groups. The next youngest group, the Millennials, who were born in 1981 or later, was more pro same-sex marriage and ate more sushi than those in Generation X.

The sushi/same-sex marriage correlation is more powerful than the correlation between milk drinkers and drug addicts, but it certainly isn't flawless. Since the studies were separate, we don't know whether other questions were asked in the surveys, how the questions were asked, or whether respondents were led to answer in certain ways. We also don't know where the survey was conducted or by who, nor what other correlations existed in the studies.

Assuming that the correlation between sushi eaters and same-sex marriage supporters is valid, what does it tell us about the bigger picture? Perhaps younger people are more open-minded than older people, or maybe it's a simple matter of exposure. Sushi is a fairly new trend in the United States. Most people over 65 didn't grow up eating sushi like younger generations and therefore never assumed the habit of eating it. At the same time, gay people in the Silent Generation, born between 1928 and 1945, were much more reluctant to be open about their sexual preferences, because it was much less accepted than in later generations.

While these are plausible explanations for the correlation between eating sushi and supporting same-sex marriage, there are likely many other reasonable explanations. With a high correlation and enough ammunition for relevance, do we have causation? To determine whether we have causation, work the equation backward and ask yourself whether one correlative factor could cause the other. In this case, if a person who is against same-sex marriage eats a piece of raw tuna, will he then support same-sex marriage? Alternatively, would a steak lover suddenly desire sushi upon a newfound approval of same-sex marriage? Causation is unlikely here despite the correlation, relevance to the analysis, and interesting cocktail party conversation. If the correlating sushi/same-sex marriage data automatically reveals causation, Japan would be the most pro same-sex marriage country on the planet.

When Correlation + Relevance = Causation
Finding Patterns Through Data Analysis

Heart disease is a growing problem for people in the United States. Without modern technology, my father, who passed away just before his

89th birthday, probably would have died more than thirty-five years sooner. In 1978, he was saved by triple-bypass heart surgery, which was revolutionary at the time.

The causes of heart disease and ways to avoid it have been the subject of many articles, books, and theses. It is a major profit center for everyone connected to the medical field, especially the drug companies. Reliance upon medication, stents, and other aids have dramatically impacted our lifespans when our cardiovascular systems otherwise may have failed.

In less-developed countries with lack of infrastructure, people frequently die of myriad maladies well before they have a chance to develop heart disease. This is why a study of heart disease in more developed countries offers more comparable data. The larger and more similar the sample, the more reliable the data will always be. The following examples include large sample sizes of people with the same genetic background.

Italy

Italian-Americans have had a long-standing love affair with America. When earlier generations immigrated, there was a strong desire to assimilate and adopt the American culture. They embraced the United States as their new homeland, and as each generation became more Americanized, they fell into the pattern of working hard to become materially successful. With that drive for success came stress and a work pace that was unlike that in their Italian villages.

In his book *Outliers*, Malcolm Gladwell examines the low rate of heart disease in Italians who had recently come to America and settled in the town of Roseto, Pennsylvania. It was common at the time for towns or areas to be mainly populated with a single ethnic group. The Italians lived in Roseto and the Germans, Welsh, and English lived in nearby towns. A doctor from the area noticed that the people of Roseto were living longer than people from other towns and most notably, had a remarkably lower rate of heart disease. The difference was significant and predated the explosion in advanced cardiovascular technology.

What was the reason for the aberration? If you spot a trend such as

Italian immigrants living much longer than other nationalities, you need to look for and isolate factors that would explain that trend. As usual, ask why this is the result. By following a logical process of elimination, doctors ruled out the soil or air in the area, as other ethnic groups living in the surrounding towns did not exhibit the same health tendencies. In fact, the death rates in those towns were three times as high as that of Roseto. The local doctors also ruled out a purely Italian diet, because the people of Roseto did not use all of the same healthy ingredients as they did back in Italy. By process of elimination, they concluded that the culture of these newly minted Americans was the key differentiator. Business transactions in Italy rely strongly on relationships, and the Roseto Italians had strong personal relationships—not only with their extended family, but also with other people in the town.

While the Italians in Roseto may have cooked with lard instead of olive oil, they likely ate the same quantity of food as they did in Italy. They were also farmers and laborers who expended a lot of calories during the workday. The combination of moderate exercise in their daily activities with the appropriate quantity of food meant that the people in Roseto were unlikely to have been overweight.

Present-day Italian-Americans who have been in the United States for generations are fully Americanized. They often do not eat the same amount of food as their counterparts in Italy, even when they are eating healthy, fresh, well-prepared Italian cuisine. Layer on the ubiquitous fast-food restaurants, including pizzerias that serve food with ingredients of questionable pedigree, and you have a population that is much more overweight and unhealthy than people in Italy.

Remember, we are looking for a pattern that allows us to isolate the causes of lower rates of heart disease. We have identified a correlation between the Italians living in Roseto, Pennsylvania and a lower rate of heart disease than other immigrant groups. Just like the local doctors did, comparing the Italians of this town to other ethnic groups living nearby who had higher rates of heart disease allows us to rule out possible causative factors in the environment such as soil and air.

Which other factors may be relevant or directly cause the lower rate of heart disease? While there can be more than one causative factor, all causative factors are not necessarily equal. To determine which causative factor for the lower rate of heart disease in Roseto may be more important than the others, we look for cause-and-effect scenarios among correlating factors with a large enough sample size.

The strength of personal relationships and the old-style European village pace seem to be major factors impacting the health of the Italian immigrants in Roseto compared to current-day Italian-Americans who suffer high rates of heart disease. The other factors that may cause heart disease in modern-day Italian-Americans are the quantity and quality of the food they eat compared to Italians in Italy or recent immigrants. Here we may have multiple causative factors, although they are, perhaps, not of equal importance.

This is also a great example of the law of large numbers at play. When we think we have determined a pattern that might exist—or the probability of a pattern—large-scale numbers provide more data and offer much better evidence than smaller numbers.

Japan

Among developed countries, Japan continually has a low rate of heart disease. Japanese people eat more fresh seafood than people in European countries, but most Japanese do not eat seafood every night simply because it is too expensive. They also rarely eat beef because it is even more costly than seafood. Instead, they eat lots of vegetables, rice, and seaweed. There are, of course, some tempura restaurants in Japan that serve fried vegetables and fish, but even those items are much lighter than typical American fried food.

With such a healthy diet consumed nationwide, why doesn't Japan have the lowest rate of heart disease in the developed world? Perhaps diet is not the only causative factor here. Perhaps other causative factors exist. What other factors might prevent Japan from having an even lower rate of heart disease? Like the Roseto Italians, lifestyle dramatically impacts the health of the Japanese.

Japanese children begin intensive schoolwork and studies at age five and work hard to get into the best schools. There is a lot of competition and pressure throughout their academic careers, and then success comes in the form of a job at a prestigious Japanese company, where another competition ensues. In Japan, "kiroshi" is the Japanese word for death by stress, especially for the common "salaryman," a typical Japanese man who works at a large corporation and rises to the level of middle management. For the salaryman, the business morning often begins with long commutes in packed train cars, followed by long hours at work. No one leaves until his boss leaves, and his boss works late so that his boss, in turn, sees him as a hard worker. After work, the salarymen are expected to entertain clients and mingle with co-workers. This often involves drinking more than a moderate amount of alcohol.

While the salaryman makes a decent living, everything in Japan is expensive, mostly by design, so he is trapped on the middle-management hamster wheel of success. He is successful enough to be considered successful but not successful enough to break out of the rat race. This keeps his stress level high throughout the salaryman's working years, which is most of his life.

Based on this, the two factors that seem to prevent the Japanese from having the lowest rate of heart disease are drinking and stress. We have a vast amount of statistically reliable data with correlative factors and a few very relevant factors that also seem to be causative factors. Italians drink about as much as the Japanese, but in Italy they slow down, take breaks, socialize, and drink wine with meals. The Japanese eat the types of food that a cardiologist would recommend, which shouldn't hurt their ranking, but their lifestyles are hectic and very demanding. The major variation between Japan and Italy appears to be daily stress.

The French Paradox

Interestingly enough, a large country that also has a low rate of heart disease, often even lower than that of Japan, is France. For a country that eats Brie, steak tartare, foie gras, and pastries, this shouldn't be the case if a low-fat diet is a significant causative factor of a reduced rate of heart disease. This "French paradox" is quite puzzling. British researchers have focused on it because they find it infuriating that the French have a much lower rate of heart disease than British people, while the French embrace high-fat foods. In this case, a low-fat diet cannot be the causative factor for lower heart disease, which is consistent with a study performed by the Harvard School of Public Health on US women. It seems that the only causative factor here seems to be the French way of life. As the French say, Americans live to work while the French work so that they can live. Imagine what the lifestyle would be like in the United States if there was a law that limited the work week to 35 hours.

Blue Zones

On Sunday, October 28, 2012, the *New York Times* ran an article about the health of residents of the Greek Island of Ikaria. The statistical data in the study is remarkable. Ikaria inhabitants are more than twice as likely as Americans to live to the age of 90, and Ikarian men are four times more likely to reach age 90 than American men. The article stated that not only were the Ikarian people living longer, the quality of their health, both physical and mental, was far superior to that of Americans.

This article, while comparing Ikarians to Americans, highlighted part of a larger research project to determine why certain pockets of people, from women in Okinawa, Japan, to Seventh-day Adventists in Loma Linda, California, and several other areas known as "blue zones," lived longer and healthier than most other people. The research about the diet and living habits in Ikaria are very close to what was found in the Italian-Americans living in Roseto.

The typical Ikarian day starts much later in the morning than in modern America. The island's doctor doesn't even open his office until midday, because there is no need to open earlier. The Ikarians live off the land to a great extent, very often from their own fruit and vegetable gardens that they plant and care for. Not only does this give them access to fresh, healthy, unprocessed food, but also, tending to their own garden keeps them active every day. Although most Ikarians have jobs, they experience very little stress. Multiple generations live together, and they socialize daily with friends and neighbors.

Three factors exist that, either independently or taken in combination, might account for the surprisingly good health of the Ikarians: diet, genetics, and lifestyle—most specifically, a lack of stress. With this information at hand and the goal of finding a pattern in order to better predict the outcome, we need to look for

1. Which of these factors, if any, correlates to living longer, healthier lives
2. Which correlations are relevant
3. Whether any of the factors directly cause longer, healthier lives

The Ikarian diet consists of a low intake of saturated fats from meat and dairy, olive oil, goat's milk, fresh beans, potatoes, greens, and seasonal vegetables. They also drink wine on a regular basis while socializing with neighbors. At first glance, it may appear that the Ikarian diet alone is the cause of their superior health...until we look further.

Eight miles away on the island of Samos, people have the same genetic background and eating habits as the people of Ikaria, but the Samosans live no longer than an average Greek person. Their genes and diet are the same as those of the inhabitants of Ikaria, but the resultant lifespan is different. Why? Samosans, in general, value money and affluence more than Ikarians. Samos is populated with high-rise buildings and resorts and expensive real estate. While the article does not provide an in-depth study on Samos, it is clear that the people of Samos have a different work ethic, pace of life, and a higher stress level than the people of Ikaria.

This doesn't rule out diet and genetics as factors impacting the longevity of these two groups of people, but it does seem to indicate, when taken in tandem with the study of Roseto and the low rate of heart disease in

France, that lack of stress and greater happiness through socialization helps promote a healthier human being not only in terms of quantity of years lived, but also in the quality of life during those years. This seems to reveal three causative factors, with lack of stress being the predominant influence on having lower rates of heart disease.

Managing Vast Data

The entire goal of pattern recognition is to connect data points to find correlation, relevance, and causation. Complex issues involving tens, hundreds, or thousands of data points require an efficient approach that allows us to account for all of the data at hand.

The approach I recommend works like the often-vilified business tool, PowerPoint. I'm not referring to those nightmare PowerPoint presentations where the presenter puts every detail possible on a very long set of slides jammed with too much information. I am referring to the way this tool is supposed to distill a lot of information into a few slides of bullet points. This efficient approach begins with grouping similar data into categories. Grouping like data allows us to look at a greater scope of information at once and summarize an overall observation.

I have seen this concept used very successfully in real life. One of my former partners, Gerry Grese, who is one of the smartest people I have ever met, encouraged people to boil down everything into three bullet points on one piece of paper. After protesting ad infinitum that this was impossible because the task at hand was too complex to be summarized in so few words, they reluctantly agreed and were successful at the task.

Does this mean that everything in the world can be made simplistic and there is nothing complex? Not at all. However, the bane of intelligent people, or those who think they are, is to get lost in the weeds of the complexity of a problem and lose track of the overarching concepts.

When analyzing a large amount of data, simplify matters by first grouping like data into no more than five different categories. To illustrate, let's look at the earlier example examining why certain groups have lower rates of heart disease than other groups.

The people in our study consumed fish, meat, cheese, pasta, vegetables, fruit, and alcohol and had different gene pools and varying lifestyles. When we started the analysis, we didn't know whether food, lifestyle, or genetics would have a correlation to the outcome. We also didn't know which foods might help prevent or contribute to heart disease. We can, however, sort all of the factors into groups and make diet our first category. The second category may be gene pools or other things driven by DNA. Occupation can be the third category. Across all groups there will be farmers or fishermen and other laborers, white-collar workers, and every profession in between. Lifestyle will be our fourth category, as it incorporates aspects of daily life outside of occupation, including marital status. Some data may not fit into one of these four categories, so our fifth category can be "other."

With this PowerPoint-type approach, we have sorted extensive data into five manageable categories that can be analyzed and digested much more simply than if the data was not grouped into like factors. By doing so, we can more effectively look for patterns that answer why some people live longer and healthier lives than others.

Recap

Pattern Recognition starts with collecting all of the data you will need. Most times, this creates a large number of individual data points that then need to be connected. Try to sort these data points into no more than three to five categories. Look for correlation, relevance, and possible causation. Examine the evidence objectively, and don't begin with a conclusion in mind.

Pattern Recognition Checklist

- **The key to pattern recognition lies in determining which factors correlate with the outcome, which of the correlative factors are relevant to the outcome, and which may be causative factors.**

- **The single most common mistake in pattern recognition is confusing correlation with causation.** Determining correlation is the first step in the process, not the conclusion.

- Relevance is defined as a meaningful correlation between the recurring fact and the result. **To find relevance in a correlation, ask, "Why?"**

- **Correlation with relevance does not guarantee causation.** Information can have relevant correlation and still not reveal causative factors.

- **Causation can encompass more than one factor.**

- **Identifying causation allows us to predict results and make more optimal decisions.**

- **Categorize large amounts of data into manageable groups** in order to analyze vast data more efficiently.

- **Grouping like data allows you to see the bigger picture** and more easily identify which points correlate with the outcome, which are relevant, and which may directly cause the outcome.

DEAL OR NO DEAL – PART 2

WHAT DOES GARY DECIDE?

Now that you have learned the four-point framework, let's get back to Gary and his game show experience. When we left Gary, he was faced with the decision of whether to accept the banker's offer of $85,000 or decline the offer for the chance that his briefcase holds the $500,000 payoff. His advisors tell him to take the deal, but Gary decides to turn down the $85,000 offer (which, if you remember, is a lot higher than even the "life-changing" amount of $63,000 that the banker offered him earlier in the game). Gary says he is following his gut and shouts, "No deal!"

He now has to select another case to eliminate. The case he chooses contains $25,000. Gary and his advisors are relieved that the case does not contain $500,000, meaning that there is still a chance Gary's case holds that amount. The banker recalculates and offers to buy Gary's case for $97,000. Gary's stubborn reluctance to follow the suggestions of his advisors has now earned him an offer of nearly $100,000. While $85,000 was a very good offer, Gary says that $97,000 is a "phenomenal" amount of money. It is also $34,000 higher (over 50% more) than the previous life-changing offer of $63,000. Finally, Gary and his wife have a substantial offer. Gary's reluctance to accept the previous meaningful offers has paid off. We don't know what amount Gary and his wife had collectively decided would be their target amount to walk away with, but this certainly has to be up there.

Gary has a strong instinct that he holds the case with $500,000, but he is relying solely on his gut. He may feel that he was just extraordinarily unlucky at the beginning of the game, when the cases with the largest amounts were eliminated and that if there is a reversion to the mean regarding luck, he should be quite lucky at this time. In reality, Gary has been lucky on the last few turns and his luck isn't as bad as he recalls. Gary has progressed from a cash offer of $30,000 to a $63,000 offer. From there, he received an offer of $85,000, and now it is $97,000. He can only make a decision about this offer with the facts he has, not the ones he wishes he had. This is all about probabilities and balance.

With four cases left in the game, if Gary keeps going there is a 25% chance he will select the case with $500,000 and the next offer will plummet. Conversely, there is a 75% chance he will not pick the case representing $500,000, which makes this a classic case of risk versus reward. The chances are greater that Gary will not pick the $500,000 case, but if he does, the banker's next offer will be dramatically lower.

The $97,000 offer on the table is a lot of money to Gary and his family, but he feels he can do better. Based on what you now know, what would you do if you were in Gary's shoes and why?

Gary decides to gamble one more time and rejects the offer. The case he selects contains $50,000, which means that there is still a chance that his case contains $500,000. The banker offers Gary $129,000–an offer that is more than twice the life-changing amount of $63,000 that Gary had previously rejected.

Three cases remain in the game: a $500,000 case, a $75,000 case, and a $10,000 case. Gary's case holds one of these amounts. The $129,000 offer is either much higher or much lower than the actual amount of money in the case that Gary holds, and there is a 67% chance that his case holds less than the banker's offer. This isn't a question of Gary wanting more money. This is an issue of risk tolerance. We all like more money, but we don't like more risk.

If Gary accepts the offer and his case holds the $500,000, would he have made a bad decision? If Gary accepts the $129,000 and his case is revealed to have contained $10,000, would he have made a good decision? While the better outcome is the highest amount, remember that the decision shouldn't be based on the outcome. It should be based on the thought process of the decision.

What would you advise Gary to do now and why?

Gary has a lot to think about. He has a substantial offer of $129,000 and a 67% chance that the case he holds is worth less than that. While you may or may not think the offer is "fair," the offer is what it is. Fairness is not a consideration unless it is so mathematically out of line that it impacts the probability of getting a substantially higher offer and not a much lower one.

Gary says, "No deal!" There are three cases left, including Gary's case. He picks one of the two others to eliminate, and it is opened to reveal that Gary has just eliminated the $500,000 case and his chance at that jackpot. The two remaining amounts are $75,000 and $10,000. Gary's briefcase contains one of these amounts, and the final briefcase up for possible elimination contains the other amount. The banker now offers Gary $38,000 for his briefcase.

Certainly Gary must feel disgusted that his luck ran out. It is a natural reaction to compare the previous $129,000 offer to the current offer of $38,000. This is anchoring, as described in "How We Decide Now." His decision of whether to take the $38,000 should not be tied to his missed opportunity. Similarly, he shouldn't feel that the money he almost had is invested in this next decision, which is sunk cost fallacy.

It would be a normal reaction for Gary to decide to go for it now and eliminate the last case. In his mind, he has suffered a loss of $91,000. However, he came into this game with nothing but high hopes and certain expectations, so in reality, he lost an opportunity and not actual money. The current offer of $38,000 isn't the life-changing amount of $63,000 and only around 50% of the possible $75,000 he could chance to win, but $38,000 is almost 4 times as much as the lower remaining amount of $10,000.

In this same situation, what would you do now and why?

Gary again decides to gamble and shouts, "No deal!" He eliminates the remaining case, which is opened to reveal that it contained the $75,000.

The game ends with Gary being awarded the prize contained in his brief-case—$10,000. Was Gary's decision to accept more risk as he got higher offers a smart decision? Were the decisions made when he got lower offers bad ones?

While *Deal or No Deal* is a game show, it is indicative of a several points regarding decision making:

1. All decisions are forward looking.
2. Facts are real. If you can't change them (as Gary couldn't), deal with the facts you have.
3. Probabilities tell you the likely outcomes, both good and bad.
4. Risk tolerance is the key, not the outcome you want. Everyone wants a better outcome, not more risk. If the amount of risk is unacceptable to you, the possible reward isn't worth it.
5. Excess emotion or gut-level reactions can lead you astray.
6. Anchoring and sunk cost fallacy can negatively impact decision making. The previous decision has already taken place and should not influence your next decision. You may be happy or unhappy about your prior choice, but it has already occurred and cannot be undone.
7. There is a tendency to compare the caliber of the decision with the outcome.

THE FRAMEWORK IN ACTION

Now that you are familiar with the four-point framework and how it works, let's apply it to some important decisions. All of the examples in this next section may not apply to you, but many of them will. They range from playing the lottery to getting married and from investing to going to war.

Legalization of Marijuana

The debate regarding the legalization of marijuana continues to draw attention. Clearly, this is not the most critical decision the country faces, but it does seem to be time to either revalidate or modify the prior decision. Should marijuana be categorized with more addictive and powerful drugs like crack cocaine and heroin? Should the federal laws that apply to marijuana be modified?

If we are in a "war" on drugs, can we make a comparison between decision making about the legalization of marijuana and decision making about a military war? I think we can, but let's run through our decision-making analysis to find out. Always remember that using the same decision-making framework doesn't mean that we have to agree on the conclusion, but it will help to clarify where we disagree.

The Problem to Be Solved

Marijuana is slowly being de-criminalized or allowed for certain circumstances in a number of states. Despite this, there remains a federal law that forbids the use of marijuana at all, which means that either the federal law should be changed to make it a state-by-state decision or the existing federal law should be enforced despite the states' positions.

Should we affirm our prior decisions and continue to fight the "war" as we have in the past because it is the optimal course of action today? Should we continue the cause, no matter the cost or efficacy, because it is morally the right thing to do? Should we abandon the effort altogether and institute new regulations or change our definition of the drugs we are fighting against so that we can be more successful?

The stakes in this decision are actually quite significant. The amount of manpower and money employed to combat the war on drugs is substantial. If marijuana were removed from the list of illegal substances, we could use that savings to combat more serious drugs and other national security threats. On the other hand, if we think that marijuana should continue to be illegal in the United States, we will need to redouble our efforts because we are not winning the war against its use. Using backwardization, as we did in estimating the costs to engage in a military war, we must ask ourselves whether the goal to eradicate marijuana use in the United States is worth the total estimated cost of the war we are fighting.

Timing

As with any important decision, Timing is the first step of the analysis. The other three factors can follow in any order. Like many important decisions facing society, there is no set deadline for this. All decisions are forward looking, and this is no exception. We are not revisiting whether the decision to outlaw marijuana was correct or not when it began decades ago. We are reevaluating whether the current federal law that classifies it as an illegal drug is the correct policy going forward. Timing demands that we set a deadline to examine our current strategy.

Probabilities

We need to choose the path with the highest possibility of achieving our goal, so we need to clearly define what our goal is. I would suggest that our goal should be to have a sensible drug policy that benefits society as a whole and is realistically achievable.

How do we define a sensible drug policy? The most sensible drug policy may be either to stay with our existing laws or to change them, but let's first establish some facts. Other harmful substances are legal in America, only some of which are regulated. There are age restrictions on buying and drinking alcohol and buying cigarettes, both of which are proven health hazards. On the same note, the excessive amounts of sugar found in most sodas and trans fats in foods are not good for you, but they are still legal. With alcohol, you become a threat to society if you drink too much and attempt to drive home, so we have laws against driving while intoxicated but otherwise generally allow the consumption of alcohol by people of a certain age. The question seems to be whether a person can drink alcohol, smoke cigarettes, consume unhealthy foods, and still be a productive member of society. The answer seems to be yes.

Now let's look at marijuana. Can you use marijuana and be a productive member of society? Again, the answer seems to be yes, since some occasional users have gone on to attend top law schools and become President of the United States. Can you use marijuana to the point that it renders you unproductive? Of course, but the same is true with alcohol, which we have established is legal. A sensible drug policy would allow people to make their own choices regarding the use of a substance when that substance will not prevent them from being a productive member of society.

While it is estimated that having marijuana legalized would create additional tax revenue, the creation of tax revenue is not one of our goals but may be an effect of legalizing marijuana. The reason that raising tax revenue should not be part of the goal is that it implies that we should legalize all illegal activities just to maximize tax revenue. When dealing with matters of social and moral concern, tax revenue should not muddy the picture. We wouldn't legalize heroin, crack-cocaine, or child pornography solely to benefit from the additional tax revenue.

Pattern Recognition

In order to discover useful factors that may be correlative, relevant, or causative with our goal, let's compare our decision about whether or not to legalize marijuana use with the prohibition of alcohol and the law's subsequent repeal. For nearly fourteen years, the sale of alcohol was illegal

in the United States. Its prohibition was established through an amend-
ment to the United States Constitution, which required significant political
support.

After the law was in force, a great deal of the public still wanted to
drink. People were familiar with the effects of alcohol because they had
previously been allowed to drink, and drinking alcohol was not widely
perceived as an excessively evil or immoral act. Secret and not-so secret
speakeasy clubs proliferated in answer to the public demand for alcohol
after its criminalization, and people started making their own alcoholic
brews using homemade stills. Without government regulation, there was
no way to ensure that alcohol being dispensed to the public met any standards. During Prohibition, Al Capone, one of the most notorious gangsters
of all time, rose to great power and wealth mainly through smuggling and
bootlegging liquor, and organized crime proliferated.

When the law was eventually repealed, it was left up to individual
states to decide whether to stay "dry" or allow alcohol use. The prohibition of alcohol wasn't repealed because hard science indicated that drinking
alcohol was critical to the health and well-being of the general public. It was
repealed because society wanted it repealed, and it would take alcohol out
of the shadow of criminal syndicates. When it became legal again, alcohol
became highly regulated by various governments with identifiable standards of quality.

Proponents of marijuana legalization point to its prohibition as a
leading cause of the power of organized crime related to its production,
distribution, and use.

While you can agree or disagree with the assertion that there is a valid
comparison between the prohibition of alcohol and the criminalization of
marijuana, the point is not that marijuana should be legal because alcohol
is. The point is that a similar pattern of events and data exists related to
the sales, use, and trafficking of both substances while banned. The decision we face now is whether to continue waging this war that we are not
winning, that is costing substantial time, effort, and money, and that is not
supported by a growing number of people. Much like alcohol prohibition

in the 1920s, people who want to use the illegal substance are finding ways to do it anyway, and its societal acceptance is growing.

Marijuana did not have a history of being used legally by a large percentage of society before it became illegal. However, it has seemingly reached the tipping point in being accepted as a recreational drug. It is often comically referenced in movies and television shows and is sometimes even celebrated. Several politicians and celebrities readily admit to having used marijuana, including President Barack Obama and former President Bill Clinton. While its use by high-profile people doesn't mean that it should be legalized, the fact that their successful presidential races were not derailed when they admitted to smoking pot reveals the general consensus that having used marijuana is not a behavioral aberration that would preclude someone from being the commander in chief of the Armed Forces and chief decision maker of the United States.

If you rewrote history and banned marijuana early in the twentieth century and then allowed it again and were now contemplating legalizing alcohol for the first time, you would be faced with a similar analysis.

The symmetry in data points between alcohol and marijuana are as follows:

1. Both have been illegal.
2. Both have gained general acceptance in society.
3. The prohibition against them did not permit quality control standards.
4. Keeping them illegal forced users to interact with and empower (through substantial profits) organized crime.

When alcohol was made legal, governments gained complete control over its production and regulation, including passing laws to limit excessive alcohol use when it can be dangerous to other people. Large international corporations now produce and distribute liquor, and the profits no longer go untaxed to organized crime but to legal entities that pay tax.

Are these factors relevant to the decision analysis? I believe they are. Are any of these factors causative? If one of your goals is to regulate marijuana in order to make it safer and to undercut organized crime, then yes, legalizing marijuana will cause those two things to happen.

Gateway Drug versus Gateway to Illegal Distribution System

Now we enter an area where reasonable people could disagree. One argument against legalizing marijuana is the suggestion that, while it may not be as inherently detrimental as "hard drugs" like crack and heroin, people who try marijuana will go on to try other drugs. Thus, marijuana is viewed by many as a "gateway drug." Their belief is that legalizing marijuana will cause more people to try drugs that we all agree are very harmful to individuals and society.

Let's look at correlation, relevance, and causation. Is there a correlation between marijuana use and the use of hard drugs? Let's assume that before anybody used a hard drug, they tried marijuana first. This leaves us with a 100% correlation between marijuana use and the use of hard drugs. Even if the correlation is lower than 100% but still quite high, the existing correlation forces us to focus on our decision-making analysis. A correlation this strong would lead us to conclude that marijuana is indeed a gateway drug. However, as discussed in the chapter on pattern recognition, a very high correlation, even if it is 100%, does not immediately prove relevance or causation. If we also assume that the vast majority of people have had a can of beer before they tried marijuana, based on our assumptions above, drinking beer is a gateway to smoking marijuana, which is a gateway to using hard drugs. If this is the case, then beer should also be illegal, right? The high correlation between beer drinkers, pot smokers, and hard drug users is useful data in our decision process but does not prove causation.

Another Gateway

As alcohol did with organized crime and speakeasy clubs, marijuana introduces otherwise law-abiding citizens to some level of organized crime.

Most casual users of marijuana get their marijuana from a friend or local acquaintance—let's call him Joe. Joe, in turn, gets it from his friend Pete. Both Pete and Joe do nothing else that is illegal, so they assume that their connection isn't to organized crime. But where does Pete's supply come from? Higher up the chain, people related to organized crime are producing and smuggling enough weed to supply countless friends and associates with an ample stash for distribution. There is absolutely no question that the illegal proceeds from marijuana have provided large profits to organized crime.

Let's look at alcohol during Prohibition. Some otherwise law-abiding people went to speakeasy clubs. The profits went to organized crime syndicates, and as a result, these people might have gotten involved with criminals they otherwise would never support. When alcohol was made legal, alcohol consumption went from illegal speakeasy clubs to regulated liquor stores and bars. The connection to criminals was broken. If marijuana is made legal, the selling of marijuana will go from illegal activities to legal businesses. The gateway to the illegal distribution system will be broken.

Balance

The question of whether or not to legalize marijuana is a perfect platform for weighing risk versus reward. There is inherent risk here: If we don't change our laws, there is a risk that our war on drugs will garner even worse results. The same could be argued about changing our current policy. There is risk no matter what we do, so trying to achieve zero risk is not a realistic goal.

According to a 2008 study published by Harvard economist Jeffrey A. Miron, the annual savings on enforcement and incarceration costs from the legalization of marijuana would amount to roughly $8.7 billion per year. Does this mean that we should make marijuana legal just to save money and collect more taxes? No, but as with any war, we must know its cost, especially when it doesn't appear to be going so well.

What we should do to increase our chances of success while minimizing our chances of failure depends on your view of the current situation. I am of the view that our existing position on marijuana is failing with little prospect of getting better. In terms of war, it is a war we are losing. When you are losing a war, you revisit whether you should be waging this war and how you are waging it. Something needs to change for the war on drugs to be successful. Based on the data at hand, I believe that federal laws prohibiting marijuana should be repealed. The question of its legalization should be left to the individual states to decide. If declassifying marijuana as an illegal drug like crack or heroin does not work toward achieving our goal, we can always ban it again.

Of course, this is my own analysis. Others may have a strong case for disagreeing with me. Again, this decision-making framework won't always lead to the same conclusion, but it does allow us to think through the issue and clarify where we disagree.

MARRIAGE

Should we apply an analytical thought process to the decision of whether or not to get married? After all, choosing to marry someone is a matter of the heart, not a linear algorithm. Still, just as there is a science to the art of decision making, there should be a science to the "heart" of decision making.

Remember, we only need to Think Deeply about decisions that are important—when the stakes are high or we are out of our area of expertise. In a decision to get married, the stakes are usually much higher than we think. Almost no one is really an expert, and our society's aggregate success rate is awful. In other words, whatever decision-making process people are using (or more accurately *not* using) when they decide to get married is clearly not working. A lot of current data exists on marriage and divorce, and it doesn't paint a pretty picture.

Full disclosure: I have been happily married to the love of my life for almost forty years. While my marriage is what I would classify as "successful," the fact that it remained that way through building our careers and raising children together seems to be an aberration these days.

Problem to Be Solved

The divorce rate of first-time marriages in the United States hovers around 50%. A recent Gallup survey poll found that only 30% of married couples are happy. If we define "success" in marriage as those couples who are not merely married, but happily married, the failure rate is a staggering 70%. Of the 30% of successful marriages, how many just got lucky? I suggest that the percentage of people who properly thought about marriage before saying "I do" is less than 30%, but that is just conjecture on my part. Let's stick with the 30% number for this example, as that is already bad enough.

What is leading to the dismal statistics, and how can we improve them? How are people thinking through the decision to marry each other? Mostly, they're not thinking it through. Remember all of the tricks our minds play on us, as discussed in the first section of this book, and the problems that can stem from basing decisions solely on emotional pulls. Usually, the decision to get married is just a gut-level reaction on steroids. For many of us, it is the single biggest decision of our lives. There may be nothing more potentially impactful both emotionally and financially. It is a huge gamble with far-reaching consequences. Failure can bring heartbreak and sometimes, deep bitterness. Whole families may be affected, and the entanglement of assets, liabilities, and financial responsibilities can bring emotions to a fevered pitch.

Each year we attend weddings that are filled with hopes and dreams, clinking champagne glasses, dancing, and cake. People travel from far and wide to attend and shower the bride and groom with substantial gifts. How can over half of these marriages turn out so differently from our expectations? As we know from the discussions on probabilities and pattern recognition, the law of large numbers dictates that the larger the sample size, the better the chances are that the data tells an accurate story. Here, the sample size is immense. Where is our foresight?

In addition to the impact divorce has on children, the split of assets and future income streams is significant. The percentage may vary from state to state, but a 50% split is a good reference benchmark, and more and more states are trending toward a "no fault" split of the assets. What does that mean? It means that it generally doesn't matter if you can prove that your spouse had an affair or two or three. It usually won't dramatically change the overall economic split of joint assets.

With all of this at stake, shouldn't we approach the decision to get married more thoughtfully? As a group, our success rate is far worse than that of a coin flip, and that shouldn't be our target benchmark for a decision of this importance.

How much would you wager on a bet with fifty-fifty odds? How about one where your chances of success are less than 50%? How about one with 30%? Take everything you own in the world—all of your savings, your car, your house, stocks, and bonds, and don't forget that business or career you built. Would you bet it all on a 50% chance? If your answer is no, it doesn't mean you are doomed to be alone; it means that you need to engage in Thinking Deeply to better determine your own odds or chances for success in the marriage you are considering.

Deciding to marry someone is emotionally driven, and it should be. A decision-making framework is not meant to deny or replace emotion, nor is it meant to eliminate romance and all of the other wonderful things that couples dream about. It is meant to complement your emotions and give you better odds to work with than the current statistic. Just like in all other important decisions, your goal is for your gut reaction to agree with a more thoughtful process.

Marriage = Romance + Hunting and Nesting

There needs to be chemistry or some sort of "spark" between two people in order for them to get romantically involved, contemplate living together, and then possibly make their arrangement legally binding by getting married. While the chemistry is necessary, people frequently stop thinking about it there. What else you need depends on what marriage means to you. Here are my observations:

If two people decide to live together, they are agreeing to share in the hunting and nesting responsibilities that animals have. In the jungle, animals have to hunt for food and take care of offspring if they have any. Human beings are the same. At least one person has to hunt. In the modern world, this usually means earning money to pay for the goods and services necessary to survive and thrive. If both parties work, the nesting part can be outsourced by hiring help such as a cleaning person or a nanny if there are children. Even if there are no children, nesting includes buying food, cooking it, cleaning up, and taking care of the home. Having children just makes nesting a much larger part of the relationship. No matter how sexually attracted a husband and wife are to each other, the combined number of times they shop for food, cook, clean, take out the garbage, and handle all of the other mundane things involved in daily life will far outnumber the number of instances they have sex.

Timing

When do you have to make this decision? With a decision about whether or not to get married, your answer may be driven by other life goals. There may be social pressure at the age when friends are getting serious and making commitments. This is a classic case of priming. You may meet your future spouse in elementary school, but you don't think of running off and getting married in fourth grade. When people reach a certain age and observe others getting engaged, they start to view others as potential mates. This priming of your decision isn't necessarily wrong, but be aware of its influence.

You may want to be married for a few years before having children, and your biological clock is ticking. Maybe your deadline is based on a philosophy that after dating for two or three years, the logical next step is to get married, but deciding you "might as well" get married because you have already spent three years with this person is sunk cost fallacy at work.

These assumed deadlines will drive the timing of your decision and the timing about when you need to engage in real thinking about your decision. While countless variables that involve timing may play a part in your decision to marry someone or not, unless you're facing an ultimatum or other scenario you can point to on a calendar, there is probably no real deadline for your decision. In this case, it's important to create one of your own.

You may think that being happily married is important to you, but after dating someone for several years, you still feel no real sense of urgency to get married. Here, you should ask yourself how important getting married really is to you. As with any goal, if you take no real proactive steps toward fulfilling the goal, it probably isn't that important to you. Are you making this big bet because it just seems like the next logical step? You may be comfortable in this relationship, but are you excited about it? You should be because hunting and nesting is a lot of hard work and compromise.

Balance

In this scenario we are balancing risk versus reward—a happy marriage against an unhappy marriage or divorce. We don't want to be so afraid of marriage that we let that special person slip away, but we want to avoid a problem if we see it.

There is no way to hedge against the emotional pain of an unsuccessful marriage, but we can better avoid a bitter divorce. In the case of one partner being the majority income earner (the "moneyed spouse" to matrimonial lawyers), the financial risks are out of balance in favor of the lower-income earner. Without a prenuptial or other agreement, the major income earner runs a greater financial risk if the marriage ends in divorce. Prenuptial agreements are used specifically to lower such risk.

A prenuptial agreement may sound cold and calculating, but it can protect both parties. If your marriage is successful, the prenuptial agreement is a non-issue. It is designed to lower risks in case the marriage fails. A prenuptial agreement can cover monetary awards and visitation rights and can be used to safeguard against or punish bad behavior. Depending on the state, the prenuptial agreement might provide that if one spouse has an affair that causes the marriage to fall apart, the misbehaving spouse gets less money and fewer rights in the divorce. While you want to be fair with your potential life partner, your definition of "fair" might change if your best friend gets your wife pregnant.

The wedding ceremony is the legal entrance to marriage, and the prenuptial agreement is an exit strategy that is used only if needed. Unlike the decision to get married, the choice to get divorced only requires a decision by one person.

Probabilities

Marriage should not be undertaken unless we believe there is a very high probability of it being a success, because the stakes are high. If you believe that you that you only have a 50% chance of this legal relationship working out, why would you get married? There is no guarantee of a successful marriage, but you should at least have an extremely high level of confidence in the prospect of yours being successful.

You have to make your own very personal estimate of the chances of success based on what you know now, not what might happen in the future. If your potential mate has a core trait that is an anathema to you, don't assume that he or she will grow out of it or change.

Identify which elements will cause you to be happy in your marriage. You are looking for the few key "buckets," known in some relationship advice books as "must-haves," or "deal breakers." For the sake of example, let's use the categories of fidelity, sexual compatibility, common goals, and financial stability as our must-haves. While there may be many other things you want in a relationship, attempt to identify your absolute must-haves, which may also reveal your deal-breakers. If fidelity is a must-have, logic would dictate that infidelity is a deal-breaker. With the categories in mind, we will engage in real thinking about the relationship.

The halo effect is the most common bias that skews our perception in a relationship. We love our partner, love certain special things about our partner and are looking at a potential life together with that partner. We focus on the good things in the relationship and are emotionally attached to the possibilities, which can often cause us to overestimate the positives and ignore, or at least underestimate, the negatives.

If my partner is an aspiring and unknown artist with no other source of income than sales of her artwork and sales are unpredictable at best, my financial stability must-have is clearly at risk. The halo effect might cause me to gloss over the truth with hopeful fantasies of her early fame, fortune, and notoriety in the art world, when we would both be better served by a healthy dose of reality. This is not to say that my partner's lack of financial stability has to be a deal-breaker. The mismatch does not have to end my hopes for the relationship, but our awareness of this mismatch will allow us to seek solutions that help prevent the issue from growing into a deal-breaker. We can address the issue proactively with a healthy discussion about how long we can happily continue the relationship with one partner bearing all of the financial burdens, or my partner can agree to work part time until art sales become more substantial and predictable. It doesn't matter what the choice is as long as there is a discussion and agreement on how various scenarios will play out.

Let's apply probabilities to our marriage decision with an analogy to the card game Texas Hold 'em. The goal here is to improve your chances of winning, which in this case means entering into a great marriage. In Texas Hold 'em, all players are dealt two cards and decide to put down their initial bet based on those first two cards. Over the course of the game, each player will get additional cards that will improve the hand or weaken it.

Let's say you decide to enter a Texas Hold 'em competition that requires a bet of $1 million after you are dealt the first two cards. If you are dealt a weak hand and the required bet is $1 million, you would be foolish to stay in the game. You might get lucky and win with the cards that will follow the first two, but with a weak hand, the probability is high that you will not win. You may hope that the future cards you are dealt will improve your chances of success, but hope is not a good strategy for decision making.

When you get married, you are making a very big initial bet. The cards that follow the first two cards in Texas Hold 'em are the things that happen after your wedding and may include promotions, substantial salary increases, demotions, job cuts that are beyond your control, healthy and happy children who do well in school, children who have physical or emotional problems, and so on. You hope the additional cards you are dealt will help, but they may not. The cards are both positive and negative, and as Forrest Gump said in the same-titled movie, "Life is like a box of chocolates; you never know what you're going to get."

If you are not starting out with a very strong hand—the emotional, physical, and spiritual equivalent of a pair of queens or better—don't get married. You wouldn't bet a million dollars on a weak hand, so don't do it in real life, either!

Pattern Recognition

Pattern recognition goes hand-in-hand with probabilities in the decision to get married. Once we have established our must-have categories, we can use pattern recognition to determine the probabilities of our must-haves being fulfilled.

Pattern recognition is also a great antidote for bias here because we are looking for patterns that will help foretell the results of our decision or actions. We do this not with emotion or personal opinion, but with relevant data. Remember that in pattern recognition, correlation, relevance, and causation all focus on the relationship between facts or incidents. Marriages can fall apart because of a clearly identifiable event such as a romantic affair outside of the marriage, or the love can gradually erode away due to daily stresses and other forces at work.

How about fidelity? Infidelity is an issue that is emotional and quantifiable. It has either never happened in your relationship or has happened some number of times that can be measured. If fidelity is one of my four must-haves, I should do more than discuss how I feel about infidelity with my partner. I should look at the data. Has my partner ever been unfaithful to me? If so, how many times? Has she been unfaithful in other relationships? The suggestion here is to look for repeating data points to see if there is a pattern. Past incidents do not guarantee that a behavior will continue, but if data points exist, I should not ignore them.

In the book *The Mathematics of Marriage*, author and professor Dr. John Gottman lays out a system for analyzing interactions between couples and predicting with an amazingly high degree of accuracy (95%, according to the book) whether that couple will still be married 15 years later. His method of sizing up couples and his predictive analytics are summarized in the equally interesting book *Blink: The Power of Thinking Without Thinking* by Malcolm Gladwell. When keeping with the 95% accuracy standard, Gottman analyzes a husband and wife talking with each other for an hour. Almost more incredibly is that he can achieve a 90% accurate predictive rate when he only analyzes fifteen minutes of interaction.

Gottman's method is to pick up subtle, yet distinctive messages in words, tone, and other inflections that send a clear, predictable sign as to whether the couple will stay married over the long term or not. It isn't just about how often they argue in that time span, but the intensity and inflections within the arguments. Gottman is practicing classic pattern recognition and probabilities. While the book tracks which couples stay married and not which couples stay *happily* married, his methods have a far greater success rate at predicting results than the general public's success rate.

My suggestion is that you consider Gottman's method before you are married, or at least work through probabilities and pattern recognition as he does in as unbiased a way as possible. Rely on a few trusted friends to observe the interactions between the two of you. In a recent study, untrained university students using Gottman's methods achieved an 80% success rate in predicting the future of a relationship. If there is a serious issue before you become a legal partnership, the probability is that things will not get better when you take on a mortgage, car loan, children, and everything else that comes with real life.

Logic and a good betting instinct tell you to bet on the cards you see, not the ones you hope will come along. Don't assume your potential life partner will change for the worse, but don't assume he or she will change for the better, either.

MONEYBALL

Moneyball: *The Art of Winning an Unfair Game* is an excellent book written by Michael Lewis, whose books and writing style I enjoy immensely. The book was also made into a movie starring Brad Pitt as Billy Beane, the renegade manager of the Oakland Athletics baseball team. In the corporate world, Beane would have been known as a "change agent" for transforming the way that players were selected for this major league team.

While the decision-making process involved in building a winning baseball franchise on a limited budget does not address an issue most of us face, it does illustrate how pattern recognition and probabilities can be used successfully in a real-life scenario to achieve a desired outcome. It is also a great example of getting optimal results through a decision-making framework rather than relying solely on gut instinct and biases or making decisions based on the way things have always been done.

Moneyball is one of the best examples of thinking creatively to solve a problem, and it illustrates the four factors at work and the impact of, and resistance to, an analytical decision-making framework that utilized real data points in an innovative way.

Situation Analysis

From 1980 to 1995, the Oakland A's were owned by Walter A. Haas, Jr., a wealthy businessman who treated his ownership of the baseball team more like an expensive hobby than a business. When the team needed something, Haas funded it. By 1991, the Oakland A's had the highest payroll in all of baseball. That is quite a distinction when you consider the vast sums paid out by notoriously free-spending owners such as George Steinbrenner of the New York Yankees.

Things changed drastically when Walter Haas, Jr. died. The team was sold to a pair of local businessmen who approached their ownership of the franchise like a business, in large part, by tightening the purse strings. This meant that the team could no longer automatically bankroll the highest-paid players in the league. Instead, the Oakland A's had to field a winning team that could make the playoffs without spending big money like they did in the past and as other ball teams still could.

In most professional sports, getting and retaining great players requires huge sums of money. While owners and fans lament about how much money players now earn, the owners keep paying them. The conventional thinking is that if you want to build and keep a competitive team, you have to pay for top talent. There seems to be no other choice.

Problem to Be Solved

As the saying goes, "Necessity is the mother of invention." Prior to the budget cuts, the Oakland A's, like every other team in the league, picked players through baseball scouts, most of whom had played the game professionally at some level. These scouts traveled more than 100 days each year to watch hundreds of high school and college games. They mainly visited schools that had traditionally produced major league draft prospects or that they heard from other scouts had a potentially phenomenal player. Most scouts visited the same places and looked at the same players. In other words, they went to the usual places.

Were these scouts professionals? Yes. Were they experts in the art of spotting new baseball talent? If an "expert" is defined as someone who spends a great deal of time doing a particular task and is as good as anyone else in their field, then they can be called experts. That being said, all of these scouts seemed to rely solely on their instincts. While their instincts were among the best in the business, there was no science to the art of picking future impact players at the major league level.

The problem that went unrecognized when the team had plenty of money was the amount at stake. If you sign a ballplayer for $3,000, which was the reported signing bonus for Mariano Rivera, former star relief pitcher for the New York Yankees, and he doesn't pan out, you wasted a spot on your roster and lost $3,000. If you sign a player for $10 million and he doesn't perform well, you've wasted a small fortune. No one in major league baseball realized it at the time, but they certainly could have used a decision-making framework to understand their risk. If they had used a more analytical approach, they would have recognized that the cost of being wrong, even in their area of expertise, was too high.

Most casual poker players don't bother to learn the math involved in playing poker and instead bet on gut instinct because they play games with very low stakes. This is not a big problem when you are only betting $1 a hand, which will probably only amount to a small loss by evening's end. What happens when you sit down at a table where the stakes are $10,000 per hand? The stakes have gone up dramatically, but your poker skills haven't. This is what happened to the Oakland A's, as well as the rest of major league baseball. Market forces drove up the costs to sign players, significantly increasing the cost of being wrong. The stakes for losing had changed, but the skills and methods used in picking the right players had not kept pace.

Timing

This is the only area in which the decision-making process of the Oakland A's was not great. Just as most of us wait too long to see the doctor and only make an appointment when our symptoms and pain become severe, businesses that are thriving usually lack the sense of urgency that would otherwise force management to revisit existing beliefs or processes. So it was for the Oakland A's. Management scouted for baseball talent the same way each year because, as we know from the chapter on timing, they had "always done it that way."

When the situation changed and the bottomless budget was replaced with a more stringent budget, management was forced to rethink existing operations. A combination of two factors, lack of funds and a skyrocketing payroll, meant that they had to revisit the existing strategy for selecting talent. In hindsight, I wonder how much money the Oakland A's could have saved while garnering better results if they had changed their strategy before it became absolutely necessary.

As the cost of players' contracts slowly but steadily got more expensive, nothing changed. As happens to many individuals, companies, and governments, the Oakland A's became the proverbial frog in the pot of water that was heated slowly. Skyrocketing player contracts should have signaled a time to revisit past assumptions, but because they had ample money, they didn't set a deadline. Then, when the spigot of money was turned down to a drip, the deadline was set for them.

Balance

The old Oakland A's had the classic imbalance of relying too much on gut instinct and not enough on hard data. While you have to realize the power of objective data, you should also recognize that blind reliance on numbers is not perfect and is also out of balance.

The New York Yankees signed an unknown player from Panama who didn't have overpowering physical ability but did have a passion for baseball, which is how Mariano Rivera came to be a Yankee. They picked Mariano because of his passion and knowledge of the game and because the monetary risk was low ($3,000).

If a player runs to catch a ball but can't hold onto it when it hits his mitt, it can be ruled an "error." Errors are bad, and this data point counts against him. What if the only reason he had the chance to make that catch was that he is the fastest person in the league? A slower player would never have gotten close enough to attempt that catch, and the ball would fall for a base hit rather than an error. The faster player may be more valuable for the team than a slower player but may have more errors due to his ability to chase down more balls. In this and other circumstances like this, we need to reconcile the data and check our assumptions. We may initially assume that the slower player is a better player in the field due to the fact that he has fewer errors.

What is the risk involved in changing the way we pick players? If you believe that it is necessary to pay top dollar in order to field a winning team, the converse should also be true. If a team no longer has the ability to spend an enormous amount of money, you might conclude that they are doomed to have a losing season. Unless you are willing to settle for that result, something has to change.

There are two issues in play here: money and the way we select players. With significantly less money at our disposal (the first issue), we know that the probabilities of building a winning team are very low unless we change our selection criteria (the second issue). The risk of not doing anything differently is ending up with a predictably poor result.

The organization's risk in changing their methods is minimal. If the new method of picking players doesn't work and they lose games, they may be no worse off than if they had done nothing differently. The risks to their reputation and job security were high for the individuals who had the courage to implement what was viewed as radical change. Without enough money to successfully compete with the other wealthy franchises, the choice was clear that change was needed. The risk wasn't in change itself, but the type and amount of change.

Probabilities

As discussed in the chapter on probabilities, expected outcomes are the basis for most decisions. This is particularly true with regard to investments and sports. We want to choose the option with the highest probability of achieving our goal. If you are the owner of the Oakland A's, your overarching goal is to win the World Series. Long before you can win the World Series, you have to qualify for the playoffs. Here, the goal becomes clearer. How many wins do you need to qualify for the playoffs, and how do you plan to win that many games without the money to hire the best available talent?

The Oakland A's concluded that they needed to win 95 games to get into the playoffs. Winning 95 games wouldn't guarantee that they would make the playoffs, and winning only 94 games wouldn't necessarily eliminate their chances. Based on their research, winning 95 games would give them an expected outcome of making the playoffs. Figuring out that part of the equation was the easy part.

Pattern Recognition

Now that they identified their goal, how would they go about winning 95 games against teams that could afford the big-name talent? They would need to score more runs than their opponents 95 times, but how? While the Oakland A's couldn't predict what the score would be for any particular game, they determined that they could increase their expected wins by increasing their own expected run production (offense) and reducing their opponents expected run production (defense).

The A's looked for patterns that could predict what they needed to do to score more runs than their opponents. Pattern recognition engages us in Thinking Deeply, so before we can look for patterns to see if there are factors that correlate, are relevant to, or are causative of our desired outcomes, we have to understand the game of baseball in some detail.

First, baseball, as compared to some other sports, isn't measured by time. There is no clock. There are no quarters, halves, or time outs, nor is there extra time allotted for injuries or play reviews, like there is in soccer or football. If your team doesn't get three outs, your team stays on offense indefinitely. This became the crux of Oakland's offensive strategy. They could only get three outs per inning, so the outs were a limited commodity to avoid. Think about this a bit. They didn't have to do something spectacular to score a run. They just had to avoid making an out.

Second, there are no "quality points." In gymnastics and diving competitions, the performance is judged not only by the execution of the planned routine or dive, but also by the difficulty of the routine or dive. A bloop single in baseball (a weaker-struck ball that drops between the fielders for a single) counts as a base hit as much as a blistering line drive that is picked up on one bounce by the outfielder, and ditto for homeruns. A ball that goes hundreds of feet over the fence is a homerun, but so is a ball that drops one foot over the fence.

Third, in baseball, scores come in whole run units only. If, in the first inning of the game, the visiting team hits a home run that barely leaves the park, they get credited with one run. If, in the bottom half of the first inning, the home team gets its third out while the bases are loaded (players on first base, second base, and third base at the same time), they don't score three-quarters of a run; they get zero runs. Like the Oakland A's, in real life you need to think of all of the aspects of the pattern before you can focus on which factors are most crucial to solving your problem.

Oakland's organization challenged all known tenets about baseball and baseball players when they switched their way of picking players for the team. This relates to the need to revalidate preexisting absolutes. "He looks like a ballplayer," in reality, doesn't matter.

For the 2002 season, the A's management correctly predicted that the team would score between 800 and 820 runs, while their opponents would score between 650 and 670 runs. Based on that range of run differentials (the total accumulated runs scored by a team in a season over the number of runs scored by its opponents), they estimated that the team would win 93 to 97 games and probably get into the playoffs. But how did they know which players would get the run differential they wanted? They figured this out by examining statistics that would help determine each player's "expected run value" per game and then built the team based on these statistics.

This is a core concept that plays out over and over again in decision making where there is enough data to support the analysis. *Moneyball* provides an enjoyable but useful analysis demonstrating that if a batter leads off an inning with a double, the value of that runner being on second base with no outs is 0.55 of a run. As we all know, there is no such thing as 0.55 of a run, but that is the concept of expected value. The 0.55 run statistic means that the runner on second base will probably score, but by no means is this certain.

Because the first rule was to never make an out, the A's coaching staff trained their players to have more discipline when looking at pitches from the opposing team. While not as impressive-looking as hitting a line drive, getting a walk (a free pass to first base) when the opposing pitcher throws four pitches outside of the strike zone would still put a player on base without making an out.

By having disciplined players with higher-than-average expected run production based on statistics, they increased their chances of producing the desired run differential and increased their chances of winning the targeted 95 wins. This increased their chances of making the playoffs, which increased their chances of winning the World Series. To this day, the Oakland Athletics continue to be one of the most successful teams in all of baseball, even though they radically changed the way they chose players.

The story of *Moneyball* represents not only an endearing and funny sports tale, but also an analysis that should extend beyond baseball and other sports. It is a perfect use of pattern recognition and probabilities, two critical factors of decision making.

After Oakland pioneered this way of managing a baseball team, other teams followed suit in an attempt to emulate their success. Today, most sports pages include a column dubbed "run differential" alongside the list of baseball teams' standings. The correlation between the run differential and the team's overall winning performance is almost 100% accurate. If the team has a negative differential, meaning that its opponents have scored more runs than it has, the team usually has a losing record. If the differential is positive, the team usually has a winning record. The team with the largest differential is almost always the team that is in first place.

THE UNITED STATES OF MONEYBALL

This example is unlike the others and is broader in context. Here, we are taking the principles established by the Oakland A's in *Moneyball* and applying them to the United States of America.

There are two major points. First, at the end of this example, I hope to establish that large groups of people can be predisposed to adopt the same solution to any problem because they have always solved their problems that way. As pointed out in the first part of this book, this is the exact same mistake that a medical doctor would make by treating all patients with chest pains the exact same way. It is attempting to apply one simple solution to a complex problem.

Second, and this applies to all decisions including those in the business world, money alone is never the solution. Money can be a useful tool in implementing a well-thought-out decision, but it is never the sole answer.

The section of this book titled "How We Decide Now" detailed how individuals can be influenced to make a tentative preliminary decision based on various heuristics and prejudices. There are numerous articles describing how group decisions are made. The dynamics of leadership styles, the varied interests of different stakeholder groups, and personal and organizational politics all play a large role in reaching a decision.

Strong bias, particularly after rousing political speeches, can lead us to a predetermined end game just like other biases and heuristics. It becomes a unique group heuristic. Psychologists usually focus on the biases that we have as individuals but don't have the same depth of research and writing on large group biases. Post World War II, decision makers in the United States have had a strong tendency to view every domestic problem as solvable by money. If it doesn't get solved, we throw more money at the problem until it eventually collapses under the mountain of money sitting on it.

US decision makers also try to solve too many international problems with force, which former Defense Secretary Gates referred to as the "creeping militarization" of US foreign policy.[18] This doesn't mean that the country doesn't need money to solve certain problems or that it doesn't need to use military force in certain international situations. It does mean that the United States overuses these two preordained "solutions" far too often.

As detailed in the book *Moneyball*, the Oakland Athletics had to change the way they drafted players and signed free agents because they no longer had the money they once had to spend on acquiring talent. They examined the data, challenged long-standing assumptions, and got creative. They didn't just wake up one day and have an epiphany. They were forced to suddenly make a change because of a dictate from the owners.

Money Is Not the Answer to Problems

In the post-World War II era, the United States has most often held a position of dominant military and economic power. While that is an overall advantage, the downside is that foreign policy problems have a tendency to be solved through military force and domestic problems have a tendency to be solved with money. It is the typical tendency to solve things easily with the advantage you have, but it is also a classic example of an advantage becoming a liability. This tendency shortcuts a good decision-making process, because it is a classic case of group heuristics and Thinking Lightly operating at both an individual and an institutional level.

The budget deficit in the United States has been an issue for decades but has recently become the subject of a hotly contested debate. Like the

---

[18] Tyson, Ann Scott. "Gates Warns of Militarized Policy." *The Washington Post*, July 16, 2008.

Oakland A's under the prior management, the country has always acted as though we have an unlimited amount of money to throw at a perceived problem. Why use thought and creativity when politicians can announce a beautifully-named solution (using framing) for a problem and allocate huge amounts of money to that problem? If after some period of time the solution doesn't actually work, it is often concluded that its failure was due to not spending enough money on it. What do we do then? We spend even more money on the problem than originally planned.

If a person has only one way of solving a problem (like threatening people with termination if they don't meet sales quotas) and that solution is temporarily successful, he won't know when to change it. There is an old expression in business, "If all you have is a hammer, every problem starts to look like a nail." That feeling of being a powerful and feared boss is like wielding a mighty hammer.

When you have (or think you have) exorbitant amounts of money, every problem looks like it can be solved solely with money. As the R&B group the Temptations sang in the 1970s hit "Ball of Confusion," "Politicians say more taxes will solve everything, and the band played on." The United States needs to become more creative in using money, like the new Oakland A's did and stop behaving like the old Oakland A's, hence the name for this example, "The United States of *Moneyball*."

Again, money may be the tool we need to best implement a solution, but it isn't the solution. Money itself should never automatically be part of the solution without an appropriate answer to the following question: What are we going to use the money to accomplish? An over-simplified or unspecific response such as, "We are going to use the money to fix the problem," is not a real answer.

It has been reported that the Bill and Melinda Gates Foundation donates money with clearly established benchmarks targeted. If you donate $1 million to cancer research, you feel good about yourself but may have no idea how the money will actually be used. If you have met with cancer researchers who can clearly demonstrate that the highest probability of finding an effective cure is through a specific area of research, you can allocate your $1 million to fund that specific area of research. If you don't know exactly where your money is going, it could be funding something that is not a good bet but reflects the pet project of some scientists involved. After all, the well-intentioned researchers are still mere human beings who possess biases, gut reactions, and heuristics, just like the rest of us.

Framing the Question

As a nation, we are coming to the conclusion that we need to change our educational methodologies so that the typical American high school graduate can effectively compete with similar graduates from other countries. We often hear, "We need to invest in the children." This statement is perfectly framed by politicians, because disagreeing with it would suggest that you are against investing in our children, or worse, against the betterment of children's lives.

The word "invest" immediately makes us think of money. If our initial reaction to this question is that we do need to help the children, and this psychologically equates to pouring more money into the educational system, that means we are in danger of coming to a conclusion before we think. We may, in fact, need to invest substantially in our educational system, but if we don't Think Deeply about both the problem and possible solutions, we will be using our usual aggregate thought process of seeing money as the solution to the problem instead of being a tool to effectuate a well-thought-out solution.

Ask yourself what you are going to spend the money on. For education, the categories for improvement are likely to be people (teachers and other staff), process (how we teach and what we teach), and capital expenditures (technology and buildings). Regardless of the conclusion you reach, it must be well thought out. Money is simply a necessary tool to effectuate that well-thought-out conclusion.

EDUCATION IN AMERICA

As Americans, we pride ourselves on having a culture that is open minded and creative. The vast majority of the most meaningful technological developments over the past fifty years has come from people and companies in the United States. In recent decades, the American West Coast has been a particularly fertile ground for new thinking and innovative ideas—"disruptors" of how things have always been done. However, we seem to have a real problem with our educational system. Many other countries are much better at graduating high school students who are more competent in many core areas, particularly math and science.

Situation Analysis

In this competitive global environment, we are constantly reminded that we are losing ground to other countries in terms of test scores in the areas of math and science. For instance, in one recent survey, the United States was ranked seventeenth in the world in math.

Why are we falling behind? Our best students can compete with anyone, but the same cannot be said for the average American student or those nearer to the bottom of their class. The brilliant and groundbreaking innovations that have come from America really emanated from relatively few creative thinkers.

We have business owners in Silicon Valley lobbying Congress to change immigration rules so that they can hire non-US software engineers because the immediate problem for these companies is a lack of available local talent. They want to grow their businesses, but can't. I would suggest that this is a symptom of a much larger problem. Why can't these companies find enough competent software engineers in the United States? After all, this is the country that fundamentally invented software.

Problem to Be Solved

How do we improve education in our country to produce the most competent workforce possible so that they, and the country as a whole, can compete and excel in the global environment?

In many countries, the school year is much longer than it is in the United States. In Japan, for example, the typical school year is sixty-three days longer. Sixty-three more days in school equates to Japanese students spending about 35% more time in school than American students. All else being equal, one would expect the average Japanese student to perform better in math than the average American student simply because a lot more time is spent learning math. To put it another way, it would be very surprising indeed if a Japanese student did not outperform an American student. If American students began outperforming Japanese students, the Japanese would need to examine their system to determine what to fix.

Some would point to education funding as the culprit in the United States, as it is uneven from state to state and from school to school in the each state. But remember that money is never the solution to any problem. Money may be the critically important tool necessary to implement the solution, but we still have to know what to do with the money.

Timing

Just like many important decisions, this one has no set deadline, but the decision to implement changes to improve the overall education of our children is unlike other decisions that can be implemented quickly and will show immediate results. Changing the educational system in America will take time, and seeing results will take even longer.

Important goals that take a long time to implement or produce results should be made a priority. If the goal is to improve the educational outcomes for all high school graduates, launching initiatives that begin with high school students who are 14 or 15 years old and have been in the school system for a decade or more is not going to be an optimal approach. We need to start with pre-kindergarten children and work with them all the way through the end of high school so that they don't have years of conditioning from a failed system to overcome when reforms are introduced. It also means that we won't see the complete results and won't know if we are truly successful for about 14 years after implementation.

When there is a long timeline necessary to see results, the sooner we begin implementing changes, the better. The sooner a deadline is placed on planning and implementing reforms, the sooner we will bear the fruits of our labor. Our timing here is driven by how soon we want to begin pursuing our goal with a longer vision of when we want to start seeing results.

Balance

As mentioned in the chapter on balance, there is a risk in doing something and a risk in not doing something. This seems to be a relatively easy part of the decision-making process about changing educational outcomes in America. We are losing this global competition, and there is nothing to suggest that we won't continue losing this battle unless we have meaningful change. Here, the greater risk seems to be in not changing anything at all.

If we do nothing, our students as a whole will continue to fall behind a number of other countries. High-paying jobs will be lost to outsourcing, wages will fall without those high-paying jobs available to American workers, and the economy will suffer. We must have a constant and reliable supply of well-educated students. We don't want to nor are we capable of entering into a contest that results in lower wages for our workers. Neither our current economic system nor our collective pride would support such a drastic paradigm shift. We will only have a successful economy and a large, thriving middle class if we compete on the quality of a product and not solely on the lower cost of a product.

Balance will come into play in determining how we measure the success of our actions. Will it be measured strictly by objective data points like test scores, or should it, and can it, be measured on a more subjective scale or by data other than test results?

What happens if we do nothing and continue to produce a less-educated workforce than our competitors? The less-educated worker will earn less his entire life, and the economy will suffer, as well. The only possible argument against a massive overhaul of the system is the cost.

Probabilities

We want to choose the option with the highest chance of achieving our goal. In order to do that, we need to be very specific in stating our goal. It can't be something general like "better-educated students." We are in a global competition for educated talent. We need to accurately predict the skills needed both now and 25 years in the future and work to teach those skills. When we say we want students who are better educated and can compete in a global economy, do we mean that we need to produce students with stronger math and science skills? What about other skills? We need to clearly articulate a specific goal; otherwise, we will not be able to measure whether we are on track for success or how near it we are.

Prior to World War II, Germany was considered a developed country. After the devastating effects of World War II, Germany aimed to become a developed country once again. The people of Germany realized that they would never regain world economic power by making T-shirts and coffee mugs, as that would force it to compete against the very low wages of the many developing economies around the world. They instead decided to focus on manufacturing, which would create high-value products that command high prices. I'm not referring only to expensive cars produced by large companies. Smaller manufacturers are capturing niche markets like stained glass for churches, which is expensive to make, hugely profitable, and required to be of high quality. The German people take great pride in graduating engineers, have built an international reputation for producing high-quality products, and are able to charge higher prices for that perception of quality. The result is a robust economy with high wages for its workforce.

I am not suggesting that we should try to replicate what transpired in Germany, but we should examine those developed countries that are producing excellent students in a healthy economy and search for the factors that will produce our desired outcome. The process of identifying like factors and looking for causation is part of pattern recognition, but in complex issues, pattern recognition and probabilities are usually intertwined. We have already started to conclude what we need to do by pushing STEM (Science, Technology, Engineering, and Math) education in middle school and high school, if not earlier.

Pattern Recognition

Is it possible to find factors that correlate, are relevant and may be causative in such a subjective area as education? As we know, the larger the sample size, the more reliable the numbers—as long as we validate the underlying assumptions. What reliable data do we have? Let's examine some stories and see if we can spot predictive trends.

New York City

Author Malcolm Gladwell recounts some interesting studies in his book *Outliers*, which could be called "Pattern Recognition in Everyday Life," but his title is catchier to sell. One particular story focuses on KIPP Academy, a middle school in the South Bronx, a tough inner-city neighborhood. KIPP Academy schools are special not only because of the results and opportunities they offer children in areas that are academically disadvantaged, but also by how they achieve the results.

Anyone living in the Bronx can apply to attend, and students are accepted to the academy through a lottery system. Almost all of the students are African-American or Hispanic, and about 75% come from single-parent households. The children start at KIPP Academy at the beginning of fifth grade. Four years later, at the end of eighth grade, the vast majority of students are performing at or above their grade level in math. This is almost the inverse of their performance level when they first came to the school.

There are a number of unique things at the KIPP Academy; most notable is the much longer school day compared to other middle schools in New York City. The KIPP school day starts at 7:25 am. While all of the usual subjects are taught throughout the day, students also take a mandatory orchestra class and a 30-minute course called "Thinking Skills." The school day ends at 5:00 pm, and then the students go to homework clubs or sports practices. KIPP students also go to school on Saturdays from 9:00 am to 1:00 pm and for three additional weeks in July from 8:00 am to 2:00 pm, while the rest of the New York City public school system is on vacation.

The key differentiator between a regular public school and the KIPP Academy seems to be the amount of time that KIPP students spend learning, which equates to more than 150% of the time spent in most American classrooms.

An additional factor could be that these students, possibly at the urging of their parents, want to attend KIPP because of its reputation for producing graduates who are far better off academically and have a much greater chance of upward economic mobility than students at regular public schools. KIPP students are willing to make the extra effort to learn, something that cannot be discounted.

So far, we have two possible factors for the differences in this example:

1. Extra time spent learning
2. Positive attitudes toward learning

Economic disparity is not an issue, as the students are generally all from the same socio-economic backgrounds.

Baltimore

As Malcolm Gladwell also recounted in *Outliers*, a researcher at Johns Hopkins did a study on students in the Baltimore public school system that showed some interesting differences among students from low-income, middle-income, and high-income families. When the students began first grade, there were differences between the three groups. The low-income students showed poorer performance than the middle-income students, and the middle-income students did not do as well as the high-income students. At first blush, it seems that the high-income students have some advantage due to their access to better resources and better-educated parents or other factors. The problem was that, as the students progressed to fifth grade, the difference in performance levels among the socio-economic groups more than doubled. Why didn't the initial gap stay stagnant or widen just a little bit? With real data (test scores) at hand, we will try to determine what could have caused such exponential growth in the gap between scores of these groups.

The students were tested at both the beginning and the end of the school year because there are months between the end of one school year and the beginning of the next. If an athlete is timed in the 100-yard dash at the end of the school year in June, and then timed again in September at the beginning of the next school year, you would not be surprised that her time had changed. If she exercised and trained during the summer months, you would expect her to be faster. Conversely, if she didn't exercise at all and ate junk food, you would expect her to be slower.

The same is true with our minds. The change in scores after summer vacation shows the greatest disparity between students from the high-income and lower-income families. This is when the high-income students seem to have the greatest advantage over the lower-income students. The test scores reveal that something happens during the summer months that positively impacts the reading skills of students from high-income families that doesn't happen to students from lower-income families. What causes this dramatic increase in disparity between skill levels? It has to be something other than just money. A student from a high-income household may go on a fabulous vacation, but that doesn't necessarily cause increased reading ability.

The logical answer is that during the summer, there must be a support system in place that helps children from high-income families academically but that is lacking in lower-income families. For this reason, it seems that students from poorer families would be better off attending classes during the summer that would provide them with an academic support system in the lapse between school ending and beginning again.

As evidenced by the KIPP students, the economic disparity should not be the sole determinative factor, because the KIPP students all came from lower income families. Here again, we see numbers that support expanding the amount of time that students spend in school. In this example, the beneficiaries would be those students from the lower-income families and society as a whole.

Byram Hills High School—Armonk, New York

Each year Intel sponsors a science competition for American high school students. It is a difficult competition, and winning any level of award is a prestigious honor that increases the students' self-confidence, significantly adds to their chances of getting into a top-notch college, and gives the winner's parents invaluable bragging rights.

Byram Hills High School is a public school located in the upscale hamlet of Armonk in Westchester County, New York. Armonk has long had one of the higher-ranked school systems in New York State. Any high school student that lives within the school district is eligible to attend Byram Hills. A small school by most public school standards, Byram Hills High School's graduating senior class generally ranges from 150 to 220 students—a fraction of the class sizes at other public high schools in New York. Its top students get accepted to the most prestigious universities in the country, including all of the Ivy League schools and the top-ranked non-Ivy League schools such as Johns Hopkins, Northwestern, and Washington University.

Over the past 15 years or so, Byram Hills High School produced the highest percentage of Intel semi-finalists based on class size among high schools in the entire United States. In fact, for the 15-year period ending in 2013, it produced more Intel semi-finalists in absolute numbers than any other high school, regardless of size. Of the 300 total Intel semi-finalists in 2013, eight came from Byram Hills High School. This means that close to 3% of all Intel semi-finalists in the country came out of one small public school outside of New York City. This data reflects a high level of success and achievement in science for these particular American high school students. What caused such successful results?

Robert Pavlica was a brilliant science teacher who truly cared about teaching, had a good rapport with his students, and frequently kept in touch with them after they graduated. He taught science at Byram Hills for many years, during which time he developed a unique style of teaching and a special program that got high school students to enthusiastically embrace science. Dr. Pavlica shared with me how he was able to produce such exceptional results and recounted the "aha" moment that shifted his approach to teaching science.

One of Dr. Pavlica's former students went on to become a medical doctor and came back for a reunion. He told his former teacher that he'd never really understood science until he got involved in scientific research at the post-graduate level. He had done very well in high school, especially in science, through some natural ability and a lot of hard work. He had been able to regurgitate what he had been taught. This was Pavlica's "light bulb" moment.

While all good teachers want to make things interesting for their students and aim to enhance critical thinking, Pavlica was well aware that most schooling through the high school level is fundamentally a memory game. Simply put, the teachers teach facts; the students learn the facts through memorization and then are graded on their ability to restate the facts in homework assignments and tests. The always-thinking Dr. Pavlica saw an opportunity for change that could truly impact learning and began developing the groundbreaking Authentic Science Research Program at Byram Hills High School.

Anyone could join the program, not just the top students. Beginning in ninth grade, students enrolled in the program on a completely voluntary basis and picked a topic that interested them. Throughout the four-year program, the student researched that topic and eventually wrote a thesis and made a presentation. If a student wanted to research a particular cancer and its effects on the body, she could. If another student wanted to research the neuroscience and psychology behind the reasons people in sports get nervous and are superstitious, he was free to do that. The program matched the students with experts in the fields of science that corresponded with their specific topics to provide students with the proper guidance and feedback. Most importantly, students learned how science worked in real life and how it could make a difference to real people. There were no scores given for work. If you were performing in the program, you got an A. If you weren't, you were dropped from the program.

As a result of Pavlica's pioneering approach to teaching science, not only did Byram Hills produce a disproportionate number of Intel semi-finalists, four of them were special education students. The additional cost to the school district was ZERO dollars!

Look for factors that contribute to or cause the results we are after—high achievement in science in the case of Byram Hills. When we look for causative factors behind why Byram Hills and Pavlica's science program produced so many Intel semi-finalists, we might first look at socio-economic status. This is an affluent community. Could it be that students' access to better resources and parents who stress education is the cause? Affluence could be relevant if the competition was limited to Byram Hills and schools from underprivileged areas, but the Intel competition is open to all schools at all socio-economic levels, including the most exclusive and expensive private schools in the country. A factor which must be taken into account as highly relevant is the student's willingness to take on extra work, as with the KIPP Academy, and subject matter taught in a way that is engaging.

Are there any factors that correlate with our desired outcome of having students who can compete on a global level, especially in the areas of math and science? If so, what is their degree of relevance? Which factor, if any, do you think rises to the level of causation and directly affects the result?

Innovative teaching methods are not to be limited to science. A recent *New York Times* article titled "Why Do Americans Stink at Math?"[19] showed the ways in which Japan has revamped its approach to teaching math. What was surprising was that the Japanese educators got these ideas from American educators, but the programs were not successful in the United States because we didn't train teachers in how to teach math in this different and an engaging manner. Having students engaged in learning math gets tremendous results.

The examples above, combined with the recognition that we are in a global competition for talent and have to be mindful of what other countries in Asia and Europe are doing, show that the following should be strongly considered when reaching the best decision on how to dramatically improve our educational results:

1. More time spent in school appears to have a high correlation with better educational outcomes. It terms of the Baltimore study, it appears that more time spent in school during the summer months would be a relevant factor, if not a causative factor, in preventing students from lower-income families from falling behind, but we won't know the true impact until students actually spend more time in school.

2. More time in school during the regular school day appears to have a high correlation with results, as evidenced by the KIPP Academy. If you have two equally gifted athletes, but one spends a lot more time training and being coached, you would expect that athlete to be better at her sport. It is simplistic, but convincingly accurate. Just like athletic training, more mental training should produce better results.

3. By using new and innovative teaching methods, the Byram Hills

---

[19] Green, Elizabeth. "Why Do Americans Stink at Math?" *New York Times*, July 23, 2014.

High School method for science research is exactly on point. Instead of having students regurgitate facts and figures and perform required experiments in the science lab, they perform research on a topic they choose. Teaching students in a direct, engaging way that also shows them the relevance of their new knowledge in a real-life application increases the probability of a better outcome. Here, the desired outcome was to have more high school students enthusiastically embrace the sciences. The increase in Intel semi-finalists is an objective data point that indicates success.

4. As evidenced by the KIPP students and their families and the results of the Authentic Science Research Program at Byram Hills High School, what may be the most important factor here is the value that the students, their families, and their teachers put on the importance of learning. If the students have a strong desire to learn and see education as the best path to success and if our teachers can harness that energy and engage them, we will achieve success as a country.

Playing the Lottery

I was putting the finishing touches on the first draft this book when I stopped at the local gas station to re-fuel. The lottery jackpot was over $100 million, so I decided to buy a ticket. As I handed the cashier my money, I wondered if this was a good decision.

I am well aware that no competent financial advisor would suggest that playing the lottery is a good investment, but as the author of a book on decision making, I thought it might be of value to revisit my choice and determine whether playing the lottery was an intelligent decision or a foolish one, because reexamining my past decision will either change my mind or revalidate my prior non-thinking decision to play the lottery from time to time.

If we engage in Thinking Deeply and apply the four framework factors, will playing the lottery ever make sense? In some cases, I believe so. In other cases, playing the lottery may be a very bad decision. What makes the difference? It's not about winning. Remember that an optimal result, which in this case is winning the lottery, doesn't necessarily mean I made a good decision; maybe I just made a lucky one. Let's go through the process and see where it leads us.

Remember, as discussed in the beginning of the book, the four factors can be used in any order except for Timing, which always comes first. Here, I am putting Balance last because I think it raises the most important thoughts.

Timing

The lottery is ongoing and has drawings each week. If you are playing for a specific jackpot, your deadline will be driven by the date of that drawing. For most of us, the decision to spend a few dollars playing the lottery can be made at any time because it is a very small amount of our disposable net income. There is no final deadline for this decision, so use the next drawing as your deadline.

Probabilities

From a probabilistic standpoint, playing the lottery is a bad decision. The odds of winning most lotteries do not warrant the purchase price, regardless of the amount of money at stake. According to the official lottery website, the current odds of winning Powerball or Mega Millions are approximately 1:175 million.[20] In comparison, there is a 1 in 700,000 chance you will be struck by lightning this year, which means that you are 250 times more likely to be struck by lightning than to win Powerball or Mega Millions.[21] Like most people, you don't expect to be hit by lightning any time soon, so you can't reasonably expect to win that big jackpot any time soon either.

What if you're a wealthy person who wants to get wealthier? Let's say the jackpot rises to $500 million. If you can afford it, you could guarantee a winning ticket by purchasing all possible combinations, which will cost you $175 million for tickets that cost $1 each. For a game that charges $2 a ticket, you will have to pay $350 million. The problem is that you need to pay cash upfront for the tickets, and the jackpot is paid out over multiple years. While there are differences among lottery games for discounted interest rates, if you want to receive cash immediately instead of

---

[20] Power Ball and Mega Millions are two of the lotteries sold in New York. These odds are constantly changing as the games change.

[21] "Flash Facts About Lightning," National Geographic, accessed September 17, 2014, http://news.nationalgeographic.com/news/2004/06/0623_040623_lightningfacts.html.

as an annuity over a number of years, you will only get around 65% of the jackpot amount—and don't forget that lottery winnings are taxable.

Let's say you paid $175 million to guarantee that you will have a winning ticket and the lump-sum payment on the $500 million jackpot is $325 million. Seems like a good bet, right? Not necessarily. The same combination of numbers can be sold more than once, so there could be multiple winning tickets. You will have a winning ticket, but you may not have the only winning ticket, which is something beyond your control. You might have to share the jackpot and will have lost money.

So far, the odds suggest that it's a bad decision to play the lottery, but let's continue with our quick analysis.

In Probabilities, you want to pick the highest possibility of achieving your goal, so what is your goal? If your answer is that you simply want more money, consider this: If you planned to spend $10 a week on the lottery and then choose not to play the lottery for a year, you will have $520 more (net, after taxes) at the end of the year. While you *could* win the lottery if you did play, the odds are overwhelming that you will not win. If your goal is just to have more money, the better option is to not play the lottery.

If your goal goes beyond just having a bit of extra money to having more money than you could ever earn by working for your entire career, playing the lottery gives you the hope that you can win big and change your lifestyle. If you are stuck in a minimum-wage job with no realistic chance of improving your economic condition through hard work, with a $1 or $2 bet you are buying hope. After all, the best thing about having a huge sum of money is the freedom from having to worry about having enough money to pay for housing, travel, medical care, education, and everything else. Essentially, we play the lottery to win an enormous amount of money, which we believe will allow us to live a happy, non-stressful life. After we bought our tickets but before the numbers are drawn and we realize we didn't win, we are dreaming about freedom from the treadmill of daily life.

For a dollar, we buy hope, but is this a wise decision? If your goal is specifically to have a lot more money, based on the probabilities, playing the lottery seems nonsensical. The financial advisors are right. Still, while your chance of winning is extremely remote, you know you can't achieve the same wealth in your current career, so the lottery appears to be the only way.

Pattern Recognition

While it is highly improbable that you will win the lottery, you can improve your chances of winning big by examining the winning numbers that have been drawn in the past, which is easily accessible public information, and choosing different numbers. While these previously-won numbers can be picked again and again, there is a better chance that numbers that have never been selected will be picked in the near future. While a professor in statistics and probabilities will tell you that each selection of the numbers is random and unrelated to the previous drawings, he will also tell you that the same numbers being chosen over and over again is improbable. If we examine rolling a single six-sided die, there is a one in six chance that the number five will come up. On the second roll, the chance of rolling a five is still one in six, but the chance of rolling a five twice in a row is actually one in thirty-six. Numbers that haven't been selected many times before are more likely to be selected than those that have appeared frequently. Picking numbers that are more likely to be chosen should increase your chances of winning.

Balance

If you are hoping for a less stressful, more comfortable life, playing the lottery may be a good idea, since it's the only way this might happen. Again, you are seeking to balance a number of things, but the key ratio here is risk to reward. What is the risk-to-reward ratio, and does it balance out? Let's say that you are buying a ticket for one dollar. The one-dollar risk is small compared to the possibility of a huge monetary reward, even if it is a very remote possibility. The non-monetary reward is your hope to be able to quit the daily grind that wears you down. While the chances of you winning are almost zero, the temporary hope you will have in the time between purchasing the ticket and the numbers being drawn is nearly guaranteed.

If you can afford to bet the dollar and get enjoyment from playing, I think playing the lottery is a good decision, but what about increasing your bet? If you think that betting one dollar is okay, then what about betting an additional dollar and increasing your total bet to two dollars? A two-dollar bet still seems reasonable. What about throwing in a few more dollars to make the bet an even five bucks? This is probably still a decent risk for most people, but at some point the balance tips so that not only is the risk greater, but the rewards will start to diminish. This is when playing the lottery turns out to be a bad decision.

Let me demonstrate by going to the extreme. A person decides to take his life savings and use all of it to buy tickets to next week's lottery. Here, we have a bad decision. Why? As noted earlier in "Probabilities," buying a lottery ticket is not a sound investment, even if you buy multiple tickets to increase your chances of winning. The risk of losing your life savings is now extremely high. Your remote chance of financial reward has not kept pace with the increased monetary risk, and, in fact, the non-monetary reward is likely to have diminished. The hope that you bought with a one-dollar ticket is more likely to be replaced with stress or despair from risking everything you own. If the person who spent his life savings on lottery tickets actually won, would we call it a good decision? No. We would say that he made a poor decision and got very, very lucky.

What is the sensible amount for you to bet on the lottery if you do choose to play? The point at which the balance tips too far is not set in stone and will vary with each person's economic status. A $10,000 lottery ticket purchase is significant for almost all people, but a $5 or $10 bet may not be. Since what you are really buying is a positive emotion (hope), perhaps replacing the money invested in the lottery with something else you do for enjoyment, such as enjoying a latte at the local coffee shop with friends, is feasible. If you decide to play the lottery, trade the latte for a less-expensive regular coffee and spend the difference on the lottery ticket.

This way, you haven't spent more than normal; you have reallocated the money you spend on small enjoyments from latte to lottery. Anything that is outside of your normal spending habits is not advisable.

I make small bets on the lottery only when the jackpot is large enough that the after-tax lump sum will be meaningful to the lives of my children and grandchildren. I think my decision to play the lottery for the small amount I bet is a good decision for me. If others disagree and come to the conclusion that the lottery should not be played at all using this four-point framework, I could not tell them I am right and they are wrong. Maybe they'd prefer to save the $10 each week and have a guaranteed extra $520 at the end of the year that I would have wagered on tickets that are likely not to win. The important thing is to consider all of the four factors and empower yourself to make a thinking decision with known risks of which you are in control.

An Open Letter to My Friends in Silicon Valley

As my friends know, I am an unabashed fan of both the people and the innovative culture in Silicon Valley. I have spent some time out there, and both of my children currently work in tech start-ups. If you have colleagues or friends in the area, you know that there is a communal pride in maintaining an ecosystem that creates and nurtures creativity. Instead of just looking at tweaking existing products and procedures in minor ways, they dream of better ways to get things done and then invent the mechanisms to achieve those goals. They have disrupted the way that things normally get done, whether we are speaking of a social phenomenon or a business operation.

Once you get used to using a new concept or gadget, you quickly forget how you managed without it. Everyone in my family, including my mother, who is in her late eighties, uses a smartphone. News aggregators on our computers, smartphones, and tablets have replaced newspapers in our driveways. Streaming videos have revolutionized the way we watch television and movies. The same goes for how we buy and read books or make airline, hotel, or dinner reservations.

In Silicon Valley, if someone starts a project, other people will offer some helpful initial feedback, but you rarely hear, "That can't be done." When there is a naysayer in the group, especially if it is in relation to the economic potential of a start-up, others respond with, "That is so East Coast."

However, as mentioned earlier in the book, even Google had

decision-making hiccups. Being smart and creative doesn't mean you are better than others at making decisions. Almost all growing organizations, as well as some developed, large organizations, have decision-making problems. As the company grows, there is an even greater need to agree on how decisions will be made and establish protocols for communication between the board of directors and the company's senior executives, most notably the CEO.

One of the greatest technological advances of the past hundred years was the development of the automobile, formerly known as the horseless carriage. Not only did it disrupt the established transportation business, it radically changed everyday life, especially in the United States. It allowed people to travel, and the invention of trucks allowed for the transportation of food from farms to cities. Without this development, cities would not have been able to grow in population like they did because food sources would be limited to what could be delivered fresh from nearby farms. If I asked you to think of an area of the world that is associated with innovation, many people would think of Silicon Valley, but just about no one would mention Detroit.

What about the great technology companies that paved the way for the current generation of innovative entrepreneurs? What about Hewlett-Packard, Yahoo, and others? They are great companies, but they have languished a bit in recent years and are going through strategic restructurings.

Hewlett-Packard (HP) was started in a garage in Palo Alto, California and became the iconic symbol of excellence in science in that area of the country and beyond. Meg Whitman, who by all accounts is a very good CEO, is currently trying to turn HP around to regain some of its past status, yet few people view the company as a hotbed of modern creativity in Silicon Valley.

Yahoo, like HP, was formed by electrical engineers at Stanford. It still has a powerful following, but this young company has languished for a few years. Former Google executive Marissa Mayer, who was brought in to get the ship headed back in the right direction, is now running it.

Bill Gates seems to be a true gentleman and intellectual. His personal character and genius are without question, but Microsoft is not considered to be producing cutting-edge products right now and is seeking to regain its footing.

Now we have Google, Apple, Facebook, and several other relatively new companies that are changing our everyday lives. Is there anything we can learn from the not-too-distant past about these older tech companies that can help the executives at the newer tech giants? This isn't about the older tech companies specifically, as there are lessons that can be learned from non-tech companies, but the comparison hits closer to home. In fact, this is not about East Coast or West Coast ways of thinking and isn't even limited to the United States.

Smart, creative people can, and usually do, fall into the same individual and organizational decision-making traps as others. As noted earlier in the book, being smart is an advantage but not an area of expertise. You may be an extremely bright, accomplished creative or technical wiz, but you may not be the best at, or even particularly good at, mergers and acquisitions that cost billions of dollars.

Selecting the Chief Decision Maker

While there are a number of articles about the excessive compensation of CEOs, a great CEO can make a huge difference. Whether a particular CEO warrants the pay she receives is specific to that person and that company, but that CEO is the most important person in the business organization, as she can make or break the company for the next ten years or longer. One of the most important decisions a board can make is selecting the right CEO. First, you have to determine the type of CEO you need and why. Every company needs to keep improving, but if your company is already dominant in an industry, it may only need incremental changes. If the company's strategic vision is correct, it may need someone who is better at execution.

Execution is undervalued. If you fail to execute on an excellent strategy, the result is suboptimal or even awful. If the company has a serious issue and needs radical changes quickly, this requires a different skill set. It may need a visionary change agent, as opposed to a person skilled only in execution of an established vision. A lot of people mistakenly believe that they are equally adept at both vision and execution, but reality indicates there may be only a handful of people who truly are. Regardless of where the company is in its lifecycle, the CEO and the board need to agree on a strategic vision.

When IBM was hemorrhaging money and facing a serious dilemma, the board brought in Lou Gerstner, a tech-industry outsider who could lead change. The board deserves praise for considering executives without tech backgrounds; Gerstner, prior to his IBM tenure, was the CEO of RJR Nabisco. He left a company whose research and development department developed products like the Double Stuffed OREO to lead a major technology-driven company. Prior to being CEO at RJR Nabisco, he was CEO of American Express. Neither company is technology based, but he was still the right person for the job.

Defining Important Decisions and Communication Protocols

There has to be meaningful interaction between the CEO and the board on all important decisions. This sounds basic, but not establishing communication protocols upfront is a recipe for disaster. There are no more important internal communications than those between the C-suite and the board of directors. The board wants to be involved and kept abreast of all important decisions, and the CEO wants to do her job without requiring constant approvals by the board. What are the important decisions in the corporate context that should receive board approvals?

#1—Strategy

"Strategy" is one of the most often misused words in the business world. Very few decisions are actually strategic. They are almost always tactical, but "strategic" sounds more important and intellectual. This does not mean that tactical decisions are unimportant—quite the opposite. The reason that most decisions are tactical and not strategic is that there can be numerous tactical maneuvers and very few strategies. In fact, there may be only one overarching strategy with hundreds of tactical decisions to execute that strategy. The CEO and the board of directors must agree on the short-term and long-term strategy for the company. If the strategy is wrong, perfect execution will be pointless.

The overall strategy for the company is always an important decision to be made. There are no minor decisions when it comes to choosing the direction of a company and understanding the reasons behind that decision. If a majority of the board and the CEO disagree on strategy, something has to give. When it comes to strategy, there is no middle ground.

#2—High-Level Tactical Decisions

Tactical decisions are important if they are critical to achieving the strategy or are high in value. For a large publicly-traded and very well-capitalized corporation, an acquisition worth $200 million does not usually need board approval, but it should be noted at the next board meeting. Acquisitions in the billions of dollars should almost always include discussions with the board before definitive action is taken.

The biggest mistakes in the corporate arena are disastrous acquisitions, regardless of their size. The track record is abysmal when it comes to large corporate acquisitions turning out anywhere near as successful as originally envisioned. If there is a gaping analytical hole in the way most companies do numerous acquisitions, it is the complete lack of analysis of past acquisitions. Some work out better than others, some are adequate, and some are horrible, but instead of chalking this up to "not every deal works," a regression analysis should be done to understand the reasons behind the successes and failures of past acquisitions. Were the underlying assumptions correct? Was the price too high? Was all of the analysis correct, but the implementation team just didn't execute well? Keep in mind that in almost every company, the team that does the analysis and negotiation for a deal is not the same team that follows through on the execution of the merger over the course of several years. In addition to doing a regression analysis of your own deals, look at the deals made by some competitors. You can learn from your past mistakes, but it's even better to learn from your competitor's mistakes.

The CEO and the board should agree in advance on the parameters that would necessitate the CEO seeking board approval ahead of time. The board might have a tendency to want to be involved a great deal, but if you have hired the right CEO, you don't want her to be hamstrung. Let her execute the strategy you have already agreed upon.

#3—Low-Level Implementation versus High-Level Tactical Decision

There was a very large US manufacturer that was losing market share and money, and the bleeding had to be stopped. It was losing market share because the average consumer had a perception (based mostly in reality) that the manufacturer was producing an inferior product to its competition. Not only was it losing market share, it could only keep its sales going by reducing what it was charging for its product using constant sales promotions and low-cost financing. The result was mounting losses and a lack of cash.

The *New York Times* reported that in order to conserve cash, the company was closing ten plants in the United States.[22] Who should make that decision? Should the board be involved? Why not just have the accounting department select the ten plants that cost the most money and close them?

This manufacturer's industry was highly unionized and there were constant tensions between management and labor. Labor blamed management for poor marketing and inferior engineering, and management blamed labor for not caring about quality production. The article reported that one plant in particular produced quality products, and the local management

---

[22] Maynard, Micheline. "G.M. Announces Decision to Cut 5,000 More Jobs." *New York Times,* November 22, 2005.

team and union employees got along quite well. So, why was this plant being closed?

The company had a cash flow problem, but dwindling cash was the symptom, not the underlying problem. The core issue was that the company was producing a product that the public thought was inferior. If the public thought the product was great, they would buy more of it at higher prices and the company would have a lot of cash. If you have a plant that is producing a high-quality product but costs more than some other plants, what do you do?

I don't know what level of the organization approved these plant closings. If saving cash was so critical that it made sense to close one of the better-run plants, the company was in dire straits. If cash flow was a problem, but not a critical one, closing one of its better manufacturing facilities meant that the company didn't really understand its core problem.

The decision to close a high number of plants should be discussed with the board. The board would not usually get involved in the details about which plants should close and which should stay open, but this time it definitely should have been a board-level decision. If you are closing a top-performing plant, it could indicate that your basic business model is at risk. This type of decision was too important to delegate to the accounting department. It was a strategic decision—or, at a minimum, a high-value tactical decision. By the way, the company was General Motors, which years later had to be bailed out by the US government.

If you are in Silicon Valley or elsewhere and I ask you why you think these things won't happen to your now well-run company, the answer cannot be, "We have a lot of smart people here, and we just won't let that happen." Don't presume that what happened to an old-school manufacturing company could not happen at a cutting-edge high-tech company. A number of high-tech companies have had to write off the value of multibillion dollar acquisitions.

There is an old saying that the definition of insanity is doing things the same way and expecting a different result. If you want a different result, what will you decide to do, or not do, that is different from other companies who also had a lot of smart people but failed? If you have a company with great sales and cash flow, don't assume it will go on forever. Look at companies you have admired in the past but that have not fared well and ask yourself this question: What do I have to do now that is different than what they have done so that I get a different result? What happened to HP and Yahoo can happen to you, unless you take proactive steps to

- thoughtfully select the chief decision maker,
- define important decisions and communication protocols,
- and allow the board to be involved in major decisions involving strategy or high value tactical decisions.

Hire an expert outside consultant who knows the ins and outs of Pattern Recognition in order to find the types of past mistakes others have made so that you can plan actions to avoid the same fate.

WAR

Most of this book involves decisions that we might encounter in our everyday lives. The decision to go to war or not is sobering, and is not something that we think about on a regular basis. Many people have said to me that it is a decision that is made by other people at a higher level (in the White House, Congress, and the Pentagon), so there is no need for the average American to think deeply about this. I disagree. While you are not the commander in chief of the Armed Forces, as a citizen you should have a well-reasoned opinion about whether or not we should go to war and be able to communicate your thoughts to your elected leaders. With great humility, I admit that only in writing this book did I become fully engaged in real thinking and apply a suitable thought process regarding the decision to go to war.

The United States has been involved in armed conflicts or threats of armed conflicts ceaselessly since World War II. Some major examples include:

1. Tens of thousands of troops stationed in former West Germany to prevent an invasion by the Soviet Union in Western Europe and troops stationed in Okinawa to protect and monitor Japan after World War II
2. The Korean War
3. The Cuban Missile Crisis
4. Vietnam
5. Iraq after Iraq invaded Kuwait
6. Iraq after the pursuit of weapons of mass destruction

7.   Afghanistan

8.   North Korea and Syria

Unfortunately, by the time you read this, there is a good chance this list will need to be updated. There are many other occasions when we have sent troops to assist others, or have been asked to do so, that I have not listed. During my adult life, I cannot remember a great length of time that the United States was not involved in a military conflict or direct threat of a military conflict somewhere in the world.

Situation Analysis

Let's first construct certain fact patterns. Let's assume that we can agree that if another country directly attacked our country and there was a threat of further immediate military strikes against us, we would immediately seek to protect our fellow citizens and our rights with all of our collective strength. Let's also agree that in this era of weapons of mass destruction, we may have to immediately retaliate in order to survive.

You may not agree with these assumptions, but except for these narrow scenarios, every military action is optional. With additional time to think about the multiple levels of decision making involved in going to war, the choice may still be to go to war, because dealing decisively with a clear military threat in the present could prevent a much bigger military and civilian cost in the future, but this is still a choice.

There are two basic camps that people fall into with relation to military intervention: the "realists" and the "idealists." For a good read on these two camps and current US foreign policy, read "The Consequentialist" by Ryan Lizza in *The New Yorker* (May 2, 2011). Although you may find yourself possibly switching camps based on a particular fact pattern, you have a strong tendency to be primarily in one camp or the other.

Here is the overly simplistic description of the two camps: A realist only wants America to intervene militarily when there are clear American interests at stake. An example might be drone strikes on terrorists who have stated that their goal is to attack the United States in the same way as the attack on the World Trade Center towers on September 11, 2001. An idealist has a much broader mandate. They believe that the United States should intervene when a dictator in a foreign country is killing thousands of his own people. A true idealist believes that we should intervene to stop these killings even if US soldiers may be killed in the process. Knowing my preconceived bias is that of a realist more than an idealist, I will approach the issue here with as even-handed an approach as possible.

The Problem to Be Solved

There are three decision points for a major military action: whether to strike, when to strike, and how to strike. Do we use an all-out military offensive, primarily leveraging our superiority in technology and weaponry? Do we need massive numbers of troops on the ground? Do we use surgical air strikes or Special Forces? The original decision will lead to multiple subsequent decisions that must be continually reevaluated and revalidated because despite the depth of intelligence gathered before the decision is made, facts change.

The term "fog of war" is often used to describe previously unknown developments that arise. Perhaps our potential adversary has commenced further aggressive action that, coupled with prior events, now makes military action advisable when it wasn't before. If we originally decided to take military action and facts have changed or new data has surfaced, will our previous decision be altered? As mentioned earlier in the book, war is the classic example of game theory, albeit the most perilous, most costly, and most impactful example of game-theory analytics. If we take an action, how is our opponent likely to react? Based on that reaction, what will we do?

Timing

The decision to go to war usually does not have a set deadline, so one should be set. Once a deadline is set, relevant facts should be continually revalidated. Setting a deadline does not require a rush to judgment;

rather, an appropriate self-imposed deadline trains you to make decisions in a timely manner. If you decide to go to war, timing also forces you to consider another component: when. If it can be managed, the most opportune time to strike is when you have the greatest advantage and your opponent is weakest. A surprise strike without a prior public announcement would appear to be one of the more optimal choices.

Balance

> *"He who wishes to fight must first count the cost."*
> — Sun Tzu, *The Art of War*

It is not an accident that this same quote was used in the chapter on Balance. It is here in case you are reading this as a stand-alone example and forgot the importance of balance. Also found in that same chapter was the quote from former Defense Secretary Robert Gates saying that the United States typically underestimates the costs of going to war. Balance is critically important in the decision to go to war. We know the reasons (benefits) we might choose to go to war, but what is the price (cost)? The cost to focus on is human lives, both in quantity and quality. Monetary cost is also a valid concern, but it is a distant second to the mental and physical well-being of our soldiers. If you conclude that we need to go to war regardless of the cost, you have skipped the all-important balance part of the analysis.

Through backwardization (also addressed in the chapter on Balance), we first determine the end result we are after (the goal) to better estimate the optimal way to achieve the goal or to decide whether the goal is truly worth pursuing. When deciding upon military action, ask yourself if you would support this military action if it cost the lives of 100, 1,000, 10,000, or 100,000 US soldiers. This backwardization concept is important to military action because it forces a focus not only on the benefits of the proposed military action, but also on the costs. It also forces an avoidance of sunk cost fallacy and determines in advance when you will implement your exit strategy, and unless you plan on attacking and permanently taking over another country, you MUST have an exit strategy.

How many lives should we have risked in Somalia or in Iraq? The only proper analysis involves accurately estimating the country's total cost to engage in a military action. Then, and only then, can we look at ourselves in the mirror and conclude that the mission is worth undertaking. While protecting our rights and the lives of our citizens is paramount, the decision to go to war still demands balance.

Ask yourself whether you would be willing to send your own son, daughter, or other close relative to fight this war. If you are not comfortable with that idea, then you should not be comfortable sending someone else's son, daughter, or other close relative to fight the war either. This is not a case in which you seek out the highest remote possibility of success. Your confidence level in your chosen course of action should be high. It should not be a goal of getting it about right more than half of the time, as once said by a US President. It is a classic case of balance. Is the benefit of the war worth putting your child's life or mental health at stake? If it is, then you genuinely believe in the decision to go to war. If you wouldn't risk your own child's life, you have decided that it is really not worth the risk. Here, the personal risk makes you think hard about the reward of military action.

Probabilities

Whether the goal is to achieve a positive outcome or to avoid a negative situation, any military action should have a clear goal in mind. When deciding upon a course of action, you need to set a clear, specific goal. If dealing with a threat, your goal will be to defuse that threat, which may involve economic sanctions or diplomatic missions and possibly include other countries as mediators. It might also mean military action. You can't make the decision that gives you the highest probability of achieving your goal if you can't define your goal with absolute clarity. Even if you decide to engage in war, without a well-articulated and well-thought-out objective, how will you know when your actions have been successful?

Establishing a clear and precise goal will also help direct you on how achieve it. If your goal is to defuse a threat, perhaps it can be achieved through the use of a cruise missile or drone strikes. If you need to deploy combat soldiers, the specificity of your goal will determine how many troops you will need. In World War II, the military theaters staged around the world were brutal, but the goal was clear: unconditional surrender of the adversary. Most wars, especially in modern times, don't have such clear goals.

The metrics of success in war today are different. For centuries, the leading indicator of whether a war was being "won" was the number of bodies on the battlefield. If your goal is to kill 100 of your enemy for every soldier you lose, then a body count is the appropriate metric. If you want to establish a different type of goal, the number of casualties your opponent suffers may be relevant but does not define "winning."

Once we have a goal clearly defined, we can identify the best ways to achieve the goal in the most efficient manner. Our decision-making framework will allow us to pick a course of action that maximizes our chances of success while minimizing our losses and perhaps strike a balance between the two. You may end the war when your goal has been achieved or when it is clear that your goal cannot be achieved without risking further substantial losses of lives and resources. A clear goal forces you to rethink your original decision and revalidate the decision of whether to continue with military action or to strategically retreat.

Pattern Recognition

Humans have been warring with each other on some level since the prehistoric days of competing tribes. Unfortunately, regardless of how many times these conflicts take place with ever-increasing destructive efficiency, they continue to happen. How did World War II follow so closely after World War I and involve mostly the same countries?

As mentioned earlier, there is a highly selective program at Yale that teaches the history of histories to a group of potential future decision makers who may be in the position to meaningfully influence the outcomes of US foreign policy. I think this program is great, and the people behind it should be commended for putting it together, but I wonder why the entire public isn't being taught to recognize patterns in international relations by having a similar course in high school.

Pattern Recognition illustrates that the real value in learning specific facts is to help us recognize cause and effect. If we expect people to learn from history and not repeat the same mistakes over and over, this is the only approach to teaching history. We need to determine whether there is a recurring pattern that can predict why, where, and when there will be concern for an event triggering a potential military conflict. As noted in "Pattern Recognition," the purpose of learning specific facts should be to identify predictive patterns, not merely to impress people with your encyclopedic knowledge of trivia.

Recognizing patterns can help predict the best tactical approach to an armed conflict. Rarely is a war fought on neutral ground. The land being fought on usually belongs to one of the combatants. War historians or an armed forces training center like the US Army War College could look for trends by studying past invasions and their results. How often were the invading forces successful? At what cost? What type of conflict did they wage?

Data would reveal that forces will most likely fight with greater intensity if the battle is in their homeland. They have nowhere else to go, but the invading forces can always go home. To put it in sports vernacular, "home-field advantage" counts for a lot in war. This is why the US revolutionary militia was able to defeat the British, who had vastly superior military forces. For the British, the Revolutionary War turned out to be a war that just wasn't worth fighting.

INVESTING

It is staggering how many people who have earned a lot of money are horrible at making investment decisions. I'm not talking about financial professionals but about successful small business owners, doctors, dentists, lawyers, and so on. If you own property; dabble in the stock market; have an IRA, 401(k), or other retirement account; or are owed a pension, you are participating in investing. Whether you are directly participating in the decisions or are depending on an expert to handle your money, your future financial well-being and post-retirement lifestyle will be directly influenced by the investment decisions you make now.

If you have money that is invested somewhere and is being handled by someone you don't know without any direction from you, you have surrendered thoughtful decision making to blind hope and reliance on luck. Hope is a powerful emotion but not a good strategy for effective decision making and neither is relying on luck. While you can invest in real estate, commodities, stocks, bonds, and derivatives on all of those, buying stock is an investment example that is familiar to most people, so I am going to use that asset class as an illustration.

You may not be a financial guru like Suze Orman or my friend Larry Trainor, a former partner at Spear, Leeds & Kellogg and Goldman Sachs, but you can and should do some basic research to improve your knowledge whether or not your occupation involves investing, economics, or finance.

There is a premise so basic that it shouldn't be necessary to state but is so vitally important and frequently overlooked that it must be said: ALL prices are determined by supply and demand, not just stocks. If there are more buyers than sellers for homes, we can easily predict that real estate prices will rise. Conversely, if there are hardly any buyers but many sellers, real estate prices will drop. A home's market value is not determined by what it cost to build the house or what it was worth five years ago. Supply and demand directs the price. It is the same in the financial markets.

Timing

Making money through investing usually requires two good decisions: a good decision to buy and a good decision to sell or not sell. The only way you make money is to buy at the right time and sell at the right time. To keep the analysis simple, let's assume that you are considering buying a particular stock in the US market.

This is another classic case of a decision without a set deadline. You don't have to decide whether to invest in the stock today, tomorrow, next month, or even by the end of the next year, but if a year goes by and you have still not decided one way or another, you have made the decision by default. Don't rush your decisions, but don't avoid them so long that your inaction becomes the decision. Take the time you need to gather and analyze the information relevant to your decision, and act only when you are ready to do so.

Timing affects many investment decisions, including:

1. Whether or not to invest.
2. Who will make your investment decisions, you or a financial advisor.
3. How long your target investment period is.
4. When to buy the investment.
5. When to sell the investment.

Whether your decision is to invest or not, rethink it on occasion. It might have made sense to be in the stock market at one point, but when global markets are riskier, it may make sense to sit on the sidelines until things settle down.

In order to determine the right investment strategy, you may need to work backward (backwardization, as described in "Probabilities"). When do you anticipate needing the money—at retirement or when your child goes to college? Will you need the cash over a period of time for the rest of your life?

If you buy stock at $100 per share and it increases to $200 per share, how much more money do you have in your pocket? The answer is none. You may feel a bit wealthier and happier because on paper your investment has gone up in value, but until you sell, you haven't made a nickel. Everything is a theoretical gain or loss until you sell the stock. Therefore, timing can be the critical factor in determining how good or bad an investment you have made.

Balance

Investing is the quintessential example of risk versus reward. This puts the concepts raised in the chapter on Balance front and center. Everyone wants very little risk with great reward, but it usually does not work that way. On rare occasions, opportunities like this can happen if you spot an aberration in the marketplace between the inherent value of an asset and its current price, but that situation, if it does exist, doesn't last for long. If Goldman Sachs develops a trade that makes a lot of money, JPMorgan Chase and all of the other major competitors will copy that trade, driving the profit margin down.

Most people focus on how much money they want to make with their investments, but the real focus should be on how much risk you are willing to take. Let's say you would like to earn a 7% annual return on your money, which is a modest but decent return in the current market. Most people, if asked whether they would like to earn 8% instead of 7%, would immediately answer yes, but if the same group was asked whether they would like to take more risk, not everyone would be as enthusiastic.

Decide how much you are willing to risk with your money and be as realistic as possible about the potential risks you face with each investment.

Take inventory of your risks. In the stock market and other investment arenas, there will be potential risks as well as positive developments that are beyond your control and ability to predict. Negative Black Swan events such as wars and other geopolitical events could occur. Positive Black Swan events might include technological advancements and other unforeseen developments that could benefit your investment.

You can't control the fact that some dictator may launch a missile and cause the stock market to dive, but you should have a view on how these events might affect your investment portfolio and your ability to weather the storm.

What happens when your investment begins to lose money? Studies show that people hate losses more than they love profits. While risk aversion is a good thing, if we allow ourselves to be emotionally driven to avoid loss, we risk incurring a greater loss by not selling. Most good investors and professional traders know to cut their losses quickly when a trade is not going well, despite the fact that they thought it would go up. Sunk cost fallacy is a powerful emotional trigger that can cause investors to hold onto declining stocks much too long in a failed attempt to avoid a loss. The most common mistake that retail investors make is not selling stocks that are losing value.

If you buy stock at $100 per share thinking that it will rise to $120, but it goes down to $92 , what do you do? If you sell, you lock in your $8 loss, but limit your loss to $8. If the stock goes back up to $100 (or more), you will kick yourself for selling too soon. Whereas, if the stock drops to $85 and stays there, you will be happy to have sold the stock at $92 and limited your loss to $8. There is no right or wrong answer here, but you need to anticipate this scenario and think ahead of time about what you will do. It is rare that all of your investments will go up and only up.

There are two factors that drive your decision in a situation like this. First, how strongly do you believe the stock price will rise to $120 per share? For example, are you 60% or 85% confident? The second driver is your timeline for the investment. If you think the stock will be $120 some day but you are a short-term trader, your investment horizon may not extend far enough to reach "some day." In this case you should be focused on what you believe the stock will do within the next week. If you have a longer-term view, then your confidence level (which has to be revisited from time to time) will likely drive your decision. A longer timeframe and high confidence may lead you to hold onto the stock, but a short-term view and less confidence would indicate that you should sell and limit your loss to $8 a share.

Probabilities

How much money do you want to make? The correct answer is not "more" or "as much as possible." Establish a clear goal by defining how much money you want to make before you invest. If your current answer is "as much as possible," you need to be more specific. If you don't know what your goal is, you won't know when you've achieved it and may hold on to the investment too long.

My brother, who is a smart guy, worked in the Silicon Valley area when technology stocks began to boom. He had a little money to invest and bought some tech stocks. One in particular did quite well for a while. He bought it at $8 a share, and in time, it went all the way up to $56 a share. When the tech bubble burst, though, it dropped back down to $8 a share. When I asked him why he didn't sell at least some stock when shares reached $35, $45, or $55 a share, he said, "I thought it would still go up."

Unfortunately, his story is all too common. If he had sold the stock at $24 a share, which was three times his investment, he would have made great gains but, as it continued to increase past $40 and $50 per share, he may have felt foolish for cashing out too early and losing the chance to further his gains. The problem is that he didn't have a target goal; he didn't decide beforehand the price at which he would sell some or all of his stock to hedge part of the risk. If he had sold a third of his stock holdings, he would have recouped all of his investment and still had two-thirds of his portfolio intact.

Retail investors often fall into this same trap. You need to begin with a goal that when reached will trigger a decision process. For example, if your ambitious goal is to get a 30% return on your money, a decision process should start the moment your stock approaches that value. With your goal achieved, you should immediately consider selling some or all of the stock or placing a "stop loss" order that triggers a sell if the stock dips below a certain price. If you do nothing and hold onto the stock, you risk the stock dipping back down and not reaching your goal. If you don't have a goal, you won't know when you've reached your desired outcome and when you need to rethink your position.

While you or your advisors can do all of the best research and analysis possible, you can never be 100% certain that your investment will produce the outcome you want. You may hear a pundit on television or your friend on the golf course say, "I bought the stock at $100 and knew it would go to $120!" Of course, this proclamation comes *after* the stock has gone to $120, validating his investment decision and publicly affirming what a smart investor he is. Having worked at some of Wall Street's most noted global financial institutions with a lot of smart people who are experts in this area, I can tell you without a doubt that in reality, no one knows what will happen until after it happens. They will, however, make big bets on things with which they are familiar based on the probability that it will result in the outcome they want. The more you research an investment in a thoughtful manner, the more you increase the chances that you will reach your desired outcome.

Pattern Recognition

Pattern recognition is critical to investment decisions. Whether you are a short-term technical investor who examines trading patterns in a company's stock or a longer-term fundamental investor who looks at the underlying values of companies, you will be looking for patterns that are predictive of the future value of your investment.

You or your advisor should have a clear view on whether or not the stock of the company has a fair value of $100 when it is trading at $80 (fundamental investing). You should also have a clear view on the trading pattern of the company (technical trading). This is often demonstrated by experts on television using graphics that show bands of support (the price the stock will normally not drop below) and the resistance level (the point at which the stock seems to peak before it drops again). There are a lot of successful short-term traders and algorithm-based computer programs for trading that only look at the technical charts for the company's trading pattern and are largely indifferent to the fundamentals of the company.

If governments around the world pump incredibly large amounts of cash into the economies to make borrowing costs very low, it causes stock markets to increase in value. If you have decided to invest and can't make any money with your bank or the bond market, you have little choice but to invest in stocks. This lifts the stock markets up as more investors buy stocks because they have limited options.

There is a readily available treasure trove of data regarding investments that experts have scoured for years in attempts to discern which factors will predict the future of the economy, the market in general, and specific stocks. The challenge lies in the overwhelming amount of data available and in the necessity to distinguish data points that are predictive from those that are irrelevant.

At the very least, familiarize yourself with the following five key categories:

1. Global
   If you are buying stock in a company that does significant inter-national business, as most big companies do, you need to realize that a bad economy in China or Europe will affect the earnings of the company.
2. United States
   If you are buying stock in a company that gets most of its revenues from the US domestic market, national economic condi-tions will impact the price of the stock.
3. Industry

Not all industries react the same way or have the same potential for gains. Utilities and technology have nothing in common. Decide which industry you think will do the best over the time-frame in which you are planning to invest.

4. Interest Rates

   Interest rates have a lot to do with stocks. If interest rates increase, it will be more expensive for companies to borrow, which reduces their earnings. The other double-hit is that investors will then look to invest in bonds instead of stocks, because bonds will have better yields. Since everything is driven by supply and demand, there will be less demand for stocks in general and the overall stock market will weaken. The opposite is true if interest rates decrease or stay very low.

5. Currency Exchange Rates

   Most large, publicly-traded stocks have international exposure. If the US dollar is going to appreciate against the Euro, you need to factor this in. If the US dollar appreciates 5% against the Euro (a quick, meaningful move), that means that a US company doing business in Europe will have to sell 5% more product just to break even with last year's performance in Europe.

This list might seem complicated for an average investor, and it doesn't include all considerations. However, if you don't know the most-likely answers to these questions, you need to hire someone who does.

How to Pick a Financial Advisor

Many of us don't do 100% of our investing ourselves. In fact, most people actually do very little investing on their own. We rely heavily on financial advisors to make our investment decisions. If we are going to outsource our investment decisions to someone else, the selection of that advisor becomes of paramount importance.

When choosing a financial advisor who will make investment decisions on your behalf, it is critical to pick someone whose integrity and competency you can trust. Will she look out for your best interests rather than her own (integrity)? Does she actually know what she is doing (competency)? After all, you only want to hire someone who is better at investing than you are.

The most important thing to understand is the advisor's strategy. If he is using the same basic investing model that he has used for the past 30 years, ask him why. If the past 30 years reflected mostly normal financial markets, why would you continue to use the same model in a current market that is far from normal? If the prospective advisor cannot explain his decisions quickly and clearly, don't hire him.

Be aware of the biases that might be influencing you. If you find yourself enamored by his looks or his charm, ask yourself what you are really focused on in your decision. Are you paying handsomely for the privilege of association? This is the classic halo effect. If you are attracted to him, ask him out and spend $200 on dinner. Don't make an investment decision based on something that has nothing to do with his financial acumen. Don't be dazzled by a large office building with a commanding presence that exudes security and stability. Ignore the rich mahogany tables designed to give the impression of wealth and success. That is classic "priming."

A good financial advisor will ask you how much risk you are willing to take and assess what you can reasonably expect to earn based on your risk tolerance. He should present you with a hypothetical portfolio and stress test it. A stress test shows the impact on your investments if one of the key assumptions changes. You need to know what happens if the United States raises interest rates or if the Eurozone crisis grows worse. If your financial advisor is unable or unwilling to run scenarios like this for you, find someone else.

MEDICAL DECISIONS

Choosing which type of bandage to use is not a life-or-death decision, but it is staggering how many people choose important options regarding their health without much thought at all. When people think of important medical decisions, they conjure up images of being wheeled into an emergency room with a team of medical professionals whirling around and performing life-saving procedures. There is no time for reflective decision making at that point; you are relying on the experts. They are checking your vital signs and hopefully referring to their checklists for emergencies.

How many times have you decided to visit a doctor, take medication, or have surgery? How many times have you made the choices to start exercising, stop smoking, or eat a healthier diet? These are all important health decisions. Compare that to the number of times you have had to take an ambulance to the hospital. The reality is that we have more than enough time to think about almost all of the important choices we make about our health.

Your goal is to avoid the ultimate negative personal Black Swan event—getting seriously injured or dying before it should happen naturally. There is a 100% certainty of death. The only questions are how and when you will die. On a personal level, there may be no goal more important than the remaining quantity and quality of your life. Health-related decisions certainly fall into the category of important decisions.

Most health-related choices can be put into three categories. The first of these is long-term preventive care. This usually relates to lifestyle choices, including not smoking, drinking in moderation, regular exercise, and managing stress. The second relates to mostly midlife choices, which may include things like deciding whether or not to start a suggested drug protocol like Lipitor to reduce cholesterol, using physical therapy to rehabilitate a physical ailment, or resorting to a surgical approach. The final category involves very short-term decisions or decisions for major medical issues. This would include choices about how aggressive to be in dealing with an advanced form of cancer or whether to undergo open-heart surgery.

The decision-making analysis will vary depending on which category you are in, so I will try to address them separately. A lot of medical choices can come at different times and therefore won't fit neatly into these three categories. I chose three categories so that the four factors can be somewhat tailored to typical fact patterns within those categories.

Much of the focus in these examples will be on probabilities and balance, but you always need to consider all four sides of the framework for a proper decision-making analysis. No matter what the decision is or which category it falls into, like all other important decisions, timing is always considered first.

Timing

Long-Term Preventive Care

The further away we believe we are from a crisis, the more time we believe we have to make a decision. Here also lies the greatest opportunity to delay and waste time. Most of the types of decisions we make about our health do not have externally set deadlines, and as we know from the chapter on timing, if we don't have a deadline, we need to set one.

Let's start with an easy one: lifestyle choices that we make even though we know they are bad for us. Are you waiting for some sort of sign that will catapult you into action to change your behaviors? Take, for example, a middle-aged man with a large potbelly who is 50 pounds overweight and works in a stressful job. This man has a medical issue, not just an aesthetic issue of carrying a few extra pounds or not being in great beach shape. He is putting undue stress on his heart and his lower back. If he is aware of this but does nothing to change things, is he assuming that his first heart attack won't be severe, or is he ignoring the probabilities and just hoping it won't happen to him?

The best medical decision you can make is to take proactive steps to avoid having to confront a medical crisis. As a hospital CEO once told me, unless you work in a hospital for a living or are there to give birth or visit somebody, your goal is to never be in the hospital. Doctors and nurses in hospitals can save your life, but that is the prevention of a negative thing. It might be a very reasonable assumption that you will live at least until you are 85 years old, but it is important to revalidate that critical assumption every once in a while by getting an annual physical.

Use backwardization here. Imagine you are being wheeled into that emergency room and that things are touch and go. Wouldn't you regret not watching your diet or maintaining your health before that moment? If you smoke cigarettes, you know that smoking is bad for you. You may intend to quit someday, but at some point, "someday" has to become today.

Put your health goal on your calendar to set a firm deadline. If you have an electronic calendar, add an alarm. Put it on your calendar two additional times, as well—two weeks after the first date and two weeks following that. If you miss the first deadline you set for yourself, you will see it again in two weeks. If you miss the second self-imposed deadline, you will see it once more two weeks later. If you fail to take action after all three, there are two possible conclusions: You don't have the self-discipline to take the proper course of action, or you have consciously decided that the unhealthy behavior is rewarding enough to risk the serious problems it may cause you later. You are choosing to tolerate the risk.

Midlife Choices

You don't have to be in midlife to be confronted with some of these problems, but it is rare to find people over 60 who are not taking some prescription medication, getting surgery, and/or having physical therapy for a knee, shoulder, back, or other joint problem. At this point in life, there is still enough time to ponder the alternatives, but not as much time as for the 30-year old who decides to actually buy and use that gym membership.

The typical midlife decision relates to some ailment that will likely need to be addressed in the next few years, but the pain from it is not sufficient enough at that moment to create an immediate burning platform that necessitates a clear time for a decision. Typically it is something that can be deferred, like knee surgery.

The timing question will be injury-specific, and the resolution will revolve around whether the postponement of fixing your knee will make your problem worse or not. No one likes to undergo surgery. Even common outpatient surgery like arthroscopic knee surgery carries a risk of complications and infection. If your problem is not severe, you can defer surgery and try physical therapy. If your problem is severe, deferring it may lead you toward knee replacement surgery. Knee replacement is common today, but there is a greater risk, a much longer recovery time, and lower success rates than arthroscopic surgery.

If you need a total hip replacement, you and your surgeon may want to defer it as long as possible so that you can get it done once and not have the device wear out when you are much older and the risk of further surgery is quite a bit higher.

In this category, the best timing decision will involve the following analyses:

1. Will deferral of my decision make very little or no meaningful difference to my health?
2. Will postponing the decision exacerbate my problem so that the future solution will pose a much greater risk to my health?
3. Should I try to avoid or delay surgery like hip replacement in order to gain an important advantage to my health?

Major Medical Issues

Here, I am assuming that there is a more immediate or short-term need to come to a decision. Most people get the timing part of the decision-making process right in this scenario simply because the decisions almost always have to be made right away. These can be life-or-death decisions or quality-of-life decisions. If the decision can be deferred, it may not be for long.

Probabilities

All decisions are based on the highest probability of achieving your desired outcome. Medical decisions are tough, but they force you to realize that your risk of getting a bad outcome is never zero. You can't balance risk and reward if you don't know the chances of the good outcome occurring and the chances of a bad side effect happening. Without knowing the odds of each outcome, you are flying blind. Probabilities also force you to be specific about your goal. While your overarching objective is to have the highest quality and largest quantity of life, the choice you are facing is usually much more specific than that. Use probabilities to help you clarify your immediate goal.

Long-Term Preventive Care

When we think of medical decisions, we often think of times we are already ill and are contemplating the choices to best rectify the situation, but most of the important decisions about our health are done well before we are sick. A chain smoker can live a long life without getting lung cancer, bladder cancer, experiencing heart failure, or any of the numerous bad outcomes associated with smoking cigarettes, but the probabilities are against him.

Conversely, a person that never smoked can develop cancer or heart disease. Dana Reeves, the wife of actor Christopher Reeves, died of lung cancer at an early age even though she was not a smoker. A person who is looking for an excuse to keep smoking will cite these examples, but it is abundantly clear that the heavy smoker has greatly increased his chances of developing a serious disease and dying prematurely. Very few smokers think they smoke as much as they actually do. The smoker might get lucky, but as we know, hoping to be lucky is not an intelligent decision-making strategy. This is all about probabilities. Lifestyle choices do not guarantee a good outcome or the avoidance of a bad outcome, but when you make the right choices, you are deciding to play the probabilities in your favor, which is a smart choice.

Midlife Choices

In the United States, we are often frustrated by the amount of red tape that delays the introduction of new and useful drugs and procedures. We might conclude that while we in the United States are slow, we are also safe, but that isn't always the case. There are frequent recalls or mass torts against drugs that have proven unsafe, even after approval by the Food and Drug Administration (FDA). Based on a US government document, the *Wall Street Journal* reported that over 27,000 heart attacks were caused in four years by a popular arthritis pain medication, but this doesn't tell you what you need to know. While there is almost always some risk of negative reaction to any kind of drug, including common over-the-counter pain relievers, what you need to know is the percentage of users who have negative reactions, especially dangerous ones.

When you see an advertisement for a medicine that might help you, the ad always lists the possible side effects. While the commercials and magazine spreads are usually high-dollar productions, the lengthy lists of possible side effects are almost laughable. We may attribute this need for disclosure to our litigious legal system, but the commercials don't tell you the chances (probabilities) of the potential side effects you risk by taking the medication. The drug companies do have this data. There was a *New York Times* article about a possible law that would clearly disclose the probability of something helping you and the probability of that same drug or procedure harming you. Think about that. Without knowing the probability of something bad happening to you, you really can't make an intelligent, informed decision.Let me present a hypothetical situation: You have allergies that are more than merely annoying and ask your doctor for an anti-allergy medicine. He tells you about a drug that can help you and prescribes it for you. You get home from the pharmacy with your new prescription, and before you take your first pill, you turn on the television and see a commercial for that medicine. The television advertisement touting the drug claims its outstanding relief from allergies and mentions a few side effects, including an inability to control your bowels and possible depression.

We often dismiss these as required legal disclaimers that are not likely to happen. If the percentage of instantaneous diarrhea is one thousandth of one percent, it is extremely rare. You could easily and correctly assume that it is highly unlikely this would happen to you, so you swallow your first pill.

Let me change this hypothetical situation a little. You take your first pill and then see the television commercial. During this advertisement, the spokesperson notes that the chance of you spontaneously losing control your bowels is 33%. Would you take the second pill? Would you go out to a party later in the evening?

This is a hypothetical scenario, but it is done for a purpose. Without knowing the probabilities, you can't make a good decision. Most of this information is known when the drug or procedure is approved by the FDA, so even if it isn't announced on television, you can ask your health care provider.

Before the FDA put a stop to it, the company 23andMe offered a service aimed at determining whether you have a genetic predisposition for certain diseases or ailments based on your DNA. Did this predict with certainty that you would contract the affliction or disease that you were more susceptible to according to your DNA? Of course not. As genetic testing procedures improve in subsequent years, the accuracy of these types of tests and their results are inevitably going to improve, but if your probability of contracting something is higher than that of the general population, you should consult with your regular health care provider to stay a bit more vigilant than you otherwise would be if you were not predisposed to the condition.

Major Medical Decisions

When it comes to surgery, the probabilities of success, failure, and complications should be made clear to you before the surgery occurs, but you can improve on some of the data you are given by asking a few critical questions. Let's assume that these are the percentages you are told:

There is an 80% chance that the surgery will return you to the same healthy condition that you were in before the malady hit you. There is an 18% chance that it won't help as much as hoped, if at all, and a 2% chance of something catastrophic happening during the surgery. Clearly, the predominant chance is that the surgery will reap the benefits we seek. If your outcome falls within the 18% category, you have incurred the expense and physical pain associated with surgery and recovery, but you are generally no worse off than if you didn't have the surgery. The 2% risk is the personal negative Black Swan event.

Before you make a decision, let's consider the assumptions behind these data points. Your doctor is an ethical person, but she is getting these percentages from medical research journals or the FDA, not from first-hand knowledge. When there is a trial for a new surgical procedure, usually involving some medical device, the manufacturer of that device approaches the top-rated doctors in that specialty. The doctors usually operate in a highly rated teaching hospital. Your doctor may not be one of these particular doctors, but how relevant are these probabilities in relation to your particular situation? After all, that is really what matters to you.

How is your doctor rated? How is the entire medical team rated? This not only includes the surgeon, but also the anesthesiologist, nurses, and others involved in the operation. What about post-surgical care? What about the hospital where the surgery will take place—how is it rated?

Ian Thorpe, the Australian Olympic swimmer, is by definition a world-class athlete. He went into the hospital to get surgery for his shoulders, and as a result of an infection he picked up in the hospital after this surgery, his agent said he is unlikely to ever be able to swim again at a highly competitive level. What makes you think this can't happen to you? At least Ian gets to live, which is not always the case. The data is clear that many people die unnecessarily from infections they contract after surgery. It doesn't matter if you die in surgery or after surgery from an infection. Do hospital employees use a medical checklist to prevent infections? Make sure you ask about the infection rate in the hospital where the surgery will take place. It is critically important.

Ensure that all probabilities you are given are accurate for the specific surgery, your doctor, and your chosen hospital. The data you are given may be accurate based on clinical trials in special hospitals, but unless you are using the same team at the same hospital as the clinical trials, the reality is that your probabilities may be dramatically different. As discussed in the probabilities chapter, ensure that the key assumptions underlying the data are correct.

Balance

Long-Term Preventive Care

You should lean toward mitigating the risk to your health as much as possible, but you can never get your risk to zero. There are a number of balancing acts with regard to health. First and foremost is that for everything we do, there is a physical or mental health cost. You can physically be the healthiest person you know with unfathomable self-discipline, eating only the right foods and exercising every day, but what about mental health? Remember the example from the chapter on pattern recognition about the health of the people living on the Greek island of Ikaria? They ate fresh fish and vegetables and got moderate exercise by merely walking around their villages instead of going to a health club, but it seemed that lack of stress was relevant to their healthy longevity, if not the causative factor.

Most doctors will tell you that a glass of wine with dinner is fine. About the same number of doctors will tell you that if you have two glasses, that's probably okay too. It is hard to find a competent doctor who will tell you that drinking an entire bottle of wine by yourself each night is good for you. It is all about balance.

If you have ever become ill while travelling in Europe, you have witnessed a distinct difference between the medical cultures in Europe and in the United States. In the United States, if there is any doubt, doctors have a tendency to prescribe (and patients have a tendency to want) some prescription medication to cure patients' maladies sooner. In Europe, there is a hesitancy to prescribe pills. Which approach is right? It depends on the circumstances; a case can be made for either one. Why have someone suffer needlessly or have a simple infection progress into a more severe one when there are pills that are likely to stop the simple infection in its tracks? On the other hand, overmedicating does not allow the body to build up its own natural immune system and can create a natural evolution of stronger diseases that are resistant to current medication, sometimes creating fatal outcomes.

Midlife Choices

There is almost always a choice when it comes to surgery. Do you enter into aggressive surgery to stop a problem when it occurs or wait to see if you can regain your health by non-surgical means? Do you go for knee or shoulder surgery or try to use physical therapy to rehab your way back to health? It depends on the severity of your injury and your lifestyle.

Perhaps you are an avid skier and don't want to miss the entirety of next ski season by trying physical therapy instead of going directly to surgery. There is a risk that surgery won't go as well as hoped and that you will not be better off afterward, but there is also the risk that physical therapy won't mitigate your issue and you will have to have surgery anyway, so why waste six months of intensive exercise without a positive outcome? If you are a professional athlete or someone else who depends on physical ability to earn a living, you might not be able to see if physical therapy alone will work.

Major Medical Decisions

The gravest risk-versus-reward scenario occurs when you are seriously ill with heart disease, cancer, or a similar life-threatening plight. These situations present the starkest choices between a more aggressive treatment and a less aggressive treatment. If you choose surgery or chemotherapy and radiation, you may improve your chances of survival but are certainly taking on risks, including the associated risks of having surgery or the unpleasant after-effects of chemotherapy and radiation.

This equation may also be impacted by your age. If you are 88 years old, you might opt for a less aggressive path in order to maintain the quality of the years you have left. A person who is 38 years old might pick the more aggressive procedures, striking a balance in taking more risk because they have more to lose. There is a balance between quantity of life and quality of life.

There are no clear answers or easy choices when it comes to the risk versus reward in medicine. The only time the answer may be easy is when a procedure or medication has become so reliable that there is very little downside to gaining the additional quantity and quality of life that this choice offers.

Pattern Recognition

Pattern recognition is extremely important for the creators of a new drug or procedure but not particularly relevant for the layperson. If the government or your trusted healthcare provider tells you the odds are 87% that this drug will help you and there is only .01% chance that you will have a negative side effect, you take the information at face value. You are not in the position to do the research yourself and challenge or validate the underlying correlation, relevance, and causation that support the efficacy of the drug.

While you can never foretell which factor will cause a good outcome or a bad outcome, as we know from "Pattern Recognition," research shows that stress and the quality and quantity of food you consume directly impact health and longevity. These types of causative or relevant factors apply to a large sample size and may or may not cause any particular outcome in an individual. In this case, all of the causative and relevant factors determine the probability of whether your choice will improve the odds of your desired outcome.

If you are wheeled into the emergency room and are unable to communicate or in a state of mental shock, the doctors will decide what is best for you. The same is true if you suffer from a debilitating mental condition in which your capacity to make a well-informed decision is absent. Hopefully, in that case you have an executed health care proxy in the hands of a loved one who knows your wishes. Absent all this, the decision maker is you. All of the other people involved, even the best-trained and trusted doctors, are your advisors. They advise and you decide. Don't be afraid to ask intelligent questions, Think Deeply, and then decide for yourself.

AFTERWORD

Before writing this book, I thought I had a pretty good handle on the best ways to invest my money. In the past, I had done reasonably well and always had a positive return, but my decision-making process was unstructured. I had been involved in the financial industry my entire career and thought that I just had a good *feel* for the markets. I was doing well, but thought I could do better.

In the first three years after formulating the four-point framework, my investments earned a better return than 98% of all professionally managed hedge funds. I didn't read any more books or articles than I did before. I didn't take a course or buy a new software program, and I certainly didn't listen to people's advice at cocktail parties. I simply applied the lessons I had learned while doing the research for the book.

After doing the research, I was much more aware of the various influences that could make me too emotional and erratic in my decision-making process. I am human and felt the emotions related to the gains or losses, but I didn't let them drive my decision making. When losses happened, I no longer let sunk cost fallacy drive me to hang on to that investment. I knew I couldn't undo my first decision to buy that stock, so I simply looked at what I thought the stock would do going forward.

With my newfound approach, I also set profit targets. Before I bought a stock, I knew at what price I would sell it, and as soon as it hit my target price, I sold it. I didn't look back if the price went up after I sold it. I looked for other investments.

Most importantly, if after applying the four-point framework I wasn't sure what to do, I made the decision to do nothing. Rather than being indecisive, from time to time I made an affirmative decision not to invest and instead sat on the sidelines until the market settled.

Ever since I became trained as a lawyer, I see everything through a different lens. Whether it is a television show or a high profile case in the news, I view situations through a different perspective than the average non-lawyer. After doing the research, interviewing people, and writing this book, I view decisions differently. When I watch a sporting event or the news on television or read an article in a newspaper or magazine, regardless of the topic, I analyze the decision-making process. Prior to knowing the result, I judge them as well-thought-out decisions or non-thinking gut reactions.

Now that you have read this book and learned the four-point decision-making process, I think that you will also view all important decisions from a new perspective.

I hope you take this framework and apply it to the important decisions you face in life and in work. You won't always get the result you want, but your decision-making process will never be wrong again, and your chances for getting your desired outcome will increase significantly. With a structured decision-making framework, not only will your results improve dramatically, but also you will make decisions with more confidence and less stress.

CPSIA information can be obtained
at www.ICGtesting.com
Printed in the USA
BVOW09s1019191117
500802BV00001B/149/P

9 780986 130618